For the Love of Long Shots

A Memoir on Democracy

by
Shawn Casey O'Brien

For the Love of Long Shots: A Memoir on Democracy

Cover art by Martin Sweeney.
Photograph of Shawn by Slobodan Dimitrov.

Published by Pumpkin Seed Publishing
c/o Evan "Bones" Kendall
PO Box 803, Whittier, CA 90608

This book is a work of art. The story is based on actual events in the life of the author, but artistic license has been taken. Names have been changed and character likenesses have been altered.

ISBN: 978-0-9798934-8-3

For Sacha Lilie,
Her Grandmothers, Marie and Tessa,
and her Great Aunt Julia

It is the mothers who teach the first lesson of democracy.
They teach us to count.

You never know when your lunch counter moment is going to come. I sure didn't see mine coming, nor was I looking for a fight on that otherwise gentle sunny morning at the beach. All I was asking for was a cup of coffee while awaiting my friend. Instead, I was being served up an all too typical bully, one who was busy exhibiting the true smallness of his spirit first thing in the morning...which was probably his worst mistake. I mean if you're going to give me grief in the morning, at least have the good graces to let me have a cup of coffee first.

There was that much sought after cup of coffee and then there was the chain, the chain that was now denying me the ability to park my sputtering Ford Granada in the café's handicapped parking spot, the very spot that was next to the walk-up window where I was supposed to order that simple, soothing cup of coffee. If they'd unlocked the chain and allowed me to use their handicapped-parking zone, none of what was about to pass would have occurred. None of it.

But, then, bullies never think of the true consequences of their actions or how it's their small, petty insults that often lead to much bigger, more important battles. Just like the lunch counter sit-in at a Greensboro, North Carolina Woolworth's in 1960 or Rosa Parks refusing to give up her bus seat, often it is the small indignities that ignite major movements of change.

At that moment though, I wasn't thinking that my simple request would have anywhere near those kinds of hallowed outcomes -- I was just waiting on my friend Sal and wanted a cup of mighty java while doing so.

Looking back, I now think it ironic that's exactly what those four brave young men in Greensboro had ordered back on that February afternoon in 1960. A cup of coffee. Like them, I too was more than willing to pay for that privilege.

Unlike them I hadn't set out to be a glorious and necessary troublemaker. For they had been picked specifically to provoke a non-violent battle with the whole of the segregated South, a fight that would change this country forever. I just wanted to park my car in a handicapped designated zone and have a cup of coffee. The only thing I was interested in changing that early morning was my still groggy consciousness.

My consciousness did get changed that morning -- just not in a way I anticipated.

"Why chain off a blue zone during business hours?" I wondered as I got out of my car, grabbed my crutches from the back seat, and walked up to the wooden counter that hung off the side of the walk-up window, the counter that would, in large part, change everything, the counter where I made my simple, appropriate request.

"Coffee please, my friend," I said to the server.

Automatically he put a cup on that counter in front of me and filled it. He was Hispanic, a young man, working hard for little money. Just one pleasant peasant giving another a cup of coffee.

From my fatigues, I pulled out a dollar and tossed it on the counter top. "Thanks," I said as he grabbed the buck. "And would you please unlock the handicapped parking spot?" I asked, pointing at it with my crutch to emphasize the fact that I am one of the anointed.

His smile went suddenly sad, and his eyes rolled up at me the way people do whenever they have to do or say something that they don't particularly want to say or do.

When he told me, "No, no, señor," I could see he was not proud of it.

Again I thought it weird, but, then, perhaps it was a communication problem. With my heaving Ford Granada doing its own form of percolating in the narrow alleyway of Venice Beach, this was no time for misunderstandings.

"Manager, por favor," I said, hoping to speed things up.

Off he went as I poured a little cream in my coffee and wondered if my attempt at Spanish was in bad taste.

As I stood there stirring my coffee, I slowly surveyed my surroundings. Venice Beach, or "Venice of America" as it's better known to the rest of the world. It was my most agreeable, if not offbeat neighborhood. I took a deep breath of the ocean air and watched some Asian women in bathing suits Rollerblade down the boardwalk with the same rhythmic grace as the deep blue Pacific behind them.

I exhaled thoroughly and contemplated how I was going to get my steaming cup of coffee over to one of those ubiquitous plastic white table and chair sets that one too many home improvement warehouses have foisted on us. My lower back hurt just looking at them, but I figured I could endure breakfast. Once again, hunger pangs beat out physical pain. It was, after all, a picture postcard day with a breeze that would keep both the acrobats on the boardwalk, as well as the ones on crutches, cool, calm, and dry. "Count your blessings," I reminded myself, "you live here."

I blew on my coffee with some contentment. I treasured my waterfront neighborhood, having lived nowhere else as an adult, and I was happy to have one more blue zone in it. It would make this café an even cooler place to breakfast with friends and family. If I could just get the heaving Granada parked, my contentment would be complete.

I was about to sip a little off the top of the cup in preparation for a landing at a nearby table, when John the manager came around the corner on the other side of the pick-up window.

He sported greasy blond hair and bad teeth. From the skeletal remains of John, one could tell that he worked at a hamburger stand...and probably did a little too much speed. He was agitated from the start.

"What's the problem?" he asked roughly, wiping his hands on a dirty dishrag.

"No problem," I answered, setting the coffee back down on the counter. "I just wanted to use your handicapped parking spot and have a little breakfast."

"Can't do that," he said.

"No, I'm a patron," I explained, pointing to my cup of coffee in front of us.

"This is private property. No one's allowed to use the parking lot," he said putting an even nastier edge on his voice. Shades of the Greensboro 4.

I dropped my head in disbelief, keeping one eye squarely on him as the BS detector in the back of my brain went off like the bell of a prizefight. In spite of all my previous contentment, I felt the frustrated boxer in me gearing up to dispute this clown.

"This is a public accommodation," I said with all necessary emphasis. "I am the public -- that is a handicapped parking spot," I said, pointing to it again. "I'm handicapped," I said indignantly, stepping back so that the whiz kid could get a full view of my magic sticks. "And that spot was put in place to facilitate handicapped citizens' patronage of this establishment. To give us an equal opportunity to have a cup of coffee at this counter," thumping my index finger on it for emphasis. I ended with a very irritated, "Thank you very much."

Okay, I was perturbed and sarcastic, but under the circumstances, I didn't see that as such a sin. After all my mother had always taught me to say thank you. "Even to your adversaries -- as they often bring out the best in you," she told me more than once. She's also the one who taught me about the Greensboro 4 and Mother Parks and Civil Rights.

Those teachings and Speedy the skeleton were about to bring out the best in me by messing with those civil rights. I seriously thought about giving Speedy a deeper appreciation of the Americans with Disabilities Act, explaining how that law, via that blue zone, guaranteed me an equal opportunity to enjoy a cup of coffee and all. But, considering the chemically addled masses of his brain, I knew such truly high ideas and worthy intentions would be lost on him. Accordingly, I opted for the much more emphatic, "So unlock the chain, dude!"

He was somewhat startled. So was I, as it all came out so smoothly, but I didn't let on.

"We know how to deal with people like you," he snarled.

"What'd he say?" I asked myself. "People like me? People like me!"

The nausea began to kick in. The discomfort of it made me realize, as always, that I was dealing with another truly unjust punk. Yet again, I faced a bully. And worse, previous experience told me that if I wanted relief in both my gut and conscience, I'd have to deal with the belligerent knave head on.

I couldn't just walk away. I had learned that early on.

In the next microsecond, my mind flashed back to my first bullies, those petty little thugs Big Mike and Victor, my hearty childhood tormentors, who not only beat upon me regularly, but would, when the opportunity presented itself, throw me into any handy garbage can and kick it down the nearest steep hill.

The dizzying ride and my already screwy equilibrium brought on the worst nausea -- that feeling I hate above all others -- and of course, on my way down the hill, I would throw up in a whirl, my tormentors running off scared when they saw my garbage-encrusted, vomit-covered carcass crawl out of the can and fade into the grass.

It wasn't just the vertigo and sickness either; ultimately I would have to crawl back up the hill in my forlorn condition and (hopefully) find my crutches. Yeah, I knew something about bullies. Ultimately, like it or not, you have to stand up to them, and just as the top of the hill was always better than the bottom, sooner was always better than later.

Quite amazingly, when I finally did hit Big Mike squarely over his head with a crutch -- taking a blow or two myself in the process -- he and Victor left me alone. Fancy that, two for the price of one. Yep, they could still kick my crippled young butt, but now, if they did, there was a price to pay. Win, lose, or draw, I wasn't afraid to fight. Whack!

The whack brought me back to the bully at hand.

"People like me?" I said aloud. "No, man, you don't know how to deal with people like me," I assured him sternly.

He got all offended, as bullies are apt to do whenever you stand up to them, turning themselves into the instant victim.

"Are you threatening me?" he said, flinging the dishrag to the counter.

"Threatening you," I laughed. This guy was a real prize. "No, John, I don't make threats, I make promises, and I promise -- that chain is coming down!"

I successfully fought off the urge to knock over my untouched coffee and create a mess, knowing that the guy who would have to clean it up was my original sad-eyed friend. No justice there, either.

I stormed off, back to my car. As I drove around looking for an unobstructed parking space, I became even more enraged at how unnecessary it all was. The distinct pettiness of it.

All they had to do was unlock the chain. A simple act of no more than a few seconds, given a steady hand and an ounce of empathy, yet they wouldn't do it. What cretins! How many others were they doing this to? I wondered. How many other hungry cripples did they chain out of that blue zone?

It was a beautiful blue zone, too, perfectly up to code. They'd have never gotten their license to open the café if it were not -- yet here they were callously chaining it off. There is something inherently incoherent about a chained off handicapped parking zone, and I grew even madder at the thought.

A handicapped parking zone is supposed to be a bright blue beacon of inclusiveness and accessibility, something that brings people in. Yet here these barbarians were chaining it off and keeping people out. In my own neighborhood, too! Damn! I knew I couldn't live with that.

As I drove around trying to find a parking spot in my tourist town, now more famous than Disneyland, it was hard for me to believe that there had even been an argument about it. What, with my plastic blue placard hanging in the front window of the Granada, attesting to the fact that I was a medically recognized cripple in the eyes of the state, the café's actions were not only illegal, but also illogical, begging all common sense and decency.

And I was a paying customer, too! "Hey, wait a minute," I wondered, "did I get my change back?" I realized I never did. Talk about salting the wound. Nor, come to think of it, had I gotten a sip of coffee. I had left it steaming on the counter.

Now I was steaming as I parked in front of the non-functioning gas station on Windward Circle, that now-paved-over Grand Canal of early Venice with the weird green swoosh of sculpture haphazardly plopped down in the middle of it, serving (just as haphazardly) as the center of town.

I made my way back over to Sal's apartment, which ironically overlooked the café, giving me a bird's eye view of the chained off zone as I commandeered his phone.

I called everyone, and not by choice, either. The Mayor's office referred me to Disabled Access, who said they handled only "on street" parking spots, and told me I really should be talking to Building and Safety, who, when I did, weren't sure if handicapped parking was "within the purvey of their authority," and thus told me to call the Mayor's office -- circle completed.

I was sadly amused at the way no one accepted responsibility for enforcement of such an obvious violation of the law. But being an optimist, I preferred to believe I'd started a blizzard of faxes within the bureaucracy, and consequently, someone would go out and let Skeleton John and the gang know that chaining off handicapped parking wasn't only illegal, but in extremely bad taste.

I even told the responsibility-shy bureaucrats who made up the circle of hearty buck passers that I didn't even care if they ticketed the guy. Just make him take down the chain during normal business hours. That's all.

Simple.

I figured that the battle was then over. That some City official would do the right and simple thing -- like enforce the law. After all, this wasn't Greensboro, N.C. in 1960, was it?

Of course, looking back on it, perhaps I had been picked for this particular battle all my life.

Just like those four young men in Greensboro had to be blessed black to be picked for their battle, I had to be blessed a cripple to be picked for mine. So be it.

Thanks, Skeleton John.

* 2 *

The good Doctor Stanford was the first to explain my blessing to me.

"It is like a light bulb that is loose in the socket," he said coolly, "and making only sporadic contact, it flashes off and on erratically." In this case, my brain, or at least the damaged part of it -- the thing the doctor was making the light bulb analogy to -- was sending messages that were making only sporadic contact with the muscles in my legs, flashing off and on as it were, making my balance erratic and uncertain at best. He confirmed my first hand experience.

"Your cerebral palsy affects your brain and your balance like that loose light bulb," he finished, glancing over his chart at me.

Easy enough for a twelve-year-old to understand. I now knew why I walked on crutches, why I was the way I was...the loose light bulb theory.

I also knew I was lucky. I was dealing with one flickering bulb that capriciously illuminated my balance, but my speech and cognitive ability were virtually untouched. Being a "special ed" kid, I had many friends with CP. Most had to deal with a number of flickering light bulbs. Light bulbs that more often than not, liked to flicker off and on all at the same time, tying them in spastic knots.

That was the amazing thing about Cerebral Palsy, or "CP" as we living illuminated refer to it. Every case is different. Virtually unique. I now call it the "fingerprint birth effect," because no two cases are exactly alike.

The good doctor's light bulb theory helped me understand why. Everyone's got a different mix of loose bulbs and out-of-contact sockets. I always appreciated that Doctor Stanford took the time to explain this minor mystery to me. Coming from him, it had a validity that no one could dispute. He was a specialist. Even at my early age, I could see how people deferred to him.

He was the first authority figure, outside my family, that I can remember dealing with. Even more imposing, he was an authority figure who literally sliced into the back of my legs. He cut, stretched, and sewed muscle, skin, and tendons, and then he made me walk better. Not perfect, but better. As such he had great credibility!

He could be surgeon cool and aloof -- and then show incredible kindness.

Maybe he knew what I did not the last time I saw him. That it was in fact to be our last time together. Having entered puberty, the time for operations on my legs was over. It was now time to be thankful for what "took."

Because of the good doctor's abilities, I now walked flat-footed, and my right leg "scissors" out more than in when I ramble around on my ever present crutches. The left one didn't take.

Such is life. Everything was right, more or less. Better, not perfect, just like my walking. I learned from such experiences that in real life that's about as close as you get to perfection. You get it right, more or less. The fact is, I was better off because of Dr. Sanford and always looked forward to seeing him.

We chatted as he tapped my knees to test my reflexes. I was telling him, between taps, how I'd fallen out of a rubber inner tube and into the shady green gray waters of Lake Huron and almost drowned. An alert camp counselor pulled me from the big drink at the last moment.

The doctor looked at me with a smile.

"I don't worry about you," he said. "You're tenacious. You have an ingrained will to survive."

"I was glad to survive Lake Huron," I told him.

"You would have gotten your head up," he said seriously. "You're a fighter. Didn't anyone ever tell you about your birth?" He sounded somewhat surprised.

"No sir, it's never come up. What happened?"

And so Dr. Stanford filled me in on my birth, as well as my current condition.

That is, he filled me in as well as he could. He was not the attending physician at my birth, but knew Dr. Cuzo well, having consulted with him more than once before putting me under the knife.

As it turns out, I was born two and a half months premature, weighing in at three and a half pounds, and was a silently screaming blue gray sliver that was struggling for life and air. There was some serious wonder at the fact that I was born alive. In the emergency situation of such a premature birth in 1956, they had prepared my family for the worse.

Unwrapping my once life-giving, now life sucking, umbilical cord from around my scrawny neck, they threw me into an incubator and flooded it with oxygen.

The doctor informed me that that may have been the point at which the brain damage happened, that first second that CP entered my life. "There's a good chance that's when it occurred," the doctor informed me, "to go from no oxygen to total oxygen in seconds is a bit much for the human brain. Today, we give oxygen gradually."

"So that may be it," I wondered aloud

"Yes, that may be it," he agreed. But that wasn't the end of it. "You were touch and go, and during your strenuous birthing process, you managed to give yourself a double hernia, which had to be repaired three days later, and, to top it all off, like many preemie babies, you had yellow jaundice."

"So I was pretty sick and ugly?"

"Your parents loved you," he assured me, "and again we had prepared them for the worst. Your chances of making it were not good, maybe twenty percent, but you were tenacious, and you beat some very long odds. Guess you were meant to be here."

How was that for a confidence booster? I was a long shot from the start.

I asked my Ma about it some time later, and she assured me it was just as bad as the doctor had told me it was. And she added that it was "very, very, frightening" for her, as I was her first child. But what scared her more, she began to joke, "was what they had me feeding you to fatten you up once we got you home."

"What?" I asked.

"Oh god, it was awful, but you loved it."

"What was it?" I asked genuinely intrigued.

"Ohhh," she rolled her eyes at the memory. "I would grind up raw lamb, mix in heavy cream and Karo's syrup and that was your primary formula."

"Raw lamb?" I said shocked

"Yep," she laughed.

"That didn't kill me."

"Nope, you loved it," she laughed. "I had to cut a larger hole in the nipple of your bottle so that the lamb could get through -- you wanted it so bad. You were persistent. You wanted every drop."

Every drop of raw lamb, heavy cream, and Karo's syrup. Hard to believe.

Well, Doctor Stanford had said I was a survivor and tenacious.

I thought about the doctor when I went to make my second set of calls about the chain, which, after too many weeks to remember, still remained around the Blue Zone at the café.

Tenacity would be called for.

Evidently these small-hearted people at the café didn't know whom they were messing with. A raw lamb, heavy cream, and Karo syrup sucking man. If I could handle that bad taste, I could handle the one those jokers were now leaving in my mouth.

Not only could I handle it. It would make me stronger. I had to give thanks for that!

Thank you, Mom. Thank you, Dr. Stanford.

* 3 *

It was hard to believe that common sense and human decency hadn't carried the day over something so simple. I was amazed to find that, of the ever-widening circle of bureaucrats I had called to plead for relief, not one of them saw fit to call or visit the café and tell them to stop harassing the local cripples and to just unlock the chain during business hours.

It was more than an annoyance. I could see the blue zone held hostage every time I drove down Speedway Ave., the alley that masquerades as an avenue in this town, and the route I often used to get to Venice Boulevard east and on into Los Angeles proper.

Months went by. The chain remained. Talk about psychic pain.

To be treated like a second-class citizen in your own neighborhood really is the depths of powerlessness. I do not like feeling powerless. No one does, really.

To overcome the feeling of powerlessness, and forgo the fantasies I was having of blowing the lock and chain up, I did something to promote power.

I went to the law library. To know how to properly access and use a law library is a great psychic balm and it is truly empowering. Every serious citizen/activist should take a short afternoon trip to their local law library and become familiar with it and its staff. They are most anxious to help the serious and the oppressed.

Don't be blown away by all the size and number of books, either. The key to good legal research is to focus on what is the most important issue at hand. Once you figure that out, 99.8% of the books in the law library are of no interest to you -- so forget about them. If you're in a situation like mine -- your opponents help clarify the issues, anyway.

When I walked into the law library, I knew I was dealing with handicapped parking, so the rest of the library be damned, until, of course, it is needed.

Always remember the first law of laws: common words have common meanings. With that and a 5th grade reading level, you'll do just fine in a law library.

If you do get lost or confused, fear not, all kind of books and pamphlets have been written to help you (and less than stellar law students) understand the law and how to apply it.

Lawyers hate that I am telling you this, but if you want to be influential in all matters, private and public, learn how to properly use a law library.

The truth is every high school should have a civics class where, as part of the curriculum, they teach all students how to properly use the local law library.

Every citizen a lawyer! Sound a bit radical? Perhaps, but reasonably literate people can do 90% of their own law. Talk about revolutionary change.

One last word: The vast majority of law libraries were built and supported with taxpayer's money -- your money! You own the joint. Use it! Learn how to read a citation, check out a law's legislative intent, and "Shepardize" a case, which is to check past court decisions for relevance on a current case.

Do that and you'll understand any law thrown at you. Better yet, you'll have one to throw back. Or, as in my case, about a half dozen.

Beginning with Title III of The Americans with Disabilities Act on the federal level, there was also California's Unruh Act (the state's equivalent of the ADA), and numerous municipal violations, as well as my personal favorite from the CA Vehicle Code Sec. 22705.8, which had all the power and majesty of a one-sentence law:

"It is unlawful to block, bar or otherwise obstruct a handicap parking stall."

There it was. The one simple law they couldn't argue with. The ADA and just what is "reasonable accommodation" could be debated ad infinitum, but the simple direct language and intent of the Vehicle Code cut to the chase.

Who could argue with me, now? I had the law on my side. And a simple one at that.

"Now the bureaucracy would move," I thought to myself. "Now they could right this simple wrong and everyone could get on with their lives." I was happy in my small way to be the one who spurred them on. Let the law deal with the bullies.

Making the circuit once more, I felt like a good citizen as I called my bureaucratic buddies -- this time, spouting the law, and playing up that one sentence miracle in the Vehicle Code. Everyone was very nice, full of, "You don't say?" and asking for faxes, which I was all too happy to oblige. All but one guy at Building and Safety. He wasn't happy.

He started yelling at me, right off. He asked me what right I had to be messing in other people's business.

When I tried to explain that using a public accommodation in my own neighborhood was my business, he began to yell so loud that I could hear him spouting and cursing when I held the phone at arm's length.

It was shocking because it was such an overreaction. Didn't this guy like to do his job or what?

I wished him a terse good bye and told him I would not forget him. The bastard. Still, after all the calls I made, along with having the Black Letter Law on my side, I thought someone would do something. Somebody would do their job. Right?

As I faded off to sleep that night, I was still pondering what nerve I had hit with the screamer at Building and Safety. Was he on the take or something? Oh well, at least I didn't overreact. I didn't go off, and I believe at that point, I could have. From the recesses of my tired mind, I could hear the stern words of the wise old physical therapist who'd literally taught me to walk.

"Keep your balance, buddy, keep your balance," I hear Ms. Bass say.

And as always, I remember it is wise to follow her advice -- so many years later.

Sleep came as I silently thanked that tough old woman one more time.

* 4 *

I have never been able to maintain my physical balance for more than a few shaky moments without aid. Lacking crutches, humans, or walls, my balance is brief. Without supports, I walk a tight rope at best, and do so poorly. In my never-ending battle with gravity, I always tumble. And I never have a net.

By now, loss of balance is a given. I know how to fall. I was taught to fall. And the most important thing about falling is getting back up.

The first real lesson I learned in this life was how to get back up. Thanks to crutches, I not only became an expert in how to minimize my falls, but as the inevitable nose-dives did occur, I also learned how to stay in complete control... most of the time.

So many "Temporarily Able Bodied" types, poor "TABS," take gravity for granted, and upon loosing their balance, they lose a bit of consciousness, as well. I, on the other hand, count falling as a great skill of mine and have learned to remain lucid throughout the descent and am merely looking to crash land without hitting anything or anyone.

I remember always that any crash landing that can be walked away from is a good one.

Luckily, I get up and walk away a lot. So it's not hard to see why I've come to believe, philosophically and physiologically, that in all things, it all comes down to balance. When you really understand balance, you gain the ability "to take a fall" in all other aspects of life.

This art of getting back up was taught to me by fate, in the form of Ms. Bass, my first physical therapist. A stern, but loving hickory stick of a woman, she taught me to walk and unbeknownst to her (and me) she was the first practical philosopher I ever listened to.

Just goes to show that you can find the philosophy of life in a lot of strange places and through some very unexpected sources, such as Ms. Bass. And she had such a sage soul that even seven year olds got it. That's how deep that Bass ran.

"Keep your balance. When you fall down, get up! Get back up!" Through this direct philosophical approach, she also taught me to walk using crutches -- my beloved magic sticks -- with which I hardly ever fall. When I do...no problem. I know what to do.

Avoid hard objects and self-pity, and prepare for the epiphany you're about to have when you land safely. Nine times out of ten.

Nine times out of ten being what it is, life has also taught me that nothing is a sure bet all the time. As my daughter used to say when she was a toddler, "Sometimes, you go boom." Sooner or later the odds catch up with you due to the cluttered environment, the surging crowd, your lack of moderation, etc. and you "crash and burn," as her proud father likes to say.

You still get back up, but you do so a little less for wear. Your brains and mettle are thoroughly tested as you ponder just what the hell happened? As you shake it off you realize that it's the odds.

Even for professionals, like myself, there's always the deadly skid. A crutch tip hits oil or plastic on asphalt, and suddenly I have a skateboard under my arm and everything happens much faster than a mere fall. All I can do is prepare to take the shot, usually to the ribs, which, because of the slide, are very exposed.

As I lay there doing a body check after a quick skid, I comfort myself by remembering that one needs these calamitous moments to appreciate the 99% percent of the other moments when I fall properly and get right back up unfazed.

A Buddhist monk I once fell in front of, while hitchhiking to California, exclaimed, "What a way to participate in divinity!"

Whenever I fall now, whatever the outcome, routine or not, I remember that I am above all else participating in divinity and in that none too divine tone she used to take with me, I hear Ms. Bass' booming voice commanding "Get up, boy - keep your balance."

And the poise ascends again. Thank you Ms. Bass.

* 5 *

You always know you're on to something when people can't quite believe what you're telling them. The reaction was universal: "Who would chain off a handicapped parking space at a public restaurant?"

"Petty, cold-hearted jerks," I would explain to my disbelieving friend or neighbor.

What really hurt, what really made me feel like a second-class citizen, is that nobody in local government gave a damn or did anything about it -- in spite of the law.

"Yeah but it's so simple," my duly outraged friends would say. "Unlock the damn lock, and allow disabled patrons to use it. What jerks! It doesn't make any sense."

No, it did not. Neither the café's illegal conduct nor the institutional failure of the city to do anything about it made sense. Most able-bodied people focus on the individual discrimination and miss the larger problem...the institutional discrimination. The fact that the local authorities completely failed to protect the rights of disabled citizens in reality meant we have no rights. That's what most TABS missed. They were outraged and bemused at the absurdity of it all...and without fail they all asked, "What are you going to do about it?" Every time I heard that, I got that weird feeling again, that I had been picked. What was I going to do about it?

I was going to spend the summer studying the similarities between Buddhism and Stoicism, but now I realized, I was going to live them. It was an ethical dilemma. What was I going to do about it? All my disabled friends were outraged, as well, but none too surprised at the actions of the café or the inaction of the authorities. At least most of them asked, "What were we going to do about it?"

Well, Thompson and I were drinking. That's what we were doing about it.

I wish I could say that it started out all high-minded and rational with clear minds and sober judgment.

But, alas, we were suffering. And in that tried and true ritual of relief and redemption we were drinking...heavily. We were trying our best to drown our mutual outrage, while conveniently forgetting the age-old rule that "Outrage floats," from one drink to the next until revelation or unconsciousness.

Either would have suited us. Both did, the first night we came up with the idea.

Thompson was a wild man. He fell out of a tree as a kid and cracked his spine, leaving him partially paralyzed. Like me, though, he's another durable cripple. He was strong in his upper body and is made mobile by chair. As a blue card holder himself, he found the chain to be as offensive as I did, and in that keenest of senses.

The sense of dignity.

"Not letting us use blue zones is not only messing with our dignity, it's taunting it," Thompson succinctly, if somewhat drunkenly, put it.

"You got that right, bro," I agreed. "The only thing disabled about that parking space is the chain they put around it."

"Ain't that the truth, and if they're messing with you," he went on, "how many other disabled people are they messing with? Denying them the right to park, eat or take a piss?"

How many indeed?

"You know," he said, " the ones who can't get out of their vans or cars in the narrow alleys of Venice -- think about that -- for a lot of gimps, just seeing that chain across the blue zone forces them to drive on."

"Excellent point, bro.'"

We were two mighty blue card holders who for the moment didn't feel so mighty. And we were guzzling from the big bottles of malt liquor as we struggled with our apparent powerlessness.

"I just can't get over it," Thompson finally said. "After all, it isn't like we're asking the café to knock down walls and retrofit the damn place with ramps. Just unlock a simple fucking chain. No expense, no real hassle. It's almost weird."

"The guy's just a bully."

"We could always blow the damn thing up!" Thompson offered. I told him of my fantasies, and we agreed that there would be some momentary satisfaction of the Huck Finn variety in that, but we knew that the satisfaction would be all too fleeting, to say nothing of playing right into the owner's hands.

"He probably wouldn't have a hard time getting those local authorities, called the police, to do something about that," I drunkenly offered.

"He has rights 'cause he has property," Thompson said. "We have rights because some book in a law library says so, and, as any school kid knows, rock rips paper. Property rights rip civil rights."

"I'll drink to that god-awful truth," I moaned, the strong brew and the recurring revelation of our powerlessness hitting us in unison.

We took gallant gulps. Thompson yells out, "Regardless of what it says on paper, it's not really the law -- it is just paper!"

"Yeah, right..."

"Laws get enforced, papers get ignored," he snarled. "If they had a sign out front that said 'NO BLACKS OR JEWS ALLOWED,'" Thompson ventured, "all hell would be breaking loose. The ACLU would be screaming. Politicians would be up in arms. Such a thing wouldn't last a day."

I agreed, with another healthy slug of the Bull. "But you see, man, they're organized, and we're not. They can move politicians. We can't," I offered, without enthusiasm.

We hunkered down. We shared a little more brew, then we shared an epiphany.

"Why can't we? Hey -- why can't we? Why can't we move the politicians?"

"There must be thousands of disabled citizens of voting age in L.A. alone," one of us said. "Tens of thousands, I'd bet," the other offered.

Between more copious sips of malt liquor, and the drunken visions they imbued, we began to discuss the possibilities.

Thompson was an engineer for a public affairs radio show, and I was an old saloon singer. In our knocking around "the community," we knew that: one, citizens with disabilities were the largest minority group in the country, and two, disabilities cut across all other groups, no matter how you break them down, be it by class, race, culture, gender, or sexual orientation.

There are a lot of us, and we are everywhere, which are two good things to consider when you're talking about taking power. Numbers and territory: we had them both. That much we knew.

Civil Rights were just a starting point. You didn't have to be a political genius -- and we weren't -- to see that when it comes to issues like good health care, affordable housing, and education, disabled citizens had a direct interest in promoting these things, to better their lives and everyone else's too.

That's a lot of common ground to organize our vote upon. Best of all, voting is one of the few things that disabled citizens can do for themselves. That's powerful stuff, in a community where so much is done for us.

"Yeah, but you know how we love to fight amongst ourselves," Thompson said, showering himself and his chair with another over-enthusiastic bottle of beer.

True enough. The disabled community (at least in Los Angeles) loves to fight with itself. Blind can't speak for deaf, sticks can't speak for wheels, and on and on, arguing ourselves into individual powerlessness and mass oblivion.

On that bright shiny night, we realized that if we could get disabled citizens to stop defining themselves by their distinctions, and start to define themselves by their common interests, we'd have a voting block and, perhaps, a movement that really could take and justly exercise real democratic power.

That's when it occurred to us, the way it does when you're drunk on really big ideas. In order to vote, one has got to register. As such, what was really needed was a voter registration project.

"Voter registration, huh?"

"Yeah, if you want them to vote, you've got to register 'em."

"What would you call it?"

We wondered aloud. The League of Disabled Voters? No, too much like the League of Woman Voters, and if we used the terms "disabled" or "handicapped," we'd undoubtedly piss off some politically correct gimp.

The disabled community loves to argue over what to call ourselves. That's a big part of the reason we never get anything done -- we can't get past the first task of what to call ourselves.

Disabled? Handicapped? Crippled? Or the term universally despised within the community, "physically challenged."

"I don't know," said Thompson, well aware of the problem. "We're all so damn unique."

The poet in my brain staggered fourth. "That's it, old buddy, we're all unique people."

"What?" he laughed.

"No matter what your disability", I laughed, "You're unique. So, let's call it Unique People. The Unique People's Voting Project. It has a ring." My years of being a rock and roll singer with a knack for naming the bands had paid off again.

"Unique People. Unique People," Thompson was saying over and over. "U-P, U-P, UP!"

"What?" I asked.

"Unique People. U-P, UP!"

"U-P," I said to myself, "Unique People. Wow. UP!" Could there be a more psychologically powerful message for disabled citizens than that? I wondered. "The Unique People's Voting Project. UP! Damn cool, Tommy! It's time to get UP!" I yelled.

We were laughing and chugging. We were getting UP!

UP was powerful and it got us around the whole hassle of the crippled, disabled, handicapped debate. We were none of those things. We were all of us, unique people. Best of all, it was so damned inclusive. We could cover anybody, regardless of their disability, as well as include our families and friends.

"Because, after all," I reminded Thompson, "weren't our friends and families themselves unique, just by having us in their lives? Hasn't the experience of our disability colored their lives, too? Weren't they concerned with the same issues we were and would thus vote accordingly?"

"Hell yes!" we shouted.

Again we toasted our toasted insights.

You didn't need to be a James Carville to see that anything that multiplies our vote (like our families and friends) is a good and powerful thing, as well.

"They'd vote in our best interest, I'm sure," Thompson said with a wicked smile, "but the real question is: would disabled citizens themselves know enough to vote in their own best interest?"

"I agree with President Monroe," I told him, "who said, 'People, by and large, vote in their own best interest.' And if disabled citizens get out and vote, the vast majority will do so in their own best interest, as well as everyone else's too. They will vote in their 'enlightened self-interest' as our forefather used to say."

"I'll drink to that. True democracy and whatever you just called it," Thompson yelled in a slur, lifting the mug. He looked at me with a wicked grin. "What the hell does that mean? 'Endangered self-species.'"

"You almost got it," I laughed. "'Enlightened self-interest.' It simply means doing things in a way that not only benefits you, but the whole of society as well."

"Now there's a very high idea," he cut in, only slightly slurred.

"Exactly, my brother," I said enthusiastically. "Exactly! It's a very high idea from the Age of Enlightenment; one our revolutionary founders lived by. An idea, without which, civilization itself would have never progressed. Hell, we'd never have campfires, much less communities, without enlightened self-interest. Without it, we really would be an 'endangered self-species' as you so beautifully mangled it."

"Thank you, professor," he joked. "But I wonder, old buddy, have we really progressed?"

"We're still here, aren't we?"

"Not everyone, I'm afraid, would see that as progress. Look at that chain."

"Good point. All the more reason to organize ourselves in our enlightened self-interest."

"ESI," he said. "Otherwise it's a mouthful."

"That's good, Tommy. what UP will promote is ESI, disabled people voting in their ESI. I like that!" I raised my beer yet again. "To disabled citizens everywhere, taking power and using it in their enlightened self-interest."

"To ESI."

"When you think about it, just about anything disabled citizens do for themselves benefits most of society anyway, right?" I said, feeling both my brew and the resulting vision. "Good health care, accessible society, low-income housing, not just gimps and cripples use or appreciate those things, everyone does. Disabled citizens are the damn poster children for ESI."

We laughed hard at that. "You may have a point there," Tommy said. "Fighting our fight protects everyone else."

"Them's the best fights Tommy, them's the best fights," I happily informed him. Our mood had brightened considerably.

Then it dawned on us. Some smart pols had to realize the political potential of our community long before we did, right?

What with FDR being elected president four times, and himself disabled, it seemed more than plausible that someone connected with him would have been putting this together since the 1930's. This cooled us considerably.

We both agreed that it had to be. Just because we hadn't heard of it didn't mean that someone hadn't already beaten us to the punch and was busily registering, informing and getting out the votes of disabled citizens.

So we thought, but after a few days of calls to friends in the community across the country, we were amazed to find that no one had ever tried, at least in recent memory, to organize our vote. Many we spoke with had worked on this or that piece of legislation, or had worked for this or that candidate. But no one had, to the best of their knowledge, ever attempted to organize the disabled electorate.

Lucky us. We were the first.

Yet another lesson of grassroots organizing: Don't assume that someone else is working to solve your problem. Most likely they aren't. If they had been, you wouldn't have the problem in the first place.

Whether it's Civil Rights or the meeting of an unmet need in your locale, most of the time it's up to you, the individual citizen, to initiate a process that will resolve the problem. Like we did, you become an expert by default.

As I was rolling around in my bed a few days later contemplating all this, I began to really understand the size of the task that we were attempting to take on.

Both Thompson and I were stunned earlier in the day when we got a call back from a gentleman at the Census Bureau.

Unlike our local official, the federal government was anxious to help. Max Mitchell, from the C.B., gave us the numbers gladly, telling us, "No one else had ever made such a request." He was extremely cool. He charged us nothing. Thank you Max.

Thompson and I were blown away when he told us that there were over 828,000 disabled citizens of voting age in Los Angeles County alone, and 2.8 million in the state.

That's a lot of votes by anyone's standard, and in this era of low turnouts, merely organizing ten percent, of that vote -- much less the whole thing -- could have a tremendous impact on local elections.

He also informed us that there were thirty-five million disabled citizens of voting age currently living in the United States.

"Thirty-five million?" I exclaimed.

"That's about right, we've done a little extrapolating here, but that's more than an educated guess," he told me.

"And there are at least 2.8 million voting age disabled citizens in California, alone?"

"At least," he assured me.

Think about such a large network of proactive disabled voters in a state that accounted for one fifth of the Electoral College. That is a really big payoff. On top of that, it would be a "first."

How many of those are left in the world? Not many. How much sweeter could it be? The shot was long enough, the payoff big enough.

Now for the scariest question of all.

How?

* 6 *

I wish I could remember who gave me the written wisdom. I am deeply indebted to that person. He or she, in large part, made everything that happened, happen.

Often, true wisdom is like that. It only takes a very little bit to have a very big impact.

I wonder if the person who gave me the words realized just what he or she did for us? It was a casual offering, so nonchalant in the giving, that I can't recall who handed it to me.

There was no big deal made about it, and the person took no overbearing pleasure in giving it up. There was no trying to be cool. It was after all, less than a page. A couple of paragraphs to be exact. But upon reading it, I wanted to tell that person how extremely important he or she was. For I looked at the offering as a sign from the gods, an omen to go forward and do what had never been done -- get disabled voters to take their legitimate democratic power and use it wisely.

That powerful idea and now this -- this poetry -- showing us the way to do it.

That appealed to the barroom bard in me. As one who has always listened to his muses, and believes wholeheartedly in the power of poetry, it was easy for me to be taken with this offering from the grassroots. Lyrically beautiful in a no nonsense way, I took it as a sign of good fortune that a poet, and not a military man, would provide guidance.

Goethe, the nineteenth century poet and philosopher, had come to show us the way. The great man wrote: "Until one is committed, there is hesitancy, the chance to draw back always breeds ineffectiveness. Concerning all acts of initiative and creation, there is one elementary truth -- the ignorance of which kills countless ideas and splendid plans -- the moment one definitely commits oneself, Providence moves too. All sorts of things then occur to help one that would never otherwise occur. A whole stream of events issue from the decision, raising in one's favor all manner of unforeseen incidents, meetings and material assistance, which no one could have dreamed would have come your way. Whatever you can do or dream you can do, begin it. Boldness has genius, power and magic in it. Begin it now!"

There it was. Grassroots Organizing 101.

Upon reading it, I tossed aside all doubt. Goethe is right, hesitancy breeds ineffectiveness. Like a cat in the midst of a leap, successful execution of any effort is all about fearless follow-through.

People often hesitate because they foolishly believe that they are not "great enough" to do great things. In truth, I was beginning to realize, all great things start with common people doing simple small things that they follow through on. Initiation, commitment, and tenacity are the keys -- heaven will provide the rest.

As Goethe says "Once one definitely commits oneself, then Providence moves too."

And wasn't it true, I thought to myself as I sat there re-reading the great mystic? Hadn't providence, in the form of god knows who, put his words right there in my hands? Wasn't that a sign that what the great man said was in fact true?

Close enough. When you live a poetic lifestyle, you've got to give your inspirations and muses the benefit of the doubt. I make it a habit. I also made it a habit to talk to any crip I ran into about starting a comprehensive voter registration project in the community. About getting UP.

And wouldn't you know it, once we started talking to people about taking power in the most democratic of fashions, through the ballot box, most everyone wanted to help, offering all kinds of material assistance, and, yes, some in the most unforeseen manner.

I realized that making the powerless -- the cripples, the deaf, dumb, and blind -- powerful was at its essence the genius, power, and magic of our voting project. Poor people taking power. Better yet, poor disabled citizens boldly taking power and using it to help everybody. Living ESI.

That is my definition of justice: poetic justice.

Goethe eased my mind and helped me commit to this great effort. Initiate, create, do it now! That was my job...Thompson's too.

If for no other reason than that we discovered the problem. We stumbled onto an unmet need within our community. Therefore it was up to us. It was our civic duty.

We began to understand that our little project wasn't so much a political project as it was a civic one. We didn't care who disabled voters voted for as long as they voted in an informed manner. If they did just that, the odds were on our side that they'd do the right thing. Disabled people would become, in the process, the most powerful force in the 21st century for a civilized society and a better America. I shook my head at the profundity of it all. Boy, that Goethe sure made you dream.

The reality is that if disabled citizens did just that, got registered, informed, and out to vote, we would for the first time in history be able to protect and promote our civil and economic interests. Coming from a community that generally does little without the help of others, that's a powerful idea both politically and psychologically.

I will admit I also loved the "meek inheriting the earth" aspect of it. I ask you, how many times do you have a chance to really see the last come first? Not many, and yet, here it was. Power, poetry, and I'd get to learn a bit about democracy, too. How lucky could one aging agitator be?

And so the question became: What would happen if we paid attention to the common good as opposed to partisan politics? What if we cared more about democracy than politics? We decided to do just that.

I mean, we wondered who was paying attention to our democracy. And what did it mean to be a patriotic citizen in a democracy, anyway? This little civics project had us really thinking about big ideas, high ideas...what fun!

So what if we had nothing? That only made it more apparent that we had to start with the small things, those little daily chores that would ultimately make a greater movement.

"Do what you can do today, and then go live the rest of your life." And with that, I faded off, doing what needed to be done...sleeping.

From then on I made our experiment in participatory democracy a small part of my daily life. Some days it would take minutes, some days it would be hours. But never too long, since I was just doing the small things. Small things like going down to the post office and making off with nearly all the Voter Registration forms they had on hand, as well as making all the phone calls that had to be made. And I was talking to whomever, whenever I could, about our proposed effort.

It was pretty positive, damn near unanimous. It didn't matter if I was talking with disabled citizens, their family members, or service providers. They all saw the sense and, I'm happy to say, the simple justice of it. It didn't hurt that I was registering people to vote on the spot. "Walking the walk" from the get-go.

Many with whom I spoke requested more registration forms. "You are the 'instant organizers' that are going to make all the difference," I'd tell them. "Now go home and register your families and friends." It was all pretty encouraging.

I found people were happy to explore this most unique path to power. Even if it was a chore of Herculean proportions, only accomplished by getting one registered voter at a time, it had the kind of contrasting balances that would make any Taoist smile.

Throughout this time I always remembered -- particularly when times were tough -- that that was the time to be the boldest. "Hell, yes! Together we can register almost three million disabled citizens in California and take power!" I would tell them. I would tell myself the same thing too, when in doubt.

If that didn't work, I would remind myself to be fearless and re-read Goethe. I kept a copy of his organizing wisdom magnetized to the door of my funky old refrigerator. I found that the presence of genius, along with a cold beer, tended to help sagging spirits.

I just wish I could remember who gave me the great man's words. I want you to know, your small act moved me, and providence, too. Boldly!

* 7 *

To be sure, he was one of the boldest. Be it as a political thinker, or a humane horticulturist, he lived his life fearlessly and kept an equilibrium in the center of chaos that I learned was mandatory for all good organizers. Life with haphazard able-bodied attendants sheds such grace.

That, and bringing in a crop. Like so many in the community, our love and respect for cannabis as a reliever of both physical and psychic pain makes us what we perhaps love most: outlaws. Harmless hemp hustlers, really, but outlaws, nonetheless.

Him, big and still as a mountain on wheels, growing it, and me, low to the earth on sticks, brokering it to other consenting adults, many with disabilities. We were a tribe and we helped all others in the tribe.

I admit it. We ignored the law. But I sure as hell didn't feel bad about that, after watching how the local and state authorities were ignoring a half-dozen laws by allowing that chain to remain. Six months and nothing. At least when we ignored the laws, we helped a lot of people. We gave away a lot of pot. Real outlaws do that.

We believed that Robin Hood was right. As the Mountain would often say, "You take from the rich and you give to the poor." Pot allowed us to do that, too. I say "too" because the first thing it allowed us to do was deal with our own conditions. He was paralyzed, me spastic, and both of us were bored. Marijuana relieved our aches and pain, and lifted our spirits.

The fact that growing and selling a little made us outlaws was just another silly fact of our already curious lives. Silly, since we're all basically good people.

In all the years that I hustled weed I can honestly say that I never met a bad or dangerous person, never saw a gun (unless it was a cop's), never got threatened, nor had much ripped off. That's something I can't say that about the straight business world. However, while sharing a joint, I have met a lot of pleasant people who pay their taxes in a timely fashion and work hard to raise and nurture their kids and communities.

Many, being farmers and gardeners, have a heightened consciousness when it comes to the environment and all the people in it. In other words, the vast majority of people who smoke grass are a bunch of nice people who wouldn't hurt a soul and are outlaws only because of their lifestyle. These "crimes of lifestyle" done in the privacy of our homes with other consenting adults is the only thing that makes us outlaws.

Outlaws like the Mountain. Big as one, this modern Robin Hood was paralyzed from the shoulders down, and, as I said, outside of being a grower and revolutionary thinker, he was no big threat to society, unless you consider treating adults like adults and staying out of their private affairs to be a threat. We didn't. We considered that the freedom our revolutionary forefathers fought and died for.

"They call us criminals, but we're not. We're outlaws, sweet humble outlaws." Mountain explained the distinction to me, "Criminals prey on poor people, steal from them, exploit them. Outlaws help and protect poor people. That's why so many Americans love the outlaw and the rebel, be it Robin Hood or Easy Rider." He paused to inhale from the tube I put to his lips.

"People forget," he continued, "or are never taught, that in the story, Robin Hood was fighting the Sheriff of Nottingham, who was busily exploiting and impoverishing the people of Nottingham.

"Remember," he exhaled, "John Dillinger's heyday was during the Depression when bankers were foreclosing on family farms and businesses. A fair amount of loot from these outlaws -- imaginary and real -- was given to the common poor person. Why do you think Robin Hood and John Dillinger were so hard to catch? They had a lot of help and the support of a whole lot of poor people. And they paid for that help."

So, true to our outlaw creed, we helped a lot of poor people too. Robin Hood was right!

The Mountain was a great organizer for another reason, too, one that was deeper than mere ideology.

Let's face it, any guy who, though paralyzed, can still get in a large crop of marijuana is one hell of an organizer and one I could learn from.

He, it turns out, was organizing disabled citizens, too. This epiphany came to me when I looked up at all my brother outlaws involved in cutting down the Mountain's last half dozen "good plants" and realized that everyone I was working with had a disability.

We were more than outlaws; we were a band of cripples. How joyous!

There was of course, the Mountain, directing and selecting from his wheelchair, slightly atilt on the backyard lawn. Then there was The Captain, who, burned and scarred in a fire at an early age, had a highly customized false arm and hand, a most clever contraption that gave him some semblance of a thumb. Next to him was an enthusiastic Mexican guy from the 'hood, who, as a kid, had jumped off a garage roof, missed the mattress, and shattered his leg; he had a prosthesis from the knee down.

And there was me, stumbling through the last of the crop on crutches. The Mountain's mighty gang of outlaws.

The Mountain joked, "It almost makes you want to get busted. Don't it? Can you see the cops trying to haul this gang in?"

That made me chuckle. Our experience had taught us that cops don't like incarcerating cripples. We're a real hassle.

In jail we've got to be segregated, watched, and walked everywhere, and everybody in the joint is so afraid we're going to slip, fall, and sue that all any of them want is for us is to make bail and beat the rap. See, inside the joint -- prison, that is -- with all our "special needs," exercise, and care, we're an even bigger expense and pain in the ass.

So all you crippled pot farmers and dealers out there, don't kill anybody and be polite in custody -- most likely they're looking for a way to keep you out of jail. Secure in such knowledge, we spent a relaxed weekend harvesting and trimming the Mountain's crop.

It was a warm late October morning, with pot dust, baskets of garf weed, and drying bud all about us. The Mountain and I were enjoying late coffee, having slept in after a night of manicuring the nine-tenths of the crop that we had picked earlier.

With The Captain still snoring on the couch, Mountain and I took coffee and bong hits and adjusted to the heat of the day by philosophizing about power, pot, and voter registration.

He genuinely liked the name we came up with and the acronym it produced. Nice thing, too, that I didn't have to explain to him how democracy could, with a little organizing on our part, work miracles for the disabled. He already knew.

He also knew voter registration was a critical first step. He told me the story of how he had been trying to get the public utilities to turn unused homes on land they owned in East L.A. into low income housing for seniors and disabled.

It was an idea bred of necessity, as the Mountain was, himself, in need of a home. Shrewd and well educated, he not only got himself a home, but he got a lot of other people housing too. Talk about enlightened self-interest! Ultimately he turned his solo effort into an ongoing program, run through the East L.A. Independent Living Center. Nice old people, nice old houses. Much like the one we were sitting in then, with the smell of fresh-cut marijuana and fresh-made pot smoke mingling with the scent of fresh-brewed coffee and toast.

"Voter Registration is what did it," he said, between hearty tokes off the accessible bong. "No one would return a phone call or give us the time of day, until we started registering voters. It was amazing. The minute the local political idiots heard that we had registered about three hundred people and were getting those three hundred to register their families, everything started to happen. The city got involved, the utilities took us seriously -- 'cause the city did -- and within the year we had our first eight houses refurbished."

He thought for a moment, then, "And I don't care what people say about noble causes and good community PR; it was the votes that moved the whole lot of them," he laughed. "No matter what you're doing or fighting for, organize your vote! Only then will you be perceived as a threat to the political establishment and, therefore, be taken seriously. That's how it works."

"Our votes have got to hang over their heads like the sword of Damocles," I agreed.

"Oh yeah! A little bit of fear means a whole lot of power," he chuckled, enveloping himself in smoke.

"That's why we've got to be non-partisan and issued-oriented, so we can attract all disabled citizens," I urged.

"That's right," the Mountain agreed, "one big tent."

"There's no power in partisanship," I said, slugging back a little coffee. "Think about it, Mount, whoever you're partisan for takes you for granted and whoever your partisan against writes you off, so, consequently, you have no power or influence with anyone really."

"However," the Mountain said, seeing the point clearly, "if the powers that be have to deal with you on an issue by issue basis, you always retain some power and influence."

"You got it!" I exclaimed, "Exactly why UP has to be ruthlessly non-partisan!"

"I like the way you say that," the big guy offered, "Ruthlessly non-partisan." He said the words slowly, letting them roll off his tongue, like a threat. "What if we did throw partisan politics aside and let the chips fall where they may on the issues?" he asked rhetorically. "Think about that."

"I have," I told him.

"Now that would be a threat."

"I see it as more of a promise than a threat," I said, thinking of Skeleton John for a brief second, "which, when you think about it, is the worst kind of threat and the only real power that counts, right? The promises you keep. We've got to get the disabled to promise to register and vote and then keep that promise, come what may."

"That, and using the permanent absentee ballot to mail in their vote and you've got a revolution. A god-damned democratic revolution for the price of a postage stamp?" he laughed.

"That's right, Mountain," I said, surprised I hadn't thought about it earlier. The permanent absentee ballot for disabled citizens was just the mechanism we needed to deliver that vote. I was already using one myself.

Like a bolt out of the blue, sometimes, you get so caught up in the big picture stuff that you forget the small stuff right under your nose. "The permanent absentee ballot for disabled citizens comes before every election and would effectively take care of the 'come what may,'" I said, "in addition, the PAB gets our vote out early, always a plus with politicians."

"Yes, it is," he replied.

"You're right though, my friend, for the price of a postage stamp disabled citizens could have real political power." The pot was making me euphoric, "Damn, bro, we've got to do this," I sighed, seeing my future. "It's too cool."

"It's the drugs," he replied.

"And I thought it was the philosophy," I said with mock sadness. "You know, democracy, poor people taking power, using it justly, et cetera, et cetera."

"Taking power and using it justly," he repeated between bites of toast being fed to him by his attendant. "Oh man," he said suddenly, "you're dangerous. You're talking about organizing poor people!"

"Yes, I am! And ain't it grand? And we're dangerous," I corrected him. "This is a democratic movement and there's no 'I' in democracy. We're in this together, brother!"

"I was afraid of that," he said, a cool breeze scattering his graying locks with crumbs of toast.

"If you can't count on your outlaw buddies," I teased him, "who can you count on? You're the one that told me Robin Hood was right. Remember?"

"Who else but you would take it seriously?"

"I don't know, all them other poor people," I offered.

"Probably," he said.

"So you agree it's a good idea to start a voter registration project to register, inform, and get out the vote of disabled citizens?" I asked him.

"You mean empowering the powerless?"

"Basically."

"Hell, yes," he said. "Should have been done long ago. Just thinking about millions of gimps voting together, of wielding that much power, is almost too much."

"Bigger than the NRA," I said, toasting him, clinking his bong with my coffee cup.

"And much mellower," he said. "Only thing bigger and mellower than our vote is the pot vote."

"I think they're just about one and the same." We laughed at the truth of the statement.

"Could gimps and grass cause a progressive sea change in the politics of the 21st century?" I asked him.

He thought for a second. "The face of the electorate is changing. It's got more of a bug-eyed shit-eater's grin on it," he said, grinning bug-eyed at me, as his attendant unhooked his bib and dusted away the last bits of charred bread with it.

"The Sixties generation is growing up," I ventured, finishing my coffee.

"About time," he said. "I don't know if gimps and grass can save the world, but I do know the possibility of it will keep quite a few right-wing think-tanks up at night...and that ain't all bad."

For a couple of old outlaws, the future looked grand, and with the unrelenting zeal of Robin Hood in search of his merry men, we woke up the Captain and went back to manicure the last tenth.

* 8 *

In spite of all the big ideas, tasty marijuana, and bug-eyed conversations, the truth was we still had nothing outside of a democratic idea and a blatant need to protect our rights.

We had no money. No political connections. No power.

Okay, so we had nothing tangible. We did have 828,000 good reasons in the form of voting age disabled citizens living in L.A. to give it a go -- to organize the last great minority group of American society, the one group whose needs, when met, would also provide for most others. We had the promise that friends, disabled and otherwise, would offer us help to start -- however we were to start.

Whenever I am a little overwhelmed by a certain task, or the long odds of a necessary outcome, I return to philosophy and, most importantly, I remember the Four Noble Truths of the Buddha.

Whether you give these "truths" religious significance or not, I find that Buddha has, at the very least, given us the best test possible to soothe our often aching human psyches. This best test of modern psychology, now as then, is simple to understand and utilize.

Noble Truth One: All life is suffering.

Yep, we disabled understand that better than most.

Okay, All life is suffering. Get used to it, or as Buddha goes on to say: "Escape the suffering, by giving up Noble Truths 2, 3, and 4." Fear, ego, and desire, respectively. It's that simple.

Stop being afraid. Do not be driven by pride or hubris. Give up expectation and anticipation.

Consequently, whenever I am burdened, hesitant, or confused, I ask myself, "What am I afraid of?" Usually, very little is worthy of real fear; that's a real life lesson from someone who has lived with what some would call a severe disability his entire life.

Nearly fearless, then I ask: "Is my ego hurt? If so, why? Does it really matter what others say or think about me?" Consider the source, of course, but you'll find that usually such things don't matter. Carry on. And don't take things too personally.

And last, desire brought on by lingering anticipation and unmet expectation. What do I want that I do not have? The greatest angst of western man.

Most sweet and wicked desire. Western thought really gets Buddha screwed up here, because we tend to see desire in terms of denial. We are virtuous because we deny ourselves the wine, women and song. That kind of thing.

Problem is, Buddha wasn't into denial. He had tried that route early on, becoming a rotting ascetic for three years. Finally, he realized that this was a sure fired way to dizziness, not nirvana.

When Buddha says give up desire, he means give up expectation and anticipation. When you do that, you give up disappointment. When you give up expectation and anticipation and thus disappointment, everything you receive is a windfall. Buddha, as far as I can tell, was much more into shedding disappointment than promoting denial.

Seems he was saying, "If the wine is there, drink it. If the woman is there, love her and then sing your song." The point of "giving up desire," as the Buddha instructs, is to be just as happy the next night...when you have no wine to drink or woman to love, but just a song to sing.

When your happiness is not contingent upon what you have or don't have, but on your state of mind, regardless, then you are transcending suffering, and Buddha and I both drink to you, whether we have wine or not.

As you can tell by my customized Buddhist beliefs, I am no official Buddhist. But then, I read somewhere that when people came to the Buddha and asked him 'The Way,' he would respond, "I cannot tell you the way. The way is the way you find it, when you give up fear, ego and desire." So, I have a feeling Buddha wasn't much of "official Buddhist," either.

From what I know, it got "official" about 600 years after his death with the monks. Before that it was all fairly free-form spontaneous love and compassion -- like the Buddha himself.

To save myself from any hassle whatsoever when it comes to stating spiritual preferences, I have taken up that worthwhile habit of Woody Guthrie's. When I fill in the box on any form that asks for "Religion," I put the word "All." I think Buddha would have been cool with that.

Then it came to me, the idea of no expectations or anticipation. Steady progress alone was a basic truth of grassroots organizing, particularly when it came to the disabled.

With a singing Buddha crooning in my head, I remembered that old Buddhist maxim about fear. When one is afraid, turn, face the fear, and walk directly into it.

"Be fearless," I told myself. "Minimize disappointments." Screw-ups, setbacks, and mistakes are inevitable. Fading off, I realized how lucky I was. The disabled community, screwed up and blessed mistakes that we are, have a very deep understanding of setbacks and overcoming them.

We have a living, breathing, real life understanding of the inevitable.

In the West, it would be ironic. In the East, harmony. Such is the lullaby of a failed Buddhist.

I committed myself to taking the first step.

* 9 *

I could hear Goethe laughing at me, for no sooner did I commit than I was told how to do it. And from the wildest quarter -- the U.S. Government, in the guise of the U.S. Postal Service.

Our first real stroke of luck came out of the blue, just like the call I awoke to from my friend Carrie.

"I heard about your voting project and I'll be on your side of town. I have something for you," she said pleasantly.

"Okay," I said, half awake and half surprised.

"Meet you at the Rose café at three?" she offered.

"Okay," I accepted.

"Go back to sleep."

"Okay."

I didn't. I just wondered until three what she had for me. Carrie was a much-admired social worker who cared more about civil rights than case management. She created more proof of that over coffee and cake as she told me about "the free franking privilege for blind and disabled."

"The what?" I asked.

She pulled out a photocopied page and read: "Free material for the blind and the physically handicapped. Postal regulation E040 allows disabled and blind citizens and organizations to mail educational material postage free as long as the type is 14-point or larger," she said with cheerful nonchalance.

"It allows disabled groups to mail educational material for free?" I asked, catching my breath at the potential, "and all I have to do is print it with 14-point type?"

I was more than a little shocked, and happily so. Such a "franking privilege" would be of immeasurable help to us in terms of getting the word -- and materials -- out to the greater disabled community. I could see UP mailing every voting age disabled citizen in California a voter registration form as well as an application for permanent absentee ballot status.

"You're sure about this?" I asked.

"Yes, check it out," she urged, handing me the sheet.

There it was, in profound black and white; I was looking at the actual text.
Still, such luck was hard to believe because this was so big. Being a US Postal Service regulation, it was good all over the country, too.

I realized that the free mailing privilege, coupled with the mail-in ballot, greatly enhanced our ability to foster a most democratic social movement, with disabled citizens truly in the lead. "Wait 'til I tell Mountain about this!" I thought to myself.

"Now there's a chance! A real one-two punch for democracy!" I told Carrie. "With this free franking privilege, we can register and educate our vote, and, with the permanent absentee ballot for disabled citizens, we can deliver that vote. Unbelievable!"

I was astounded by the simple implications of it all. "You know, Carrie, with these two privileges at our disposal, now there are no excuses for disabled people not taking power," I laughed.

"I thought you'd see it something like that!" Carrie said. "But please, it's hard to take a revolutionary seriously when he has chocolate hanging from his lip."

"How sweet it is," I said, doing a poor Gleason impersonation. "I want to make sure I got it right, 'cause we're talking bloodless democratic revolution here. You're saying that all I've got to do to use the mailing privilege is keep it civic and educational, and put everything in 14-point type or better?"

"Yes, I think so," she said with a cheerful firmness, sipping a frothy coffee.

"Talk about a gift from the gods," I said as I wiped away the creamy remains of my last gift from them.

"You, old friend, as a developmentally disabled adult, can use it, and better yet, UP, as an organization that works with developmentally disabled citizens, can use it," she told me as she looked at her watch.

"Oh, hey Carrie! I'm not developmentally disabled," I corrected her. "I have cerebral palsy, not mental retardation."

"You don't have to be mentally retarded to be DD," she informed me, "Just having CP qualifies you."

"Really!" I said truly surprised as Carrie delivered yet another bit of divine information, "I'm DD? I'm developmentally disabled? I thought that it was just a polite term for mental retardation."

"A common misconception," she said.

"Thanks for straightening me out...I think," I replied, only half teasing. "Now straighten me out on something else," I said, looking over the page of guidelines, "I understand why they'd make you use large type for the visually impaired, but why the physically handicapped?"

"Many physically handicapped or developmentally disabled adults need the larger type in order for their brains to recognize the letters," she informed me.

"Ooohhh... So that's why they stuck in the physically handicapped. Bless their charitable little hearts."

As I walked home, down Main Street, I realized that, due to Carrie's sharing of knowledge, there was a now real chance that we could, in fact, organize the disabled vote. It was still a long shot, but due to the free franking privilege, and the mail-in ballot, the odds just got a lot better.

"Roll the dice," I told myself. "Take your shot!" Organizing disabled citizens to take power in a most democratic fashion was now possible. We had the means. I never thought I'd be so happy to be DD either. Hell, with a free franking privilege and the PAB, I was proud to be so.

All thanks to Carrie, we had begun to figure out how.

* 10 *

Over the months to follow, I began to wonder if the gods were with me, or just egging me on. Nothing happened. Absolutely nothing. I would sit up in Sal's apartment, stare out his big picture window, and alternate between feeling like a second class citizen and summoning up the boxer in me to pugnaciously plot how to overcome that despicable neighborhood oxymoron below: a chained-off handicap parking spot.

I met Sal during my days as a rock and roll singer and all the hard partying that entailed. He was a real character. A bit unctuous and slippery in his business dealings, Sal rationalized it all away with a dog eat dog mentality, as well all the drugs and booze necessary to deal with the crueler aspects of such a mentality. An Italian boy to the core, this made him sentimental, tyrannical, and generous.

Sal liked to carry himself like a tough guy, but I think, underneath all the bravado, he desperately wanted to be loved much more than feared. He just relied on the latter, when hurt in the former. In between all that, he liked to party and do real estate deals as fast and loose as possible.

Truth is, he could be a lot of fun. Even when his definition of fun included going down to the Coastal Commission to look up conditional use permits.

Which, as mentioned, was what we were going to do the day I went to have a cup of coffee at the café and await my tardy friend. Had he been on time, I would have never tried to park in the chained off blue zone -- and none of this would have come to pass.

Talk about the dumbest of luck. Thank you, Salvador.

It confirms my belief that the Fates do strange things -- they give you weird enemies like the kooks at the café, and even weirder friends like Sal. And now it was Sal, who, standing at his big picture window, spotted the owner of the café, down on the boardwalk.

"There he is," he said, taking a drag off his cigarette. "There's your boy -- the owner, Daar."

It was funny how Sal, so instrumental in helping me, couldn't have cared less about the chain. Most people would have gotten a kick out of helping bring it down. Not Sal.

Nothing that high-minded for him. He liked to see a good fight, as opposed to fighting one, and that, I'm sure, is why he pointed Mr. Daar out to me. I walked over to the window and looked down on Mr. Daar. He was a rumpled little man from that vantage point. I needed a closer look. I bolted out the door and down the stairs, my metal crutches slung over my arms, rhythmically clanging like busted bells as they hit the concrete stairs behind me.

Here was my chance to reason with Mr. Daar, I figured. Neighbor to neighbor. As I made my clangorous way down the stairs, I sincerely hoped to appeal to his better nature and, much to Sal's regret, avoid a fight.

Daar was walking between his café and Sal's place. Hearing all the commotion he looked over as I turned at the bottom of the stairs and we stared at each other for just a second -- me sizing him up, him wondering what all the racket was about.

"Mr. Daar," I called to him.

"Yeess," he said, his speech slightly accented.

"I am your neighbor, sir," I said respectfully, "and, as a disabled citizen, I would very much like to use your handicapped parking spot whenever I patronize your restaurant."

"What is this?" he asked, surprised.

"It's a request, sir."

"This is private property," he said gruffly.

"And it's the law, sir," I said firmly.

"So, now you're going to tell me the law?" he asked, perturbed.

"No sir," I sighed, "I just hope you'll do the right thing and let me or any other disabled citizen who wishes to eat at your restaurant use the handicapped parking. That's all," I said evenly. I thought I was getting through to him, putting a face on it for him -- and a very reasonable one at that.

He looked me over for a moment rather disapprovingly, then asked, "What do you want from me? Hot dogs? Forget about all that," he said, waving off the zone with a flick of his hand. "I will give you hot dogs!" he said, ill-tempered.

I took a step back. I needed a second to think. "Did this guy just try to bribe me?" I asked myself. "And worse, did he just try to bribe me with hot dogs?"

I took another step back. I had to fight my initial impulse to punch him upside his head with a crutch. "Hot-dogs!" I thought to myself. "This audacious fool." All my diplomatic skills melted as it became apparent to me just how Mr. Daar operated. Everything was a bribe and a buy-off. No wonder no one in city government had done anything. They were all bought off. Suddenly I knew why that screaming city building inspector got so upset!

I comforted myself with the knowledge that Mr. Daar was about to find out that some people can't be bought off.

"No, Mr. Daar," I said, containing myself, "I don't want your silly hot dogs. I want that damn chain to come down. Do I make myself clear?" I had to fight real hostility.

"This is private property. Screw you!" he shouted.

"No, smart guy! This is a public accommodation," I shouted back. "And I'm going to do everything legally within my power to bring down that chain. Got that, hot shot?"

"Are you threatening me?" he asked.

My next flashback is of ol' Skeleton John, the café's manager. "These guys must practice together," I said to myself. That being the case, I figured I might as well practice my John Wayne persona one more time and give what was fast becoming my stock reply to all victimized bullies.

"I don't make threats, sir, I make promises. And I promise you that that chain is coming down." I used this as my exit line.

All the way down to Long Beach, Sal laughed about it -- being bribed with hot dogs! It really was embarrassing. Sal loved it.

"I'll have to try that next time I'm arguing with a city inspector," he said.

I sat there and said nothing.

After a time, Sal asked in his most sincere voice, "A hot dog for your thoughts..."

"Very funny, Sal, very funny," I replied.

Down at the Coastal Commission, after we pulled the permits Sal wanted, I pulled Daar's.

Turned out my "neighbor" was in violation of all his permits as it concerned parking. The chain around the handicapped spot was just the beginning. Daar was supposed to provide parking for all his patrons in his larger lot, but he had chained that off, too. He was messing with everybody.

Weird business philosophy, if you ask me.

And the paralegal in me imagined what Daar's mouthpiece would contend: "We discriminate against everybody, so we aren't discriminating against anybody. You're being treated just like everyone else."

It's the old "All men are created equal as long as they are treated the same" argument.

But I knew, as the "protected class" under the blue zone statutes, we, the disabled, were not to be treated like everyone else, for only we disabled are allowed to park in blue zones.

Thus, when Daar locked everyone out of his parking lot and tried to palm that off as equal and nondiscriminatory, he was still violating my rights specifically as a disabled person entitled to use handicapped parking.

What Daar demonstrated -- against disabled and non-disabled alike -- was what the law calls "a consistent pattern of unlawful conduct."

"Hot-dogs!" I said to myself again, "I'll bet the thing that wasn't consistent in that pattern was the hot dogs." I knew it took a lot more than hot dogs to get away with such massive permit and parking violations around Venice Beach, where parking is at an absolute premium 24/7. That had to take money. Real money. A very pretty penny, indeed. Needless to say, even though he couldn't buy me off, the hot dogs left a bad taste in my mouth. It showed the depth of his disdain for us. His complete loathing. Hot dogs, lousy hot dogs -- if it weren't so sad, I would have laughed.

As an all too failed Buddhist, I realized it was time to go to court. It wasn't just me anymore. I began to wonder again how many others, much worst off than me, had been denied. How many others never even got a chance to ask that the chain be dropped, because within the narrow confines of the alleyway they were unable to even get out of their cars or vans to make such a request? How many? It galled me to no end.

The next day I went to the law library, got out the pleadings and practice book for civil rights litigation, and did what most lawyers do. I copied the standard complaint out of

the book and (with yellow legal pads in hand) began to fill in
the blanks with my particulars.

* 11 *

I was quickly realizing you can't very well run a voter
registration project by swiping VR forms from the post office.
Fact is, you can't do any real voter registration until you make
a trip down to the county Registrar of Voters office.

"Why didn't I think of it earlier?" I asked myself, as I
hung up the phone after talking with yet another group that
wanted "someone from UP" to come out and talk with them.

I just kept saying, "Okay."

Mountain was right. You can't just talk to people.
You've got to do something with them. Registering voters is a
good first step for most people. It gave me -- and them --
something to do from the start.

I liked that. Doing what we're supposed to do, right off
the bat -- registering voters.

It also made us appear action oriented. And what's
more, action oriented in a way that really does make people
more powerful, if they take it seriously: by voting.

The power is not just in the voting, either, but in the
fact that the local political establishment always takes notice
of whoever is registering voters. It manifests clout. In the
eyes of the local elite, it is possible to deal with real
power...the people in government!

It reminded me of my old man.

"The way they see it, you're taking their power for
yourself when you're out there registering voters," he used to
tell me. He was a local politician of some repute, both ill and
enlightened, so he knew a good bit about elections, having
been cheated out of one or two.

"Every time you register some poor wretch to vote," you're literally creating power," I can still hear him say over his morning eggs and toast. "The powers that be know most people vote for the people who registered them." He went on, "They also know it often doesn't take many votes to shift the balance of power in a lot of elections. Registration efforts often produce the very votes that control that balance of power; hence your clout, my boy."

He dipped his toast deep into the yolk and savored it as much as he did his clout, which was considerable among the many Judges, County Commissioners, and State Representatives he'd helped get elected. Even while in the State Senate himself, he was a hell of a campaign manager.

"What counts is your ability to win elections, and, if you're going to win elections, you've got to register your people to vote." He smiled at the thought, for, at its essence, that was the simple strategy that got my old man elected to the state legislature. He registered and got out the vote of a wild coalition of "hillbillies and black shop workers," and, with the help of LBJ's coattails, pulled off a tight upset,

"We've both organized the downtrodden," I thought to myself. "Now, the question is," I noted, coming back to reality, "Will my oppressed people respond?"

Who could know? The only way to find out was to begin registering them to vote. "Do that and politicians will slobber all over you," dear ol' Dad used to say, "and if you register, educate..." He'd stop right there and wink at me. "And get out enough votes, you may even get a politician or two to do the right thing, maybe."

"Right thing?" I would ask, as he folded his morning paper. I wanted to know what was the right thing?

"Let's start with not stealing the election," he would say with an all too knowing smile. Ol' Dad had learned early on to register a lot of people to vote. He'd tell you in his empathic fashion, "You've got to register more rascals than they can steal." He did most of the time. With that ringing endorsement of democracy from so long ago in my head, I called the telephone help desk.

"Los Angeles Registrar of Voters, please," I asked politely.

She had trouble finding it. "It's not in L.A.," she said finally, "It's the Los Angeles County Registrar of Voters. It's in Norwalk."

"Where's Norwalk?"

"About 40 miles east of L.A."

"That's L.A.?"

"That's L.A. County."

"So that's where the other 800,000 voting age cripples in L.A. live," I thought to myself. "I didn't realize L.A. was so big," I said to her.

"Here's your num--" the automated number voice cut her off. I took down the number.

I called the Registrar and told the receptionist I wanted to come down and pick up some voter registration forms. When I told her that I worked with a small voter registration project for disabled citizens, she said, "Oh, wait a minute, you want to talk to Mr. McDougal."

"Okay."

"He works with all the independent voter registration projects."

"Okay." She put me on hold.

Eventually it rang through. Donald McDougal answered with a slight trace of a Georgian accent that had the charm of the South without the twang of the backwoods.

I told him a bit about who and what UP was, disabled, ruthlessly non-partisan, etc., and how I wanted to pick up some VR forms and any other materials that would help us do proper voter registration.

"You've made my day," he told me. I felt like I was on "The Price Is Right" as he gave me a big "Come on down!"

The next day I drove to Norwalk, and when I told Mr. McDougal that I was surprised that the L.A. County Registrar of Voters office was in Norwalk, and not in L.A. proper, he began to educate me on just how big Los Angeles really is.

"This county is 400 square miles," he said as he pulled an assortment of materials from a bulging package that he had put together for me, "largest one in the United States."

He handed me voter registration forms, applications for permanent absentee ballot status, and booklets in a variety of languages on all the different services and materials that the Registrar has for blind and disabled voters (ballots on tape, curbside voting, etc.).

As he went through it all, I realized that this was one of the few governmental agencies that had already been dealing with the specific needs of the disabled in a proactive way.

"Let me tell you," McDougal went on, "we want everyone who's legally entitled to vote, to vote, no ifs, ands, or buts about it. And I want you to know," he said with accented emphasis, "we like what you're doing."

"Thank you," I said, "we're trying to figure it out."

"Well, that's great, and we're here to help." With that, he handed me a small stack of orange papers, the Los Angeles Voter Registration Guide. This would become my voter registration bible.

"Now this will tell you everything, and I mean everything, you need to know about properly filling out the voter registration affidavit."

"Voter registration affidavit?" I asked. "You mean the voter registration form, right?"

"That's what the public calls it," he said as he sat down at his desk and picked up one of the forms. "But to tell you the truth, that there's a legal affidavit, with the full weight of the law behind it. That's why it's so important that you know what you're doing and get people to fill it out properly."

"Oh, absolutely," I agreed, "that's what we want to do."

"It's the weight of law behind them -- makes it a felony, punishable by three years in jail, to fill one out fraudulently," he informed me.

"We don't want that," I assured him.

"Well now," he said in that way that lets you know he's educated a lot of other people on this matter, "that's not really your overriding concern -- fraud that is -- if some one fills out a voter registration affidavit in a fraudulent manner, the onus is on them, not you. Your job is to get all the necessary information, in all the right blanks."

"Okay, got it, sir."

"You're not an immigration cop or a mental health official," he graciously informed me, "If someone tells you they're a citizen, or they are competent to vote, you just give them an affidavit and a little help, if they need it."

"That's our intent, sir."

"Well, good. It's all right there in the book. Call me if you have any other questions."

"You've made L.A.'s 828,000 disabled citizens of voting age very happy," I told him.

I dug old Mac right from the start, 'cause, like us, he wanted to include people, not exclude them. He made it very clear we didn't have to worry about the citizenship status of those we got to fill out forms, and that we could work with the great bulk of the DD community, particularly those voters with mild to moderate cognitive disabilities -- the ones that get counted out too often.

What he said next floored me, coming from an able-bodied person and a government worker, at that. It was so unlike the city of L.A.

"You don't lose your right to vote just because you have a mental or physiological disability, and we want people to know that. To lose your right to vote," he went on, "you have to be declared incompetent by a judge, and that," he said rather conspiratorially, "is something that judges are loathe to do."

"Really," I said, still in slight amazement.

"You've got to be pretty whacked," he said, "for a judge to pull your right to vote."

"Jeez, I can't thank you enough, sir," I responded as I stuck all the material he had given me into my bag and flipped the long straps of it over the top of my crutch.

"Then don't," he said. "Just do a good job. And don't forget, we're here to help. Say, how many disabled voters are there in L.A., again?" he asked as I headed for the door.

"828,000 disabled citizens of voting age," I told him.

"You know," he surmised, "with the last city election's turnout of 15%, you could have elected anybody you wanted to the Board of Supervisors if you would have gotten out 10,000 of those voters, which is about what?" he asked himself, "Two, two and a half percent of your vote," he answered. "You're onto something, my friend. Good luck."

Ten thousand votes! Again, I was stunned by the numbers, by how little we really had to register and get out to vote in order to have a tremendous impact in a city as large as Los Angeles. Why, the average Supervisor's district contained more people than half the states of this country and dealt with billions of dollars in allocations of money and resources. It's no small feat to have an influence on them.

But weren't they going to be running the county's "attendant care" program? Talk about a direct impact on the disabled community. Of course -- according to Mr. McDougal -- with just two to three percent of our vote in L.A., we could have a most direct impact on them. We could decide who would get elected.

"Thanks, Mac."

As it turned out, not only had old McDougal given me all the voter registration material I needed, but he also gave me a good portion of what was fast becoming my stump speech.

It became part of the mantra.

I began to sing out everywhere I could that no citizen loses the right to vote just because of a physical or mental difficulty, without a judge's permission, and, as old Mac said, judges are loathe to make that determination.

"You all count!" I would tell them. "All 828,000 of you. Don't think so? Well, let me tell you," I would say, all full of gusto and Mr. McDougal's facts, "If we could get 10,000 of us voting in our Supervisorial races we could elect anyone, including a disabled citizen, to the Board of Supervisors. Just two percent can do that."

Imagine that. They did, because I finished with, "Who wants to be a part of that two percent? Who wants to make that kind of difference? Who wants to register to vote?"

You should have seen those spastic and plastic hands fly up. Thanks again, Mr. McDougal. As I registered each of them to vote, I heard my old man's voice in the back of my head: "Just register more votes than they can steal or suppress. "

Then I realized, as I helped another sister make her "X" on the dotted line, "If we register enough of us, they'll never be able to steal another election again."

We are everywhere; our common interests are one and the same and ultimately good for just about everyone. Those kinds of numbers, and that kind of reach and reason, make any election we participate in almost too big to be stolen.

Thanks, Daddy-O!

* 12 *

I liked Thompson's place. It was a bottom floor apartment in the pink stucco monster. Once it was Fatty Arbuckle's home.

The old mansion/apartment building itself had an upstairs, but Fatty -- being a rotund man -- didn't care much for it. He lived "ranch style" downstairs, and unbeknownst to him, built the first barrier-free apartments in Santa Monica -- at least on the ground floor.

Thus, Thompson's apartment was a joy. It had no stairs. It was low, dark, and cool, with strings of small Christmas lights slung about the walls year round, the kind that, when you bump into them head first in June, cause you to catch your breath.

Doing so, I think again of the hitch-hiking Monk and wonder, as I always do whenever I catch my breath (for the Monk had told me this was a sign), if I'm just being put on notice that I'm participating in divinity once again. "Pay attention," I told myself.

As I pushed past the low slung sparkles and into the cool ambiance that Thompson prefers, I figured we were doing just that. We drank and smoked, as is the custom in such low, dark, and cool places, and began to figure out quite literally how to take nothing and turn it into something.

I showed Thompson all the materials I had picked up from Mr. McDougal.

He told me: "You read it." Then taking one of the voter registration affidavits in his well-callused hands, he cooed comically, "This is the power."

"That thing has got the full weight of the law behind it," I said, trying to sound as authoritative and relaxed as Mr. McDougal. But not.

"I can feel that," he said in mock seriousness, holding the affidavit now as if it weighed a hundred pounds. He gasped. "Guess it's time to hold a meeting."

"Now you're getting dangerous," I told him.

After some thought, and very little discussion, we realized a meeting would formalize things greatly. Making it official with "a meeting" would give me something else to talk about and invite people to when I was out and about "agitating."

"Okay," we said in unplanned unison. We cracked a few brews and looked at the calendar. This was August, and after meeting with anyone who would have us over the next two months, we figured we would have enough interest to call a general meeting.

"How about October 20th?" Thompson inquired, looking at his calendar. "Okay?"

"Yep, okay."

Shortly thereafter, I booked the back room of the local Independent Living Center. Thompson swiped a few press releases from the wastebasket at work and, copying blithely both structure and format, he filled in the particulars of our event, stuck a "-30-" at the bottom of the page and presto, change-o! A new press release. He sent it to all the local papers.

Things were picking up; more people were calling. Word was out. From the number of calls, we not only gauged interest but began to realize that the disabled community had a hell of an infrastructure in place. Because of that, they had a lot of meetings.

At these meetings they were all too happy to have me -- "a consumer" – speak, first, I'm sure, just to break up the boredom, but also because we actually had a compelling idea: Gimps unite! Democracy was meant for you! As easy as selling power to the powerless was, there were a few bumps in the road.

I noticed right off that I was getting introduced as a "consumer" an awful lot. This did not sit well with me, as the concept of "consumer" was a subservient one at best, and one I wanted to get away from. I saw that a few inside and outside the community needed to be educated.

I tried to be diplomatic. But it wasn't always easy to do so with "Staff" who've had years of kudos for all their "fine work helping the handicapped." After years of such puffery they don't always take criticism well, constructive though it may be.

If they introduced me as a "consumer," the devil in me couldn't help but start off the speech by pointing out that: "Consumers consume for the benefit for the producers," and that "Citizens have rights and responsibilities." Then I would ask: "Which term empowers you?"

In that moment most quiet disabled consumers became vocal disabled citizens, with a new eagerness to understand and utilize those rights and responsibilities.

The reaction was always the same, and it was a thing to behold, even if a few of the social workers grumbled, "We didn't mean anything bad by using that word."

Of course not. Like most of us, though, they haven't thought it through. Ask yourself when was the last time you looked at a newspaper and counted how many times they used the word "consumer" as opposed to "citizen."

We've all been a bit brainwashed. I enjoyed shaking some of that water out of their heads. It's also rather easy to sell any people on being powerful. But when these people have historically been the most powerless people, when they begin to perceive themselves as powerful...well, that's pathos -- that's the stuff of novels.

Speaking of novels, or, at least, novel ideas, I'd read somewhere that Ralph Reed's real stroke of genius was in using the infrastructure of the fundamentalist church to organize his right wing vote. The numerous invitations I received to spread the word of power politics and poetic justice gave ample proof to both the size and scope of the "infrastructure" in place to serve the needs of California's disabled.

You didn't have to be as smart as Mr. Reed to understand that in order to reach, register, and mobilize the state's nearly three million adult disabled citizens, you had to use that infrastructure.

I did. And everywhere I spoke over the next few months, I invited my fellow citizens (disabled and otherwise) to join us on Oct. 20th, to help us launch UP. Hundreds of people were expressing support through a myriad of programs and groups.

In the middle of all this barnstorming, to sober my enthusiasm and remind me of the dark side to all this, I got a call returned from the California Attorney General's office.

Luis Verdi to be exact, the assistant Attorney General in charge of civil rights, no less. He couldn't believe my story. "You're kidding," he said more than once without laughing. "He won't unlock a simple lock and let you use a properly designated handicapped parking zone."

"Nope," I said, "it's a textbook example of a continuing public nuisance," hoping I didn't sound too pompous.

"I'll say," he said with an air of lingering disbelief. "I can't believe his lawyers haven't told Mr. Daar that it's the ease with which he could remedy the situation that makes him liable for each and every separate violation, day in and day out. That's potentially a lot of money."

"I don't think he listens to his lawyers. I think he likes to tell them what to do," I offered, "a la John D. Rockefeller." I could see we were both up on our public nuisance law.

"Want to take the case?" I asked.

"I can't," he said plainly. He then went on to explain that, as he was in charge of protecting the civil rights of Californian's thirty-three million citizens, he couldn't bring a lawsuit in every case of discrimination.

I think he could hear my heart sink over the phone, because he didn't stop there. With an emphatic: "However," he went on to explain that I could sue Daar on behalf of myself and millions of other disabled citizens, using California's Private Attorney General Act."

"The what?" I asked, my heart surfacing again.

"The Private Attorney General Act," he repeated.

"Okay," I said, wanting to see light at the end of the tunnel.

Mr. Verdi explained. In California, whenever someone is breaking the law, and the proper authorities fail to do anything about it, an injured party can bring a private lawsuit on behalf of themselves – as well as any other people in that protected class of people who are similarly injured.

In this case I could bring a lawsuit forth on behalf of myself and all the other disabled citizens who patronize Venice Beach and its boardwalk cafés.

"That's literally thousands. The asphalt boardwalk is great for wheelchairs," I told him.

"Makes sense," Verdi agreed. "You also have to show that the damage done to you, as the protected class, was different 'in kind' from the general public, or else it wouldn't be discriminatory."

"Different in kind, huh?"

"You've got that," Verdi said, and went on to point out that even if we negate the fact that Daar is supposed to have public, as well as, disabled parking, it is far easier for the able-bodied general public to find other parking and walk back to the restaurant than it would be for a disabled citizen.

"Good point," I agreed.

"That was the reason for the blue zones in the first place," he said, "and yes, you bet, chaining them off harms you and your fellow disabled citizens in a dramatically different way than it does the non-disabled. I'd say that damage is different in kind."

"From your mouth to God's ears," I told him, and then quickly corrected myself, "I mean a jury's ears."

"I doubt it will go that far," Verdi said. "I mean, once you file and serve the complaint on this guy, that will probably be it. Who'd want to fight such a thing? I just can't believe he would."

"Me neither. I've already been working on the complaint," I informed him. "I'm going to hit him with a violation of ADA and the Unruh Act," I told Verdi.

"We'll give you an Attorney General's opinion, if you need it. I doubt it though. I mean, who would want to fight a lawsuit instead of simply unlocking a chain?" Verdi asked.

Who, indeed. Emboldened by Verdi, and feeling every bit like a private attorney general, I hung out at the law library for a few more days. Shortly thereafter, I went down to the Santa Monica courthouse early one morning with proof of my low-income status, got a waiver of costs, and filed the lawsuit.

That afternoon, I had Sal serve the papers on Daar, while I watched from above, smoking a fat one.

I was hoping that when Sal hit him with the complaint, Daar would realize what it was and walk over to the blue zone and drop the chain. Had he done that, this thing would have ended right there, as I would have gone back to the courthouse tomorrow and withdrawn the complaint. I held my breath.

I was actually rooting for him. Sal gave him the papers in a civil manner. He did stare at them, bug-eyed, for a moment. Then, stiffening, he turned and walked back inside the café.

The chain remained.

"Damn!" I exhaled.

* 13 *

I had envisioned dozens. But only seven people showed up at the community room of the local Independent Living Center. Okay, half a dozen...not counting myself. Half a dozen's better than none, right? I reprimanded myself for even having such grandiose expectations. "That's the quickest way not to participate in divinity," I reminded myself. I told Thompson not to pay attention to numbers either -- this is a good start.

This turned out to be no optimistic rationalization. The sixth person to show up was a staffer from our State

Assemblywoman's office. He had seen our press blurb in a local entertainment rag and had come to offer us encouragement in our budding civic endeavor, promising in the process to check out the chain as well as the ear of our State Assemblyperson when we needed it.

I turned to Thompson and said, "Hey buddy, we've hardly registered a vote and already the politicians are listening to us. Could we have been right?" Suddenly, this really was a good start. Everyone else in the room was reasonably impressed, too. It was true. Just the perception of organizing voters gave us clout. Old Daddy-O was right!

That we had seven guys in one room talking about organizing the biggest block of voters in the state was already creating a new reality. That staffer had had a glimpse of the future and it was us.

To bolster that perception, Thompson and I started things off by handing out the proverbial mailing list, and talking up the reasons and need for UP. I did what was fast becoming "the rap:" the chain, the indignity, the lack of response from the local political establishment, followed by our grand ideas about changing all that: by registering and organizing our vote, and then going one step further by getting other disabled citizens to register other disabled citizens.

"To ultimately and unabashedly take real political power!"

Those seven cheered their approval of our mission to promote and protect the civil rights and economic interest of disabled citizens through the use of the ballot box.

Everyone agreed with our simple plan to do that: Register, educate, and Get Out The Vote of disabled citizens and their families. And to do so in a ruthlessly non-partisan, issue-oriented way.

"Petty partisan politics can only drive us apart," said a guy who introduced himself as Ted. He was well-dressed and appeared to have some sort of degenerative muscle disease. His smile was sincere and his point well taken.

"Ahh! An educated man in our midst," I said, light-heartedly.

"Harvard," somebody said.

"Well he's just been volunteered for the Steering Committee -- in spite of that," I joked.

That got a laugh. "'Cause he's right, you know. We've got to organize around issues, not political parties. It doesn't matter if you're a Democrat, a Republican, or just your run-of-the-mill anarchist in a wheelchair. If you're disabled, you care about adequate health care, affordable housing, and an accessible society, regardless of political affiliation or personal ideology. It's a big tent philosophy."

Hearty agreement there. Most saw the need to use the Mail-In Ballot to deliver much of our vote and save our chained off civilization, but a few of my colleagues pointed out that many will want to go to the polls in person. Many disabled people get a kick out of going to their -- hopefully accessible -- polling place and putting a human face on our vote.

"We dig that if you dig that," I told them. "Our only point is that, when a disabled citizen uses a Mail-In ballot to cast his vote, his vote counts as a disabled citizen. The PAB is a different color and is counted separately in many counties."

"What?" more than one of the mighty seven exclaimed.

I explained that many counties in California do, in fact, count the Mail-In ballots of disabled citizens separately, thereby quantifying our votes as disabled citizens and putting a real and certain number on our vote, giving us more political clout as a voting block. That doesn't happen when you roll into a polling place and vote."

Looking for a quick compromise, I told the leery listeners: "If you want to go to the polls in person, go! Just request a Permanent Absentee Ballot before the election, fill that out, and, when you make your guest star appearance at your polling place, drop that in the ballot box. That way you can be seen by the greater community and have your vote count as a citizen with a disability, instead of just getting lost in the mix."

"Since you put it like that," the skeptic said, "give me an application for the Permanent Absentee Ballot. I'll be happy to put my mail-in ballot in the ballot box myself."

We gave one to everyone, and all applauded when our formerly skittish colleague finished filling his out.

Next came strategy. That was easy. "Just keep doing what you're doing," Ted said. He was a soft-spoken guy, with a lot of good ideas, his Harvard education notwithstanding. "Keep doing what you're doing, keep speaking to small groups, keep registering people. Keep planting seeds."

"Planting seeds," I liked his metaphor. Whenever you're starting something new and visionary, you have to plant a lot of seeds. Maybe there's something to be said for those Harvard educated guys after all. Simple and profound. Plant a lot of seeds.

Okay.

Someone else made the suggestion that we write up a little pamphlet or brochure to explain the who, what, when, where, and why of UP.

Okay.

Everyone agreed with that and the fact that a little funding would help.

Excellent suggestions all around. The group thought it best that Thompson and I do a rough draft of the brochure. Further, I volunteered to apply my legal research and writing skills to the high art of grant research and writing.

Okay!

Last, but not least, an UP Steering Committee was formed, the only requirement to join it being the interest one showed in showing up. Can't get much more grassroots than that, I figured.

Finally, handing in the mailing list, we decided we would meet again in a few months. And with that, half a dozen cripples were going to make a difference. We already had. We had the ear of our local Assemblywoman, didn't we?

As I was readying myself to leave, Matthew, the father of a disabled daughter, who, beside the staffer, was the only other non-disabled person to attend the meeting, walked up and threw some orange and yellow stickers on the table. "Maybe I can help you with that brochure," he said cheerfully.

I picked up an orange sticker. Printed on it was an UP logo that he had created. With the curve of the U and the P flowing into an upward arrow, it was very powerful.

I knew right then, we had reached a new plateau. We had a logo. "Wow," was all I could say. Thompson was duly impressed too. More unforeseen material assistance.

Thanks, Matthew.

That night I actually began to believe that we had a real chance to pull off this god-awful long shot. Little things were beginning to add up. Weren't we now an official group? With an official mission? One that had begun to attract the attention of the local political establishment, even at this formative stage? And to top it all off, didn't we have a bitchin' logo, too? Not bad for a first meeting. Not bad.

Both the philosopher and boxer in me were at peace. We really were going to do what had never been done. We really were going to fight the good fight, or "go down swinging," I said to myself in lieu of a prayer. I slept accordingly.

* 14 *

If disability doesn't kill you, or worse, embitter you, it can give you a fairly unerring ability to relate to others who struggle and suffer. It gives you the ability to empathize...to go simpatico.

As an innate underdog, you learn to drag your feet in other people's shoes -- and, to a larger than usual extent, know something of what they feel. All people, disabled and otherwise, who have really struggled, who have suffered in their perseverance to do the right thing (or, as is usually the case, have the right thing done by them), know this simple timeless truth: struggle is ennobling.

Thank god struggle counts for something besides suffering. There's so much of it...as well as so much left to do that will most assuredly be a struggle. "Count on it," I told myself. I did.

I reminded myself that when you struggle for something you appreciate it a hell of a lot more. Struggle keeps us from taking things for granted. This grace is the flip side of suffering, the balance to it. But only if you are wise enough and patient enough to find it. Now I do not recommend unnecessary suffering, but my disability taught me long ago not to fear struggle either.

As far as I can tell, struggle and overcoming struggle are the only things that build character and impart empathy. Without struggle we develop no character, no sense of feeling for "the other," no empathy. Without struggle we end up like, I don't know, someone like Dan Quayle. I prefer FDR.

With my character well developed and my empathy intact, I realized that without my alleged disability, I would never have become a hell raiser or a fighter of good fights. More likely, had I walked unaided, I would have become a boxer and joined that breed of men who do know much about suffering and the battling of bullies. Consequently, I would have either been punch drunk before I was 20, or prone to saving the world in a whole other way.

I do love Muhammad Ali.

Had I walked unaided, I most likely would not have become what I have become -- a grassroots organizer. Nor would I have found the love of books, history, and philosophy.

It was true. While the temporarily able-bodied kids played sports, I indulged more intellectual pursuits, with little regret. At thirteen, I read *Soul On Ice*, realized that Ho Chi Minh was the George Washington of his country, and got whipsawed by the shootings of Dr. King and Senator Kennedy. All that, along with a few more bullies, taught me to appreciate struggle. As well as which side to struggle on.

It also reinforced what disability had already taught me: to always look for the advantage inherent within the disadvantage if you want to give your character a break and succeed in your struggle.

There's a Buddhist riddle about it somewhere -- about finding the advantage inherent in every disadvantage and turning that weakness into a strength. If you learn to do that, how can you ever be defeated? It is not so much a contradiction as it is a Buddhist riddle. Or is it Taoist? I'm not sure.

Neither school of thought would care about the credit as long as I got the point right. With wisdom and patience, one can turn any weakness to strength, every disadvantage to an advantage. This little riddle is one that disabled people live out every day, and one that this grassroots organizer took to heart.

The paradox is particularly useful to contemplate when you're trying to raise money and when your biggest disadvantage is that you ain't got any.

It was in the raising of money, that most distasteful but necessary of grassroots tasks, that I again learned the importance of finding the advantage within the disadvantage.

It came in the form of the aptly named Dr. Deeler.

Another excited friend, very up on UP, turned me on to Doctor Deeler. It seems this good doctor was busy pulling down $300,000 grants for all kinds of disability projects. My friend thought that the good Dr. Deeler would find UP very worthwhile and would help us focus on finding funding for our project.

Thompson and I went down to meet the doctor at Children's Hospital in L.A.

We waited. The doctor was "a little tied up." Not a problem.

To entertain and impress us, the staff brought out a couple of large black folders that were filled with all kinds of information about the good Doctor's noble projects and "self help" video tapes for people with disabilities. There were flattering letters from all kinds of dignitaries attesting to the need for such projects, as well as a synopsis of a much larger proposal. Included in the impressive glossy package was an assortment of brochures and fliers from some of the groups with which she was working.

I went over each one carefully, trying to get a rough feel for her programs and the philanthropic world in general. It was all very impressive, just like the doctor, who was Japanese, pretty, and, being late, full of apologies.

We got right down to business. Thompson and I went through our electoral song and dance, and she seemed genuinely impressed with our effort. She told us to start talking to more "infrastructure people," getting numbers and names down to help us understand our target population better. No argument there. "After we get a clearer idea of who and what we are dealing with," she said, "we will began to think about funding."

Okay. A little more legwork, I thought, but if it can help us enter the non-profit world, so be it...

On her cheerful recommendation I called every Regional Center and Independent Living Center in California and began to get that "pretty clear picture" I thought we were all looking for. I wrote up my result within the week and faxed them over to the doctor.

No response. Okay, she's a busy woman; she'll call in a day or two.

Nothing.

I waited two weeks.

No calls from her...I called, left messages...all to no avail.

Then it occurred to me: the good doctor...was full of shit. It was my first indication that the non-profit world was not unlike the for-profit world -- full of bullshit artists. Evidently, the not-so-good doctor didn't even have the professional courtesy to call and, if she wasn't interested, just say so.

We would have understood; busy people understand busy people.

But, for some reason, she deemed us not worthy of such a call and caused us to waste three to four weeks -- "Waiting to see," Thompson mocked, "what the situation was."

The answer was easy. There wasn't one...just a lack of respect and concern for our time and efforts. "And she's getting all kinds of money to do advocacy work for the disabled...what a sham," Thompson muttered over beers.

"She's just using disabled citizens like window-dressing to fund her own projects," I agreed.

"Once again we're making 'the good life' possible for the able bodied," Thomas lamented.

Doctor Deeler was a wheeler dealer all right...your basic poverty pimp, all dressed up in degrees and designer jeans, attesting to both her lack of struggle and empathy. Thompson and I just kind of sadly laughed at how preposterous it all was.

"Screw her...she just uses people, probably been doing it all her life."

"You're probably right Tommy," I added.

"Good riddance," he said, in toast form, with the clinking of our beer bottles

"Damn right."

"Why do you think she went through all the rigmarole of having us down there, pulling out those folders and showing us all that grant stuff?" he asked.

"Just a show. She's a poseur."

"But why," he asked, "why not deal with us, why not make it real?"

"Ah, Tommy, she's used to using disabled people and she probably realized that you and I would not be easily manipulated, that we'd actually be involved, so she didn't want to work with us. You know how we assertive cripple types can be," I said.

"Pains in the ass," he mumbled, then asked, "What next?"

"I don't know...I was hoping that she would at least kick-start us into the world of grants and good fortunes," I said, slightly exasperated.

We sat there a minute silently drinking. In the midst of a healthy swig, it came to me.

"Wait. That's it!" I said, sputtering with burps and epiphanies.

"What?" he asked, startled.

"Helping us with the grant stuff...remember those folders?"

He just looked at me blinking.

"In those folders was a brochure about an organization that helps struggling start-ups like us get started"

"What're you talking about," Thompson wondered.

"What'd they call it?" I wondered, aloud. Trying to remember back thorough the weeks. "A, umm, incubator, Yeah! How fitting...an incubator, that takes fledgling little groups like ours and gives them all kinds of help and guidance... What was it called?"

"I don't know if I saw that," Thompson said.

I began to rack my brains. It was a little green flier. "Community... What was it... Community Purpose, Community Partners, something like that, I think. Hey, let me use your phone book." He put down his beer and brought it out from under the table. "Here ya go, Tonto."

I called information. There was no Community Purpose, but there was something called Community Partners in L.A. I took it as proof positive that the drugs and booze hadn't addled my brains that much...at least not in the last two weeks. I called.

Yes, they were a non-profit "incubator" for start up community groups, the receptionist told me. I smiled at Thompson. Thumbs up. And yes, we could set up an appointment to meet with them. When? Next week? Good. It was that easy.

I hung up the phone telling Thompson that maybe the doctor, unbeknownst to her, had done us a favor. We may have discovered a legitimate community partner, and perhaps a real entrée into the philanthropic world...perhaps.

In the meantime, it just goes to show you that even when others are less than fair with you, fate will and does come through. If you are perceptive and undeterred by them, even the disadvantage of real jerks can be turned to your advantage.

Thank you Dr. Deeler.

* 15 *

We may have been stumbling along, as befits an organization of disabled citizens, but hooking up with Community Partners proved we were stumbling in the right direction. Before them, we were seven guys and a brochure (I can't think of a better definition of the word "fledgling") in sore need of resources and support. Community Partners was more than a incubator for us, it was life support.

They helped us understand the philanthropic world and what it means to be a non-profit entrepreneur. For a non-profit entrepreneur is a much more defiant breed than a mere for-profit entrepreneur. A for-profit entrepreneur puts up the money and assumes all the risk. Brave but not fearless. A non-profit entrepreneur uses "other people's money," assumes none of the risk, but does do the risky things that the for-profit world refuses or fears doing. One becomes profitable, the other prophetic...hopefully.

Community Partner's mission was to help the prophets. And we needed their help, first and foremost, because they had credibility in the philanthropic world, whereas, we had none.

They also had Raul Vee. Because of his years of work at other foundations, funders who now gave money to Community Partner's "high risk first time projects," such as UP, knew that all the money given would, in fact, be spent as granted. Which is exactly what we wanted them to believe...it was, after all, the truth.

Better yet, when any grants came in, Community Partners did all the bookkeeping and accounting, which meant I didn't have to. My time could be spent organizing, while they dealt with the IRS. All for just 9%, a cool trade-off.

As a project of Community Partners, UP would operate under their 501(c)(3) non-profit umbrella, allowing all donations to UP to be written off as a tax deduction. It was important for us to achieve such tax-deductible status in order to start raising any serious money.

The Steering Committee agreed it was the right move to make...where do we sign up?

As much as we wanted to join Community Partners, there were concerns. A 501(c)(3) can in no way be involved in partisan politics and there were those on Community Partner's Board of Directors who were wondering just how non-partisan we were. "Ruthlessly non-partisan," I told Raul. He laughed, and said, "That's a good answer," and asked me to use it in a letter of explanation to Community Partners' Board of Directors.

Time for another trip to the ol' law library.

I looked up Section 501(c)(3) in the tax code and it most certainly said that no non-profit can be involved in partisan political activities, but, lo and behold it did allow those same non-profits to send out educational information and facts on "issues of direct interest" to our group members. Bingo! As a non-partisan issue-oriented voter registration/education project, we could in fact be a non-profit, too!

America, you're a great country!

Just by keeping it "ruthlessly non-partisan" and issue oriented, we are free to do all the work necessary to register and inform our community on issues "of their direct interest" and then get them out to vote. I was as happy as Ralph Reed!

You see, unlike ol' Ralphy Boy, we really were going to be non-partisan.

Once again, in my missive to the Board, I pointed out that anything less diminishes our power. As a voting block, we really did have to look at everything, issue by issue, and vote in our enlightened self-interest, based on the facts and not on what some political party or hack wants.

I played up our sincere wish to inspire a little fear in all politicians' hearts when it came to our vote, and explained how, if we went about this strictly on the issues, no politician, regardless of party, was going to take us for granted. A strictly non-partisan approach means eternal power.

The letter carried the day and the Board let us "on board." UP was tax deductible.

So, if you're a struggling little group with great vision and an undying energy to do the right thing in your community, check to see if there is an "incubator" in your community or better yet, call Community Partners in L.A. They'll help.

I laugh about Dr. Deeler now. Phony Dr. Deeler didn't realize it, but she had brought us to Raul Vee -- proof positive of the advantage inherent within the disadvantage.

* 16 *

Seeds. That's what they were. Just like Ted had said. In those first formative days, I had no idea how important a logo and brochure would become in getting UP "up and running."

I do now. It's the secret of seeds.

But these seeds are slightly different. Before they can be planted these seeds need to be made, so sitting down with our artistically gifted, computer literate friend Matthew, we did exactly that. We made a six-sided, three-fold brochure that was really the seed from which all else grew. It was a brochure that people could take home and contemplate in their favorite easy chair while relaxing. It's always good to have someone relaxing when you're trying to win them over.

It was a good brochure that simply told the Who, What, When, Where, Why, and most importantly, the How of how UP was going to achieve its mission -- one registered voter at a time.

With its striking logo and Matthew's font magic, it was rather eye catching as well. As Matthew told me more than once: "Neatness counts!"

He was right. Sloppy graphics turn people off right away. They figure if you can't get a brochure right, how the hell are you going to save the world?

Good question.

While Matthew did his graphics magic, Thompson and I hunkered down for another low light session to deal with the verbiage of our little brochure. In such ambiance, I couldn't help but think of the low light by which Jefferson wrote the

"Declaration of Independence," or better, Tom Paine his "Common Sense." It was definitely funny how the universe was working. By mere happenstance, I was in the middle of a biography on Citizen Paine. The right book at the right time? I don't know. I took it as another omen.

Simon Wiesenthal, the great Nazi hunter, once said that whenever people are being oppressed or suffering, they see many things as omens, if for no other reason than it keeps them going. It gives them hope.

As long as that chained up Blue Zone remained in my neighborhood, I was suffering mightily, and I picked my omen accordingly. I took as a good sign the simultaneous reading of Tom Paine and the writing of our brochure on common sense. Paine's call to throw off the shackles of the British, to take power, and to gain independence hit a similar note with UP's rallying cry to throw off the shackles of the able-bodied world, take our legitimate power and gain -- in the sweetest sense of the word -- true independence!

"What we're proposing here is a second American Revolution," I told Thompson.

"I wish we could live out the full meaning of the first one," he cracked.

"This voting project could guarantee that."

"I still can't believe that someone hasn't done this before."

"Me, neither. Let's go to work."

We opened a couple of brews. That was all the liquid inspiration we would need that night, as it didn't take long. Like any good idea whose time has come, it came fast. The fact that we had been pondering it for months and talking it up didn't hurt either. It quickly came to the page on its own. Matthew's superb editing was also a big plus.

A few days later I hit the local copy shop and ran off 300 for a couple of bucks.

For those few bucks, we had the first tool necessary to change the world -- or at least our small part of it. This "tool"

-- along with many others we naturally developed over time, like our UP letterhead, envelopes, stickers, etc. -- was exactly what we needed to create momentum and raise further funds.

At times I wondered if my little "vision thing" wasn't, in fact, personally nickel and dimeing me to death. But, still betting on the long shot, I turned a blind eye as my pockets emptied and I thought of it all as an reasonable investment in my community. That and the fact that I felt like a true visionary the first time someone walked up and stuck a $50 check in my shirt pocket after reading our little brochure of self-empowerment.

"That's a lot of new brochures!" I said to myself. And then, it happened again, and again.

After a while, I realized our little voting project had taken on a life of its own and was actually beginning to pay for itself. "Remember," I told myself every time thereafter when I had to pay for something related to UP, "this is the cost of participating in divinity."

Truth is, I knew I was getting off cheap.

* 17 *

Divinity or no, it would take a lot of brochures, because we are everywhere. Disability is the glue of society. No matter what your race, culture, class, or creed, we all break down, get sick, or bleed. Cutting across all classes, disability has no prejudices or biases. It screws, torments, and enlightens most every group.

Lucky me. As an organizer I could pretty much go anywhere, before any group, disabled or the lowly-non. Yes, the non-disabled. The arrogant healthy human psyche never thinks of itself as sick or disabled, but the truth is that 83% of all non-disabled people will become disabled at some point in their life. That inescapable fact tends to shake up a lot of non-disabled psyches.

"83%? You sure?" they'd ask, stunned, having never thought about such a thing before.

"At a minimum," I said like a cold slap of water on the unconscious. "Only those with the grace of a ballerina and the luck of the long shot artist will be spared." They would all laugh nervously. "For most of us disability is or will be an inevitable and natural part of the life cycle," I would continue, reminding them that "the medical infrastructure you help us save today, you will access tomorrow as a disabled person."

It was a quick study in Enlightened Self Interest. Suddenly the TABs, the temporarily able-bodied, realized they weren't just helping a bunch of cripples and gimps when they joined our fight, they were, in fact, watching out for their own best interest, as the vast majority of them would be joining our none too exclusive club.

"As for you well balanced, genetically sound and awfully lucky 17%, don't get cocky," I'd politely inform them. "Someone you love -- a family member, a child, a wife, a partner -- will comprise part of that 83% and rock your world. I promise."

Eighty-three percent. I'd read the figure off a poster in a dingy little non-profit in South Central L.A, a non-profit that was masquerading as a Center for Independent Living. I say masquerading because it was rumored that the director and some of her cronies were busy feeding their drug and alcohol habits with the center's funds. Needless to say, when the rumors proved to have some validity, I didn't hang around long, cause like all junkies, their follow through involved only one thing -- more drugs and booze -- and I had no time to waste.

Feeling a bit sorry for the disabled citizens of South Central, who could use a sound CIL, I knew, too, that I'd missed a unique opportunity to work in a community that not only has a high number of disabled citizens, but also had a real reason to have them registered and voting. Namely poverty.

Poverty and disability go together. More poverty. More disability. My missed opportunity wasn't in getting to work with various black and brown citizens, either. Diversity is always pleasant in and of itself, but just as disability transcends race and culture, so do most disabled people. We'd be the last people to give someone grief over something they can't physically change such as race, gender or sexual orientation.

Being permanently disabled, we know about dealing with things "you can't change."

Or, perhaps more aptly put, we know something about dealing with people who can't deal with things you can't change. That first-hand knowledge of discrimination and the strong empathy it evokes makes all such concerns irrelevant.

I think it's safe to say that in our community, if we're loved -- you're loved. It's kind of joyous like that. No hang-ups about one's mere physical specifications. Whatever they happen to be, they're yours, uniquely yours, that's all. So, no missed opportunities there.

The missed opportunity in South Central came in not being able to work with other poor people. Most disabled people are poor people, after all. And you didn't have to be a political genius to see that as the minority group that transcends and enriches all other minority groups, we have a unique ability to reach out to other low-income communities and organize with them. Get out their vote with ours. A chance to work in South Central right off the bat would have helped establish that. Damn!

Still, I ultimately counted the encounter in South Central as another blessing. Through it I had spied that poster and it had laid out that most startling of facts.

Eighty-three percent is a lot. As mentioned, that always caught the TABs' attention. "Get ready," I would tell them.

"Register to vote and then vote like a disabled person -- in other words -- like your life depends on it."

More often than not came the reply, "It does!" from a disabled citizen in the audience. This would also make the point in the best way -- it would get a laugh.

Of course for many of the non-disabled I spoke to, they already got the point. They were the families and friends of disabled people, and a good many of them had been fighting for "Jonathan" or "Susan" every since they were "Johnny" or "Susie." Many were the very people that built the existing infrastructure, which we were now using to organize their families and friends.

These folks were and are our lifetime allies and the greatest fear that many have is what's going to happen to their loved ones after they are gone? They are for the most part, already activists, their life experience with disability having already radicalized most of them, in the most humane way. They love us. Most of them understand our problems and already think, act, and would assuredly vote in our best interest. That's why we organized with them too.

They are the great multiplier of our vote...and a good 83% of them are going to join the club anyway.

I think for many of them we have quieted a lot of fears about living with a disability. We, and they, are proof that it can be done, and done well, as in living well. So, I reiterated it everywhere I could and do so now -- Register these lifetime allies to vote, too.

Like we began to tell all who were interested, "We don't discriminate. We register all citizens, disabled and otherwise."

* 18 *

If I ever had a doubt as to whether "they get it," it was laid to rest when I went to a Self-Advocacy meeting at the Valley Regional Center to do what was fast becoming my song and dance of "civic responsibility." The old "Take Power rag" as I was beginning to think of it. There was a lot of repetition involved. Slightly adapted to the time and crowd, and always passionate, it was still the same message over and over again.

Power is never given -- it is taken! Take power! Together, we really can begin the world over again! For the betterment of all, register and vote! Register your families and friends! Use the Permanent Absentee Ballot to mail in your vote. Whether you mail it in or roll it in: VOTE! It really is up to you. Join us! For it's time to get UP!!!

The power of the idea always carried me. It carried them too. It played right into what so many self-advocacy groups in the DD community were already promoting. Namely, self-advocacy.

The whole concept of self-advocacy was set up to promote good old democratic assertiveness. People standing up for themselves and their community, in every decision that impacts their life. The pump had been primed for me. They understand that the strongest form of self-advocacy is, in fact, voting.

With the help of staff and fellow citizens we got thirty-two people registered and signed up for the PAB. Handing out blank registration forms, I reminded them, again, to "Go home and register your families." Many did.

But in the meantime, the bigger concern was about whom to vote for -- the eternal bugaboo for the newly enfranchised.

"For those candidates and issues that want to help you as citizens with a disability and who support full funding of Regional Centers," I told them only half in jest.

A loud "Yeah!" of agreement came back. They liked their center and all the services it provided.

"Vote for the candidates that support self-advocacy, better housing, good medical care and an accessible society for everyone," I added.

Cheers all around.

"Who are they?" I continued, "Who are those candidates? I don't know! You're the activists and organizers out here! Start talking with your self-advocacy groups and families, watch a little news, read 'Letters to the Editor' in all your local newspapers. You'll begin to get a better idea of who and what you want to vote for."

There was a murmur of agreement.

"Letters to the editor," a guy with a hung eye and whitened arm said firmly.

"Absolutely," I agreed. "'Letters to the Editor' let you know what's on the people's minds in your hometown." Then I added, "Why, you folks could even write a letter or two, as well as have some elected officials and candidates come out and talk with you. With thirty-two new voters and your families registered to vote, it's a safe bet many of your local candidates would show up...particularly when they know you mail your vote in two weeks early using the Permanent Absentee Ballot."

This intrigued everyone. One of the staff said that that may be a good election event to put together. I offered UP's assistance.

"Hey folks, there's one last thing I want to talk with you about today concerning voting, okay?"

A collective "Okay" erupted.

"Okay," I began. "We at UP don't support campaigns or candidates. We don't care which party you belong to. We just hope that when you vote, you vote in such a way that not only helps you, as disabled citizens, but also helps all American citizens, because most of them, someday, are going to be just like us, the disabled, right?"

This bit of black humor gets laughs and the biggest series of "yeahs" yet.

"Remember, anything that helps disabled citizens, helps all citizens, so don't let anyone make you feel that you aren't entitled to whatever it takes for you to live your life fully. Remember when we can live our lives to their full potential, so can everyone else."

"To be all you can be," one of them yelled.

"Yes!" I told them, "But the Marine Corps has a slightly different slant on 'full potential.' Here, we don't want you to kill anyone."

They all agreed with this. "Do you folks know what that's called, when you think, act, and vote in a way that helps yourself and others," I asked, remembering the "ESI" talk I had had with Thompson.

"Fairness," a young woman said.

"Good answer," I replied. "That's an important part of it." I went on, "When you strive to help yourself in a way that also helps others, you are doing so in your enlightened self-interest, in a way that benefits you and everyone else. That's what 'good citizenship' is all about...Enlightened Self-Interest...or ESI as we like to call it."

I heard the murmur of "ESI" make its way through my enlightened crowd.

"It's the way that our forefathers, Washington, Jefferson, Franklin, all of them wanted us to think, act and vote, in order to help the greatest number of our fellow citizens. Think about that," I said with a hopeful smile.

They were. They were all looking at me, taking it all in. I was wondering if they got it. "Can anyone think of anything that helps disabled citizens and the rest of society, too," I asked.

"Good health care," came a response from the back.

"Good answer, and true."

"Good drugs," said one young man with a bold smile and a smart-ass edge to his voice. They all laughed.

"Yeah, he's right," I said, "the drugs that are developed to help us, help lots of other people too." Getting back a sense of decorum, I asked, "Anybody else?"

A woman in her early twenties with crooked pigtails and blue granny glasses raised up in her wheelchair and said, "Curb cuts."

"Curb cuts?" I repeated. Even I figured those were just for disabled citizens, but before I could say this, my pigtailed philosopher said: "Sure... Go stand by one and watch. Who uses it?" She asked, and with the timing of a comedian, "I'll tell you who uses it, old people, people with children, heavy set people, skateboarders, UPS guys, and, oh yeah, a couple of disabled people."

Her emphasis on "a couple" was perfect and pulled the laughs.

"Everybody uses curb cuts, not just the disabled," she insisted. "Curb cuts help everyone!"

"Wow, I had never thought of that," I confessed. "What a great observation," I said. "Putting curb cuts in does benefit the whole community, doesn't it?"

"Everybody!" she exclaimed. I marveled at it all. They got it.

I realized later that, just as the fight for an accessible society would benefit everybody, curb cuts may just be the perfect symbol for the "enlightened self-interest" with which disabled people had to vote and think.

"Curb cuts? Who'd've thought? Listen and learn," I said to myself, "they get it! They understand enlightened self-interest."

Better than most. Even better than some in the community.

Case in point -- Kenny Ball. In a parking garage a few days after that particular workshop, I ran into Kenny, an intelligent but smug disabled guy. Kenny was also on the Board of Directors of the local Center for Independent Living and thus got away with calling himself an activist. He went livid when I told him that we had been working with the Regional Centers and all of us, ILCs, RCs, and UP ought to all come together in a giant Voter Registration effort in the next election cycle.

"Those people," he said with shocking disdain, "you're organizing those people. They're retards, man. Most of them shouldn't be voting. They can hardly count. You're wasting your time."

"What the hell are you talking about?" I asked, really not surprised; this was, after all, Kenny Ball. "You don't lose your civil right to vote just because some people think you're too dumb," I sternly informed him. "Lucky for him," I thought to myself.

"Look, I'm all for fighting for the vote," he said, squinting at me in the iridescent light of the parking garage, "but if you're signing up retards, you're holding the whole community back."

"Whoa Kenny! Your prejudices are showing, man. They're not 'retards.' They are citizens, many of whom, I remind you, have no mental disabilities whatsoever. The ones that do are only mild to moderately impaired and therefore are more than competent to vote!"

I handed him a brochure. "Join us."

He stared at it. "More than competent to vote?" he said with contempt. "What are you smoking, dude?"

"Something you need, man." Snobbish bastard. "The fact of the matter is that most of the citizens in Regional Center programs that I've talked to know what's in their enlightened self-interest."

"Their what?" he said staring back at me with a puzzled look.

"They know very well what's in their 'enlightened self-interest,'" I said again, realizing I've just thrown smart guy here for a loop.

"'Enlightened self-interest?' What the hell are you talking about?" he asked, agitated.

I looked at him, realizing it's the disability in his attitude that's hurting him more than his polio. For a brief second I think about telling him about The Enlightenment, that revolution in thought and power -- how it influenced our forefathers and how they wanted all citizens of America to think and act for the betterment of themselves and the rest of society.

He was standing there blinking, waiting while I contemplated telling him how many disabled citizens already had a keen understanding of this, even ones with off-kilter pigtails.

I almost told him how most are anxious to be in the vanguard of a new non-partisan civic movement for social justice and equality, one that best protects the disabled by taking into account the needs of the whole of society.

I thought about telling him all that. I really did, as he stood there cynically shaking his head, full of himself, his self-loathing and his hang-ups. Either that or I was going to kick his crutch out from under him.

At that moment, though, I realized poor Kenny had never learned to say, "There, but for the grace of god, go I." And then I gracefully and gratefully pitched in, "Poor, poor Kenny." I thought of all that as we were standing in that garage, with him blinking, waiting for an explanation of ESI.

"Curb cuts, man, curb cuts," is all I said and walked away, a failed Buddhist, once again.

"Curb cuts," he replied, confused.

"Yeah," I shot back, "Go stand next to one and you'll get it sooner or later."

You can't win everyone over... And you don't want too.

* 19 *

Then there's the flip side. The balance. The angels. The ones who understand and provide right away, or at least attempt to...sometimes in spite of themselves. Sound paradoxical? Then you'll appreciate my old buddy, Peter.

Peter Tart. That really was his name, but he was no longer a tart young thing. Truth be told, the last time I saw Peter, we were both younger and skinnier, but he had really blossomed into a beatific state of weight.

Everybody's got his or her disability and his was food...and that name. Peter Tart. He told me his dad gave him that name to prove that he had a sense of humor. Being a rather dour prosecutor of Japanese war criminals, I guess dear old dad had to have a rather indirect sense of humor. You'd get the joke in time.

Peter told me he found nothing funny in it as a fat kid, having endured a childhood of slurs and taunts. Peter Tart knew what it was like to be called a retard.

Of course now, with age, his name had sublime sexual connotations, that every woman who had "had a little tart in her" couldn't help but comment on, he liked to joke.

But it was true. Everybody liked to joke about it. Myself included.

"Hey Peter, you old tart," I yelled when I laid eyes on him at my friend Laine's birthday party at a local Main Street pizzeria.

"Hey, man, what have you been up to?" he asked, taking a healthy swig of a large glass of diet Coke.

"This!" I say, pulling a brochure out of my gray urban camie's thigh high pocket. Happy once again, that due to our new little "money green" pamphlet, I no longer had to go through the whole rap. As he perused it, I mentioned the chain, the local government's inaction and the need for an organized vote to turn that around.

"The need to get up," he said, closing the brochure.

"Yep. All 2.8 million of us."

"That many?" he said.

"Yep. 2.8 million voting age disabled in California."

"Wow, that's a lot of potential voters. I never realized," he said taking another healthy slug of coke.

"Lot of potential," I agreed. "You sure you're an Irishman, the way you drink?" I teased.

"You sure you're a political activist, the way you drink?" he responded.

"The curse of the visionary."

"You are that, my friend, you are that."

"What? I asked "A curse or a visionary?"

"Probably both," he said with all the enthusiasm of an older brother for the younger one he never had. "Good idea," he said putting the brochure in his jacket pocket.

"Thanks, Pete."

We were friends from the Hayden for Senate campaign in 1976 and that night at Laine's birthday party, where I handed out numerous brochures to similar progressive types, it was Peter who took the most interest. He saw the sense of it right away. As well he should have, for it was the old tart that was going to impress me most profoundly.

"You know, I work for AARP now, as their Southern California political director," he said casually. At that moment, the waitress decided to see how we were doing, and as Peter ordered another large diet coke and me a beer, I wondered if I had heard him right. To be on the safe side, I gave thanks to Goethe. "AARP? The senior organization?" I asked.

"Yeah, cool huh," he said more to the waitress than me. She was young and could not have cared less. I was stunned and felt in tune with the universe all at the same time.

Peter was the Southern California political director for the world's largest senior organization. "The world's largest non-military organization," Pete pointed out, "thirty-three million members strong."

Thirty-three million seniors that understood the power of the vote.

I just laughed. Could it be any better than this? I mean if you're going to forge an alliance with those of similar concerns, it might as well the 800 pound gray gorilla of American politics. I saw the future as Peter tried to flirt with the waitress.

In truth, I felt like it was my birthday, but I didn't tell Laine. I was too busy seeing the possibilities and planting the seeds of collaboration with Peter -- even if the waitress wasn't.

"We should sit down and start working together. There's a lot of common ground between our people," I said blissfully. "Did you know that 53% of California's disabled citizens of voting age are 50 plus?"

"No, I didn't," he said, intrigued.

"Oh yeah, in California disabled seniors are in the majority. They're you're people as well as mine, amigo."

"You think you can organize them?" he asked.

"Hell Pete, we are organizing them," I told him emphatically. Okay, so the organization consisted of seven guys and a brochure, but you have to take your shots where you find them and I wasn't going to be shy with my dear friend.

"Maybe AARP and UP could work together," I offered.

"Let's have lunch. Call me," he said, giving me his card.

"I'm just a poor little grassroots organizer. You buying?" I asked as the waitress dropped off our new drinks, and the assembled guests at Laine's Birthday party were brought to order with the clanking of spoon on glass.

"Hell, this is legit coalition building. AARP's buying lunch," he winked. "One thing about ARRP," he said in a whisper, "they like to eat. They understand you can't organize on an empty stomach. Call me."

Lucky him. Peter had found his dream job. Power politics in the most politically significant state in the country and all you can eat.

As I thought of the possibilities of such an alliance, I wondered whose cup ran over more.

Hoisting my glass to his, I made a toast, "To cursed visionaries, old tarts, and angels everywhere."

I was so happy I even slipped the waitress a ten spot and told her to keep the change. As a rule, when you're on a roll, I believe you should spread it around.

Happy Birthday, Laine, and thank you very much, old man!

* 20 *

So how reasonable is reasonable? Daar was a reasonable man, wasn't he? Even if one had to use a lawsuit to bring it out of him? A reasonable man wouldn't fight a lawsuit instead of simply unlocking a chain, would he? Reason would ultimately prevail wouldn't it?

Most everyone thought so. I thought so. Lawyers I talked with thought so. Even Asst. Attorney General Verdi thought so.

"Not so," was Jimmi's response. He was a boardwalk merchant and my friend. "Daar is a shit just to be a shit," he would say with his Israeli-accented passion. "No reason needed, just to be a shit."

Jimmi had it best. Reasonable? No. With Daar it came down to no reason. Standing at his beach side stall, full of "inexpensive, my friend, not cheap" luggage and backpacks, I had told Jimmi I was hoping Daar would back down if I threatened him with a lawsuit. Jimmi's eyes brightened. "Let me tell you about this shit, my friend," he said as he straightened a few belligerent backpacks. I listened intently as Jimmi gave me his low down on Daar and reasonableness. Merchants after all, know merchants.

And as it turned out, Daar was the biggest merchant of all.

Owning a string of restaurants and store-front spaces along the Venice boardwalk, Daar came to America and through some hard work, bullying, and alleged bribes, made good his American dream, or so Jimmi told me

"Sue Daar, my brother, sue the sonofabitch. He's never satisfied. He's a sonofabitch...he screwed me in a deal...a good deal, over space, a little beach front space...he had to have it all."

"But why Jimmi?" I asked. Like Daar, Jimmi was an Israeli by birth and a beach front merchant. "He's your fellow ex-patriot? Why would he screw with you?"

"The guy is a shit, a shit! He must have all the power," Jimmi said with scorn. "He doesn't want to have a good deal -- for everybody's sake," he says ruefully. "Daar's only happy when he screws you. This is his thought of power...I know him. So does everyone else on this beach. He is a shit. Get him, my friend. You get him good." He stopped for a moment. Taking in the fresh ocean air, he said, "You want to know something else, my buddy?"

"Yeah what?" I asked, slightly amazed. I never expected the vehement dislike Jimmi displayed for his fellow ex-patriot. Surprised as I was, it was nothing compared to the appalling truth that Jimmi was about to utter. He looked at me very sadly in the bright sunshine. It was a moment reminiscent of the Hispanic gentleman man who'd served me, at the counter, the cup of coffee that initiated this whole brouhaha.

He put his hand on my shoulder. "You won't believe it," he said. "He's got a daughter who is crippled!"

"What? Are you sure, Jimmi?" I asked shocked.

"Yes, yes, worse than you, she is crippled worse than you, my friend."

In a state of near disbelief, all I could think to say to dear Jimmi was, "What a crazy world we live in."

"What a crazy man," Jimmi said. "I told you he is a bastard. Go get him. Sick bastard."

I couldn't believe it. It was almost too unreal. He, who should be most sensitive to the needs and concerns of disabled citizens due to the personal experience of having a daughter with a disability, was, in reality, thoroughly insensitive -- and worse -- a public nuisance in his treatment of disabled citizens in general, and as a way of doing business, no less.

I told Jimmi, "I can't believe it, it's all too weird."

"You believe it," Jimmi told me firmly. "He's the worst kind of shit. Sue the shit."

I assured him, I would. "What do you figure went wrong in his heart, Jimmi?" I asked.

He told me what I already knew. "He is a bully," Jimmy answered.

"You'd think he'd understand. If his daughter is disabled...."

"He should understand because he is a Jew," Jimmi cut in. "It is the highest command of the Torah to show compassion for the lame and less fortunate. He is disgraceful." Jimmi didn't mince words in English -- or Hebrew. What followed had all the authority of a curse in any language.

I couldn't shake the feeling that I was living in a B movie. The guy that was screwing with me had a disabled daughter and had tried to bribe me with hot dogs when all I asked was to legally park in a space designated for the handicapped in order to patronize his restaurant...and all this in spite of every law to the contrary, including the Torah.

Under those circumstances, how reasonable can you expect him to be?

I began to think that just maybe he wouldn't back down. Maybe this would be a long drawn out brawl. "He's a shit?" I asked Jimmi. He just nodded his head gently in the affirmative. I really wasn't spoiling for a fight, particularly a

B-rated one, with a character who was quickly becoming an ogre.

Forget common decency, the chain was proof positive that when it came to our rights, the laws didn't matter. We really were second-class citizens -- and all because of "a shit," to quote Jimmi.

Okay! If he wanted a fight, I'd take it to him. What's to lose? "Come out swinging," the pugnacious pugilist in me sang out.

"Thank you, my brother," I told Jimmi. "I'm going to get him...I promise."

"For me, brother," he said happily.

"For you, my brother," I said walking off towards Main street to meet my friend Jacob at any one of a number of neighborhood pubs. I found him at the Triangle. He's a lawyer, but when I asked him if he'd like to work my case, he said that unless I was "going to get up in court and sing and dance," he didn't want to do it. Just another useless entertainment lawyer.

Even with my growing doubts, Jacob more or less agreed that after Daar consulted with his lawyer, he'd most likely take down the chain, if I agreed to dismiss my suit...simple...but then again, "He may not want to be so simple." Jake said this with all the manufactured confidence of a lawyer who practices "settlements" more than he practices law. "Whatever he wants to be, you look so good in *pro per*, why blow it hiring a lawyer," he insisted.

"You're a shining example of that argument, counselor," I told him over the din.

He laughed and brought me a beer. "Every Man a Lawyer," he said.

I was still reeling from the revelations of Jimmi and gave hearty thanks for the blessed brew. Jacob agreed that Daar was a real jerk. With a disabled daughter and all, too. We just shook our heads. I slugged down a hard gulp of beer. "It's all so shallow, so fuckin' petty."

"Here's to shallow, petty pricks," Jacob said lifting his glass. "Think I'm shallow and petty enough of a prick to meet that blond over there?" he asked tipping his glass in her direction.

"How much cash you got on you?" I asked.

"Hundred bucks," he replied.

I looked around the Triangle, a bar long favored by bikers, ex-boxers and other tough cripples, as well as their assorted sycophants. I assured Jacob that he and his hundred bucks were sufficiently shallow enough for this crowd.

"Jacob," I said in a serious tone, "I just can't understand why the guy is fighting me so hard over this. It doesn't make sense. Why does this guy want to mess with my civil rights?"

Jacob, who is Jewish, started to laugh, "Dude, in his mind this isn't about civil rights, it's about private property...his. Daar is an Israeli. Hell, whenever he hears the words 'civil rights' he thinks of a Palestinian youth throwing rocks at him. On second thought," he said regretfully, "this guy probably isn't prone to backing down."

"That makes two of us," I said almost to myself. That makes two of us...just like in a B-rated movie.

* 21 *

To add to the low-grade effect of it all, I got one of those preposterous calls from Daar's lawyer. Assuming I'm a dummy, the first thing he did is compliment my complaint. "Nice job. Who did it?"

"I did."

"You?"

"Yea, that's what 'In Pro Per' means counselor."

"Nice job," he said again.

"Yeah, you said that... I'm a paralegal."

"It shows."

"Great! So why the call? Your client going to take down the chain? I asked. I'll withdraw the suit if he does that," I offered, thinking that's what this call was all about.

"No, he's not taking down the chain because he's not discriminating against you," he said.

"Jesus, are you serious?" I laughed.

"Yes. My client doesn't let anyone park in that parking lot, so he's treating you just like anyone else. Hence no discrimination," he said coolly.

I was right; I had anticipated their argument. "You disabled counselor?" I asked.

"No, why?"

"'Cause that reasoning is so fucked up, I figured maybe you had a little brain damage."

"Brain damage?" he asked more surprised, than offended.

"You're going to have to do better than that for me to think otherwise, counselor. I'm not as dumb as you sound right now," I said just to let him know that I was not terribly impressed with him or his perversion of logic.

"The fact's a fact," he said, now slightly pissed. "My client is not discriminating against you."

I flash back to Verdi.

"Whose kidding who here, counselor? Even if your client wasn't in violation of his permits to provide on site public parking, which he is, your argument, that 'he discriminates against everybody, hence he discriminates against no one' wouldn't hold water," I said with discernible disdain.

"Wait a minute."

"No. You wait a minute," I cut him off, "I don't have to tell you, do I counselor, that I, and all other disabled citizens in this state are members of a protected class under the law, so regardless of what your client may get away with concerning able-bodied public parking, he still has a duty to supply handicapped parking at his café. That's why he's got that big blue painting of 'Special Ed' in his parking lot, counselor. So don't play games with me. I haven't got the time."

"Well, you've done your homework," he said.

"Yeah. Do yours. Tell your client to stop breaking the law and take down that damn chain, pronto."

"He not breaking the law," he responded curtly.

"If that's your opinion counselor, I'll see you in court."

"Yes, well..."

"Good day counselor, call me if you have a change of heart. You can expect a Request for Admissions soon."

"Discovery? Discovery? You're really going to go through with this?" he asked, as though I had dropped the whole matter because he dropped a dime.

"Yeah. Under oath -- penalty of perjury -- discovery. The kind that stands up in court. See you there counselor -- and bring that twisted logic with you. I want to watch the judge laugh you out of court." I hung up.

Okay, so I was a bit of a hard ass. I wanted them to know they were in a fight, and I wasn't going to back down, no matter how outrageous their bribes or lack of logic.

"Fuckin' ABs," I said to myself, wondering once again, who in this whole silly affair was really disabled, who was really fucked up?

* 22 *

Over a lunch as hearty as himself, Peter proposed that we put on some kind of joint event.

"A Voters' Forum, you know, where candidates could meet 'the crips,'" he said between bites of a hot roast beef sandwich.

I told him that sounded good and let him pick up the check. Subsequently, I made my way out to the Mountain's farm and was now proposing to him what Peter had proposed to me.

"AARP want to co-host a Voters' Forum with UP. Shelia Kuehl is running for State Assembly from Santa Monica and Pete thinks he can get her and her Republican opponent to debate each other on disabled/senior issues. We have set it up. What'd ya think?" I asked, taking the joint from his lips.

"Sheila who?"

"Sheila Kuehl, feminist lawyer and ex TV star. Heard of her?"

"Uhh, no," he said releasing a hit.

"She use to play Zelda on Dobie Gillis."

"Really," he brightened, "Dobie Gillis?"

"Yeah, cool huh? I think we can get AARP to underwrite most of the costs, too," I said in an ascending consciousness. It seemed strange to mention Dobie Gillis and AARP in the same breath. As the "Many Loves of Dobie Gillis" was the first hip TV show I could remember as a kid. Hip and all those AARP seniors didn't seem to fit together...until I realized that in order to have even a vague memory of the "Dobster" you had to be getting pretty old.

"Can we get her opponent to debate her?" the Mountain asked.

"He's the easy one, bro. The district's a safe Democratic seat and he's got nothing to lose. He's undoubtedly dying to get on any stage with her," I said letting him have another hit.

"Do it!" he inhaled.

"Okay." I did likewise and, after a second, we coughed our heads off in agreement.

Unorganized, unorthodox and unapologetically, UP was off to do its first public event and I'm not ashamed to admit that I felt like the Maynard G. Krebs of grassroots organizing.

* 23 *

I went to see my friend Sam, a scrambling PR guy who likes to counterbalance his "brown nosing corporate gigs," with a little grassroots activism every now and then, "just to remind myself which side I'm really rooting for."

Our side. He was only too happy to help organize the debate. But quite unlike Sam's second floor office of 1940's vintage, we needed a thoroughly accessible building in which to hold our Voters' Forum. Luckily, the City of Santa Monica, unlike its L.A. neighbor was way out in front on the issue of access and we had little problem in securing the Ken Edward Senior Center. Under the wing of Community Partners' non-profit status they gave us the place for $10.00 an hour. I booked four.

Securing that, I took up minor residence at Sam's office and helped him with a celebrity golf tournament/fund-raiser that he was putting together, by stuffing envelopes and the like. He assisted me with UP's first public event, by helping with, simply, everything.

From agendas to tablecloths, ground rules to stage management, Sammy was there, bringing both a professional attitude and a yellow note pad mentality to our endeavor. The best thing he gave to me, though, was his office when he left town for Seattle to try and work out some personal problems with his wife.

Besides the influence of strong women, and her feelings of missed opportunities, she had discovered old Sammy on the bedroom floor one night, flailing away in the midst of a Grand Mal seizure. I think the acid and three sleepless nights to complete an assignment for Texaco had something to do with it. But hey, it was probably easier for his wife to deal with the medical explanation, since she wasn't into acid.

I asked the Grand Mal man if he wanted to join the UP Steering Committee. The joke wasn't seen as funny.

Such an explanation was good enough for his wife, but he feared the effect such information would have on his corporate world connections. He had a hidden disability and he wished it to stay that way. Like most of the temporarily able bodied, even the thought of a disability scared them, not so much because of the effect it would have on them, but, more importantly, because of the effect it would have on everyone else. Few, if any who are not born into it, come easily to this community.

Okay by me, Sammy.

But just in case the drugs did have something to do with it, he tossed out the remaining acid, gave me his pot pipe and told me to watch the office. Ever since his wife had come back from her "woman's retreat," she had been talking divorce, and he was going off to try and revive his marriage, which further induced a sobering effect upon him.

I asked Thompson a couple of times if he wanted to help. He said he wanted to but was overwhelmed with work. "Getting as much overtime as I can...Sorry, dude. I'll try and make it though."

Okay. Probably best that way. He'd never make it up all the stairs to Sam's office anyway.

Our Steering Committee members had me out to their various organizations and groups, and Liquid Ted and Logo Mat were there to bounce things off of and run copy by, but outside of that I was flying solo.

Alone in Sam's office I began to organize more than just myself. Dates were confirmed, ground rules set, press releases released, signs, posters, and stickers were proofed, picked, and sent to the printers. Blurbs went out to all the local disabled programs and service providers. Best of all, Santa Monica City TV, the local cable company, was more than happy to come in and film the whole shebang as part of their local programming requirements.

I spotted their office, again through dumb luck, in the back of the City Hall where I went to pay a parking ticket (what is it about me and parking?). On a whim I walked in afterwards and asked if they'd be interested in broadcasting the affair. Interested? They were anxious! Candidates, cripples, former TV stars and a little mud flinging, it had all the makings of good local access programming.

They also assured me they would re-broadcast the whole affair numerous times after the event, which would educate the community on the candidates, their positions, and best of all on UP.

Cameras often make people behave better, too.

We decided to put together a panel of "distinguished disabled citizens" with a moderator, so that while members of the audience were wheeling up to the microphones to ask questions, we could keep the program moving with questions from our esteemed panel.

Asking around, a few people told me about a local disabled professor who would make a good moderator and I went after him. He initially said yes, but as fate would have it, he had to back out at the last second due to his mother's failing health in Texas.

Under such conditions, what could I say, but that she was in our prayers and god speed.

Two days out from the gig and I had to locate a moderator. I could have done it, but I really wanted another soul to handle it, so that I would be free to handle the 101 other details that would have to be taken care of during the event itself.

Ted called me and recommended Anthony Gordon who, like the professor, I had never heard of before. But he was a "disabled mover and shaker" and I had few if any alternatives. I thanked Ted, called Anthony, and without hesitation, he saved our butts by saying yes.

We could not have been luckier. Gordon was class personified. Erudite and gracious in manner, he was charismatic with his strawberry blond hair and green blazer. He also had a bit of that low key JFK coolness that played so well on TV.

One look at the cool quad and I knew the gods were with us. I thanked them all.

Even Sammy was impressed when he got back, still married and seriously thinking of moving to Seattle. On our tight budget, and due to his likely departure, Sammy called in every favor in town and stretched every penny for us.

On the day of the event, we scrambled around picking up cookies (sugar free and regular) and coffee at the supermarket, along with other goodies and necessities.

At the Center, I hooked up with Peter, who was much impressed because City TV, having decided to do a three-camera shoot, had brought in the big production truck, and was now running cable every which way into and out of the building. Being very careful not to impede or block access, they duct-taped everything double. They, like we, did not want to trip anyone up.

Our greatest fear was that some senior or disabled citizen would take a nose dive, live, right into another disabled citizen, starting an ugly chain reaction, à la Rube Goldberg, that would become the hallmark of the event. Disability issues be damned. We got the disabled disabling the disabled, all in living color!

All night terrors aside, it was a long day, and somewhere, two hours out from show time, I was beginning to realize what a mistake I had made in not finding someone to do the floor managing for the event. With the setting up of the hall, coordinating with the camera crews, and getting all the literature, as well as food tables prepared, I was more than just a little weary by the time the candidates showed up.

Gordon went over the ground rules with them, while I went into the men's room to put on a clean shirt. While there, Mr. Brown, my AARP liaison, who had been most helpful with bringing out the local seniors, came into the bathroom in a panic.

"Look," he said in a spooky tone, "who put this out on the literature tables?"
He was holding a pamphlet with a likeness of Benjamin Franklin on it and the inviting title "An Open Letter From Ben Franklin." This "letter" then went on to describe the "Jewish conspiracy" and how Jews were "vampires." I didn't have to read more than a paragraph to realize it. "We're being sabotaged!"

"What?" Brown looked at me excited and puzzled.

"This is a set-up. Somebody's trying to sabotage us!" I told him.

The light when on. "Yes, yes! Of course," he agreed.

"Get rid of it my friend," I yelled. We raced out the door and practically knocked the literature table over pulling the scandalous pieces from it.

Guests were already arriving as Mr. Brown and I scoured the hall to make sure we got up all of the offending fliers.

This was so insidious, so evil, that I almost marveled at it. With that title and using Mr. Franklin's good name, everyone would have picked it up, become horrified and the whole event, as well as UP's future would have been stopped dead in its tracks.

I couldn't help but wonder if Daar or one of his henchmen was up to this. What better way to fight a discrimination rap then to try and portray the discriminated, i.e. me, as an anti-Semite? Or could it be someone in the community? Like Kenny? Was he so upset that we were registering "retards" that he would sabotage the whole effort? Or was it just a loon? A lone nut?

Who knows, but it did make me wonder. It was hard to believe, but even in this embryonic state, UP already had enemies. Vicious ones, too. Thanks to Mr. Brown, though, we had foiled the saboteurs at the very last minute. Mr. Brown kept his eye on the table all night, but we never did catch the culprit(s).

After such a heart-stopping start, the rest of the affair went off without much of a hitch. Between 75 and 100 disabled and/or senior citizens showed up, and acquainted themselves in a most democratic fashion, asking, for the most part, intelligent and insightful questions.

Yes, there were a few characters in the crowd, who rambled on about Lincoln or LaRouche, but the crowd quickly quieted them, enjoying the spice they added to the affair, but not the time they were eating up.

The candidates were civil and not too long-winded. Anthony was a great traffic cop and kept everything moving, and the panel, as planned, plugged holes. Both candidates were well informed and sincere. Peter and I gave them sample questions days before the forum. We wanted informed answers, not glib one-liners which often mask a lack of any real knowledge.

I wish I could give you a blow-by-blow account, some quick, concise rendering of the intellectual tussle, but alas, I was on my toes for most of the evening. I like to think of it as directing, but in truth it was more akin to schlepping. Moving this, changing that, accommodating here, adapting there.

Between cable TV's needs and those of our illustrious audience, I had a crash course in logistics. You learn a lot about the movement of manpower and resources whenever you do disabled events.

Even with the help of a bevy of friends, some like blessed Calvin, with practical stage management skills, I still caught the whole affair in a whirl of moving chairs, sweaty handshakes, lost napkins, spilled coffee, numerous directions to the johns, and a constant rechecking of the literature table. Needless to say, I missed the finer points of the debate, but in a nutshell: Sheila, the Democrat and activist lawyer, played up the 200 pieces of legislation she'd already authored, legislation that protected numerous minorities, including the disabled. Mehan, the Republican, was for "work not welfare for disabled citizens" and "everyone" was for ADA. The toothless wonder.

Citizens spoke up, as should happen in a well-functioning democracy. And, as the evening progressed, so did the level of their enthusiasm and curiosity, to the point that we had to leave a number people standing (and sitting) in line, questions unasked.

That led to a good bit of button-holing, as the candidates tried to make their way through the moving maze of disabled citizens and their machines. Machinery, used with great stealth, to corner the candidates long enough to get off another impertinent question or two. The buttonhole extraordinaire.

Sheila was admired by a slightly larger crowd -- as the Westside heir apparent -- and her questions were peppered with many salutations to the near great Zelda. Michael Mehan was part sought after and part seeking, as is often the case with candidates running their first campaign as a grooming exercise. He was an all-around good sport.

All in all, it went well. It really was democracy in action...I was proud of UP, I was proud of the community, I was even proud of the candidates.

Peter was very happy. "Good job," he said, eyeing some trim little blond sitting in the corner. "Talk to you later. And send me any last minute receipts, dude. You did it!"

I was happy, too...just to live through it. Of course, as is true in all close calls, I learned a lot...like to always have someone "on watch" over your literature table as well as double checking all materials just before show time. I like to believe that because of Mr. Brown's quick notice we not only avoided marring UP, but we also saved the good name of Benjamin Franklin.

I also learned that it's essential to have a stage manager. If only Thompson had shown up. That was not a good sign.

I had a final epiphany while I was loading dozens of untouched cookies and cans of cola back into my car: Don't scrimp and buy cheap food. If it doesn't get eaten, you end up carting it home. Your final punishment being that you eat so many damn sugar cookies on the ride home you get racked with indigestion.

And it is true hell when it's indigestion that shows you the error of your ways.

After a half a teaspoon of baking soda in half a glass of water, I was happy and hopeful again, as I lay in bed pondering it all. With only indigestion to regret, I realized how lucky we had been.

We had pulled off the event, giving the candidates, for the first time ever, a real chance to meet their disabled constituents. We informed the public of our concerns and raised UP's profile, all while dodging a bullet that could have been fatal. Not bad.

Best of all, the local community actually showed up. That's no easy feat with all the health and mobility problems disabled citizens often face.

But it was a first and they came out to be part of it! Having the support of AARP, and Aids Project L.A. didn't hurt either, but, in truth, a lot of disabled citizens made a special effort to get there. Even ol' Mountain had shown up -- late...his Universal Access ride having gotten everything screwed up. As small consolation, we smoked a joint in the the alleyway behind the center. I told him all about the treacherous misuse of Ben Franklin's name and image, and the sad fact that Thompson hadn't shown up. He was surprised by both. We finished our joint just as Universal

Access showed back up to take the big guy back to East L.A.

I thanked him for being part of the clean up crew. That was it.

In its own kind of crazy grassroots way, it had really worked. I wondered why I was so surprised. With a loud and happy belch of baking soda breath, I slept with ease, thinking we had finally made real progress.

A few days later, I received a phone call from AARP in Washington DC, wanting to know if UP had any photographs of disabled seniors.

"You want a picture of disabled senior citizens?" I asked, wanting to make sure I heard her right.

"Yes, that's right," she affirmed, to my astonishment.

"Just a moment, please." I dropped the phone from my ear, and stared at it for a moment as the realization came over me. Unbelievable as it seemed, the fact was, the largest organization of senior citizens in the world -- some thirty-three million strong -- did not have a single picture of a disabled senior.

Organizationally they were living in denial. In spite of the fact that 53% of the disabled are 50 and over, AARP's "vigorous self image" created blinders when it came to those seniors...to the point that AARP didn't have a single picture of a senior in a wheelchair. My heart sank. I realized we were going to have to educate our friends, who should know better, as well as the simply ignorant...the task was going to be twice as big,

"Where do you want the photo sent," I said, resigned to my fate.

* 24 *

They answered. A general denial. Jimmi was right. Everyone else, including myself, was wrong. Daar was going to fight the lawsuit.

Okay, so be it. Still, it was a little disheartening. For I knew I'd have to do all the initial legal work...all that time and energy. All because this guy didn't want to be reasonable and unlock a simple chain. I never thought I would meet a businessman who hassled someone who was legitimately trying to patronize his business.

Life is paradoxical. When it should be easy, it isn't.

Unlocking a chain. When it should all be neighborly, it isn't. When it should take a polite request, it doesn't.

It takes filing lawsuits and having the boxer in me aroused.

And all I had walked up to the counter for was a simple cup of coffee.

All I got was bitter discrimination.

It was looking like it was going to take a movement.

Damn, how the Fates work! I was sincerely hoping that common sense and compassion, helped along by a potential lawsuit, would carry the day. The chain would come down, the suit would be withdrawn, and a couple of tough guys would shake hands, one would park his car, the other would sell him a cup of coffee and together they would enjoy another day in the paradise known as Venice of America.

As the kids said back then, "Not!"

See what you get for living a deliberate life, I reminded myself.

"If it takes a battle," I said aloud, "so be it."

But first...

* 25 *

Downtime. Time to relax and ponder. One of the nice things about working in a voter registration/GOTV effort is you always know when you're going on vacation. It happens shortly after the first Tuesday in November. And what a vacation...a full year or better. Then, back again. Nice cycle. Power comes and goes, but elections are forever...hopefully.

When you get into the every other year rhythm of it, you find you really do have time to gear up and plan before the election, execute your plan during the campaign and then most humbly drop off the face of the earth after the election, come what may, just to relax and ponder.

Read up. Reflect. Make love to your spouse and play with the kids. All very important, if you're into social justice for the long haul. One must know when to ebb as well as flow, and election night -- win, lose or draw -- allows you in a very concrete way to just ebb away, back to your real life, your authentic life of family, friends, and hobbies.

This time of peace, reflection, and authentic living allows you to come back to the public arena refreshed and recharged. Sometimes, as they say, it's good to go home and just be.

Democracy allows you to do that.

I figured I'd do a little reading and maybe a little grant research and writing, in addition to whatever was necessary in my case against Daar. Outside of that I hoped for a little intellectual respite, a minor sabbatical. I would continue when and where necessary to register disabled voters, but at a more relaxed pace. The main aim was to just sit back and ponder. Ponder what? What else? Democracy. It had caught my attention.

I looked the word up in the Encyclopedia of Philosophy. Not only did I discover the meaning of the word, I found out what the Ancient Ones -- those first great Greeks who actually invented Democracy - meant by it.

Better still, the editors were kind enough to include a rough history of Democracy that went all the way back to the beginning. Back before Athens, before Homer, when Greeks merely came from Greece, and not some city/state within it, there was the first democracy, the "root democracy."

To understand root democracy one must first understand the root of the actual word.

The word "democracy" comes from the root word "demos," which, according to the Encyclopedia of Philosophy, when literally translated from the ancient Greek language, means the "poor people." More startling is the fact that the very word itself -- democracy -- originally meant "the rule of the poor over the rich."

It seems the first civilized thought of governance for western civilization had to do with controlling the power of the wealthy to exploit the poor by the only means the poor had at their nonviolent disposal -- their sheer numbers. And thus Democracy was born.

It was mandatory democracy. You had a duty to participate. All citizens had to vote. And what's more, all citizens had a duty to serve. Voting was just the beginning. All citizens had to serve their community in the assemblies and councils of that time. All citizens were responsible for the common good.

The Ancient Ones realized early on that, when voting is a duty in a democracy, it tends to control greed. When voting is a mere right, greed tends to control democracy. It was then as it is now.

Isn't it funny that for over 2,600 years western civilization has been dealing with the same problem the Ancient Ones faced? How do you control greed?

Needless to say, common citizens being in charge of their common affairs and, worse, being in charge of the oligarchs, upset the wealthy to no end and after a few hundred years they wised up. These "wise guys" are the much-vaunted Athenians, the modern starting point of democracy in most high school government classes today.

These Johnny-come-latelys to democracy started off by re-defining the word demos to mean the "common folks" as opposed to the "poor folks." This happened in spite of the fact that most common folks were poor folks. This redefining of the word demos was, in reality, the first spin job of western political thought.

Those tricky Athenians didn't stop there either; they began to put conditions on who could vote. No longer was it good enough to just be a citizen, now you had to have property, be educated, etc. All of these conditions worked to shrink the number and the impact of the votes of common poor folks 2,300 years ago. Talk about voter suppression. You don't have to ponder too long to realize that Americans have been following the example of the Athenians ever since.

By exporting Athenian democracy (whose written records, unlike those of the more ancient Greeks, made it through the ravages of time), the rich and powerful have been "qualifying" the right to vote ever since. This type of "conditional democracy," with its right to vote, as opposed to a duty to vote, is what allows wealth to dominate and manipulate the political system. It worked for the oligarchs of Athens. It works for the oligarchs of America.

As I closed the encyclopedia, I became a believer in root democracy. The ancient ones were right. Make all citizens participate. Let the noble, unruly mob have their say. They will, as a fully functioning democracy ensures, vote in their own best interest, i.e. the common interest.

The Ancient Ones were right in another way. Mandatory democracy virtually guarantees that the greed and the excesses of the self-absorbed wealthy will be held in check. All with no bloodshed, no revolts or prisons. A fully participating citizenry and a fair count of the votes are all it takes.

The old Greeks knew common sense and democracy go hand-in-hand. They trusted the common citizens and gave them a system that, if fully utilized, would protect the poor people from the excesses and vulgarities of concentrated wealth.

Those wily Greeks. Over 2,600 years ago, they came up with high ideas that still inspire and amaze. I was fortified. Democracy could work. Root democracy really could put "The People" in charge of their government. Voting as a duty guaranteed that. I realized that our whole effort isn't about civil rights; it's about civic responsibility. Ours. All of ours.

Like the Ancient Ones intended.

* 26 *

Root democracy might be for all citizens, but as a disabled man, it did make me step back and wonder. Did the Ancient Ones ever have my community in mind? Probably not. After all cripples weren't real successful back then. Most didn't make it past birth. So could the Ancient Ones have ever even imagined my community?

My people by definition live outside the cosmetic norm of society and are like a rolling, walking, crawling Rorschach test.

You see what you want. What your psyche needs.

Poor pathetic people, or super crips and poster children. Or just plain folks. Disability, like beauty, is in the eye of the beholder... Behold, the vibrating spastic enthusiasm of my community, eager even in this off year, to get registered. To vote. To take power.

Even during our down time we got calls and did workshops, speeches, interviews and the like, doing whatever needed to be done to just push things along. First things first though, we would always register voters.

* 27 *

Many times X actually does mark the spot. I bracket it. Above the passionately scrawled imprint the registrant makes, I write "His." At its bottom I write the word "mark," and then print his first name on the left side of the bracket and his last on the right. Just like the good (orange) book says. Some, like my friend Roy, to save time and energy have a rubber stamp of their signature made up. Some sign with a pen in their mouth or their toes...and do so beautifully. Practice makes anything perfect.

Most had no problems filling out their own registration form, or perhaps I should say they had the same problems that many people have, disabled or not.

"Can I put down my mail box address instead of my home address?" they often asked.

"No," I told them, "the Registrar of Voters needs to know your home address so that they may determine which precinct you live in and which polling place you're supposed to vote at. Of course you can forgo the whole problem by signing up for the Permanent Absentee Ballot and mailing your ballot in."

"Hey, which political party do I belong to?" another would ask. No shit...all kinds of people ask that question.

I'd answer, "I don't know. Here's a list of qualified parties and a blurb on what they stand for. You decide."

"I'll go ask my dad."

"Okay, good idea," I agreed. That's what an awful lot of non-disabled voters do, and we don't deal in double standards. "Go ask your dad -- while you're at it, ask mom, too."

Like I said, most of our families are pretty cool and only want the best for us. So, why not ask them? Are there parents who overprotect and/or downright harm disabled family members? Of course there are. I was suing one.

But at that moment, I didn't care about him. I could literally see that many disabled citizens were ready to take that first small step towards taking power by registering and voting.

I wondered if Daar had any idea, had any inkling of what his smallness of spirit, his inability to perform the simple task of unlocking a chain, had spawned within the disability community. Probably not. Hell, even in the off years, as our activities attested, a new consciousness of activism within the community seemed to be taking hold.

It was an activism that could very well be the seeds of a nationwide movement. So, for the time being, we ebbed and flowed, but never stopped. We just kept registering voters. One at a time. Face to face, citizen to citizen, in true grassroots fashion. Bit by bit, vote by vote, we helped them fill out the forms, answering each question carefully and, yes, wiping away a little drool in the process.

The saliva of real power.

* 28 *

Anyone who has lived or worked around disabled people quickly forgets they're disabled. You transcend it. You see your friend, your brother, your niece, or, if you're really lucky, your lover, and you see them not as a disabled person, but as the person you love.

People that want to do what "normal" people do.

It stunned me when the young woman with a mild developmental disability said she wanted to vote because "That's what normal people do."

I was torn. Should I tell her that in America that's not what most "normal" people do? Worse, should I tell her that I equate normalcy with mediocrity?

"Most citizens don't vote and you're the 'normal' one if you do," I told her.

"More normal than most?" she asked quite seriously.

I thought about that for a second -- for a guy that abhors mediocrity, I had to agree that that was a very unique way to put it. "Yeah, more normal than most," I said.

I am happy to say that these, the poor, profound, semi-washed masses -- these are root democrats of the 21st century. If the Ancient Ones only knew.

Don't forget, when those ancient Greeks created democracy they were also leaving disabled children "exposed" on many a hillside to die.

Yet today, ironically, we as a people and a community are on the verge of a civic revolution that will revitalize what the Ancient Ones thought wise when running government. Having the people -- all the people -- in charge and responsible. Sweetest of all, such a civic revolution will ensure that disabled people get their fair shot at living their full lives to the fullest potential, allowing them for the first time ever to be "more normal than most."

From exposure and death...to the brink of major political power. No one could deny that over the last 2,600 years, we've come a long way, baby.

Now, if we could just get that damn chain down.

* 29 *

"That's what you get when you doubt yourself," I told myself. The sad thing was, it was such a feeble attempt on their part that I could have handled it myself. Daar's squirrelly little lawyer was trying to get my complaint thrown out of court as a frivolous lawsuit. I had bet that my Request for Admissions would upset them, being that they had to legally start admitting things...things that stand up in court. That could be bothersome for the defendant.

"Admit or Deny" that Daar, now commonly referred to as "the defendant," was chaining off "said handicapped parking stall." "Admit or deny that defendant was denying disabled citizens the right to use the handicapped parking stall." It didn't matter to me which way they played it. Just admit or deny. They decided to admit. They admitted that they were breaking the law. But that's okay, they were discriminating against everybody, according to the squirrel, so I shouldn't feel left out of being left out. Right.

Somewhere along the line, though, the squirrel realized I was right. This was not their strongest argument. They started anew. Throwing aside irrationality in favor of "official sanction." The city said it was okay for the defendant to chain off handicapped parking spots and deny their use to potential disabled patrons. Mr. Daar "has never been ticketed," the squirrel was quick to point out to the distinguished silver-haired judge. "Or even warned."

Thus, my lawsuit, they contended should be thrown out as frivolous harassment. Okay, I expected that. Pretty standard. Fairly mediocre. The volatile City Inspector came to mind. "How many hot-dogs did Daar have to spend for that protection?" I wondered.
That was his standard operating procedure.

The problem was, I didn't do the standard thing that I had done up to that point. I didn't argue the case myself. I hesitated. I got a lawyer. One must remember that up until that point -- of actually bringing in a lawyer -- I had brought forth a proper complaint against the defendant. Dotting every i and crossing every t, legally speaking, I laid out the facts and the law in such a fashion that anyone who had actually read my complaint would have been able to argue why it should go forth. No matter what the squirrel over there said.

If only my lawyer had just read it.

Thank god, the good Judge had. Because the way that my sputtering stand-in for a lawyer was fumbling through the Judge's simplest questions, I believe that had his honor not had such solid first hand knowledge, he probably would have thrown the case out.

"And what have you to say counselor," the judge intoned from the bench, "about the defendant's contention that this is not a public nuisance because it has been 'okayed' by city inspectors?" Expecting the muddled worst in the form of an answer, he got it.

My poor excuse for a lawyer started sputtering and went off on some explanation about what constitutes a lock, as I slumped back in my seat wounded by the full knowledge that my lawyer, Zippo the Wonder Kid, hadn't even read the one page of Points and Authorities I had given him. Had he, he would have been able to quote from settled case law that just as "a rose is a rose," a public nuisance is a public nuisance and can't be sanctioned or "okayed" by the law. Not only that, but he could have informed the judge on just what constitutes a public nuisance and how a chained off blue zone was a textbook example of a modern public nuisance.

If he had just read the one pager. I squirmed in the back row of the courtroom, certain that his lack of preparedness was about to sink us.

I bit my lip as the judge scolded Zippo. I really thought it was over. As fortune would have it Daar's attorney started to interject, and low and behold the Judge scolded him, too.

Telling him to tell his client, no, better yet, asking if Daar was present? He was.

The judge asked Daar to stand and proceeded to give him "a little advice." In open court the good judge "encouraged" Daar to remove the chain immediately.

Daar started to plead that he had the "okay" of city inspectors.

The Judge cut him off. "You can not officially sanction a public nuisance," the Judge said, his voice flaring like his silver hair. "Plaintiff's cause of action will stand." His hammer went down. Loud. Daar just stood their looking almost as pathetic as my lawyer. I thought maybe this humbling experience and the frank judicial advice would make Daar do the right thing. Just maybe.

I had been extremely lucky in so narrowly averting disaster. The Judge, being a literate and conscientious man, had done his homework. He had read the complaint and, in spite of Zippo's studied incompetence, he had agreed with me.

I had even made it easy for the Zipster. I had laid out a one page legal memo with Points and Authorities that would have at least given the impression that he had read the complaint. He had not done even that. When I loudly mentioned to Sal -- who had recommend Zippo -- that he was ill-prepared, and a joke, Sal thought for a moment. Then he said to me, "The guy's got a learning disability."

"And you didn't think this was important to mention before the hearing?" I asked, shocked.

"Hey, who am I to second guess the disabled? Hire the handicapped, right?" he squawked.

"They gotta be qualified, dude. Hire the qualified handicapped," I said, exasperated.

He looked at me in that mock dumb way that tough guys do. "Live by the sword, die by the sword," was all he said. Some philosopher.

Zippo had died on the sword of his own incompetence and he damn near took me with him. Now there was no doubt. I fired Zippo.

* 30 *

Some organizer. As much as I was getting off on getting others involved, I was at the very same time losing Thompson.

We still drank hearty and hailed the mutual light of our vision, but where I would soar, he would dwell, as is the either/or curse of the Irish. And where he dwelled was in the blackness, in the abyss, in the place where the pirate came out.

Head dangling, one eye snapped shut, damning everyone to a fate of weakness and despair. The fear got him. The fear of the inevitable. The fear to accept his disability. With acceptance comes transcendence. This, the pirate did not understand. This, he did not accept. This, he feared.

Not to say I was without fear, I just didn't let it manifest itself on my answering machine. He did. And with his phone number on the bottom of our brochure and his manic laughing and cooing on the answering machine -- our sanity, as well as our budding credibility was being seriously impaired.

It wasn't just the drink either. Not really. If it was just that -- that could be changed. You can stop drinking, hard though it may be. Some things, though, no matter how hard you try, you can't change. That's what tormented him. See, no matter how hard you try you can't change the effects of a busted spine...not yet, anyways.

Thompson never accepted that. It was hard for him to identify with disability. He was born and lived able bodied for sixteen years, and as noble as the efforts of UP were, to totally embrace them, he'd have to admit and accept that he was in fact, a disabled man. And that was really hard for him. It brought out the pirate.

It was a pity he didn't have the good fortune to come into it naturally, as I did, from birth. Then disability would just be part of his natural flow. So, I understand why he did what he did. In some things -- and for some psyches -- it is better to not have known, than to have known and lost.

I changed the number on the brochure.

* 31 *

As I seemed to be losing more than I was gaining, I was slightly upset with myself. Thus it was only too fitting that the first I heard of the mighty Paul was that he was upsetting people with -- of all things -- humor, and Lord knows right about then I needed a good laugh.

Finding other organizers was becoming no easy task and lone leaders do not a movement make. A majority of one might be right, but it cannot take power.

Between the stupidity of lawyers and the fear of cohorts, I seemed to be stumbling backwards.

Then I heard of his upsetting people and I knew there was hope. He'd upset everyone, too. He had real potential, because he, apparently, was not afraid to upset the pretentious and excessively serious. And he had done exactly that. People were pissed. Upright citizens were outraged!

His crime? His outrage? His sin of sins? He told a joke. A joke for Christ's sake! All these all too serious cripples were upset by a mere joke. Long before I met him, I loved him for that alone. He was, to this dismal group, that most dangerous of revolutionaries -- a comic, who, happening to have a disability, made a few jokes about it. Imagine that!

Of course some tight ass crips got offended.

We, grand cripples, are of every ilk and disposition and some of us don't see anything funny about disability, or for that matter, anything else. With such people, this utter lack of humor is, of course, their biggest disability. Quite naturally, Paul took full advantage of this and loved upsetting them. "Just doing standard shtick, can you believe it," he would say, happy it took so little. "At least they are talking about me."

"Yes they are."

"Controversy sells tickets!" Paul exclaimed, full of his Irish devil.

"So says you, me, and Muhammad Ali," I told him, full of mine.

Even ailing, he was more fun than all of them put together and, while we ate the macrobiotic crap that he loved, and sipped beer through straws, I told him the rest of the story.

It was a meeting of the Westside Center for Independent Living. They had asked UP to do a little voter registration at their 20th anniversary party. Simple enough, so I said, "Sure." Over the stout objections of the Mountain, I agreed to sit in on the planning meetings for the celebration.

Mountain had good reason to be leery. WCIL had a reputation of being little more than a grant mill, a place that used its mission and target population as window dressing to keep the funds coming in. Its founding mission of citizen advocacy and empowerment were just words in proposals to grab the cash or, more likely, to hold a dinner to grab the cash. They were exceptionally good at congratulating themselves, while giving someone else a plaque.

"It's a status quo, establishment-run organization with no grassroots base at all," Mountain had told me. He should know, having worked at the East L.A. CIL for years.

The Westside Center was the sad laughing stock of the system -- laughed at because it did so little in the way of real advocacy and sad because it had all the Westside's wealth and resources at its disposal.

"We envied them in East L.A.," he said. "They have that crazy blind guy, Lelan, running the joint... Be careful, he's a nut. And I mean certifiable." Mountain never minced words.

I should have listened; instead I gave him a flip, "Yeah, okay," thinking he was being a bit hard on old Lelan. It was true that the Westside's Director was a wee bit eccentric, but, as I told the Mountain, "Who can argue with voter registration, particularly in this community? It's like mom and apple pie. Hell..." I assured him, "we'll pull off a quick little event with WCIL and then we'll use that as a model to work with other Independent Living Center's all over California. What can go wrong? This is democracy were talking about, here."

The Mountain just shook his head. "I like your enthusiasm," he said.

I began to get my first sense that Mountain may have a point as I came out of my reverie to hear the notorious Paul, whom I did not yet know, being vigorously trashed.

"And he had this wheelchair -- some kind of crazy wheelchair..." the plump and insulted board member was saying, "that lifted him straight up, while the theme of 2001 played in the background and, once he was fully erect, he made some stupid joke about being a stand up comedian who really 'could get it up,'" she exclaimed, her color rising. She steadied herself with, "And excuse me for having to say that...really!" She was mortified, the disgust rolling hard off the "R."

It was all so silly it made me laugh. I laughed alone. Quite seriously, like a bad Italian movie they all turned and looked at me at the same time, with disdain. These people weren't handicapped -- they were bent. "Sounds like someone I'd like to meet," I told them. They leered at me. "Well, I would." Why lie? I figured.

I was sternly informed that this was their "big event," their annual dinner, with no less than Dear Abby herself at the head table. Paul had been hired to give the keynote address, and he came and did jokes, "vulgar jokes," instead. Very inappropriate. And in a red tuxedo no less.

"That sounds pretty damn appropriate to me," I said. Again no one laughed.

I thought this would be a quick little event, but I was wrong, as I found out when I asked how many meetings they wanted to have before the event.

One a week! The event was six weeks away!!!

Their lack of humor only enhanced my sense of dread. I comforted myself with the fact that I had heard about Paul. Again, I couldn't help but love Paul before I met him, as he had the best recommendation...their complete disdain. These glum types were taking their little event and Dear Abby a bit too seriously.

"Six meetings?" I asked hesitantly. "Did you say six meetings?"

A firm and annoyed, "Yes," came from the plump one in unison with a couple of her minions.

As I sat there, realizing that this was the down side of democracy -- being outvoted by the humorless and pompous -- I tried to see Paul as the advantage within the upcoming disadvantage. I was deeply honored to meet anyone who pissed off the "Dear ol' Abbster." I knew he would be great fun.

When we finally did meet up at a mutual friend's place and I talked to him about helping us to organize the community, he told me that the most he had ever organized was a stand-up comedic gig, and, "Being the only one who had to show up -- half the time I made it," he said cracking a smile.

Sitting there in Helen's front room, with all the other artists and writers she knew who happen to have disabilities -- that was good enough for me. I always felt anyone who can do five minutes of original jokes in front of a live audience is really brave and crazy anyway. Just what UP needed.

The Mountain was right, too. Doing that voter registration gig with WCIL was hell. But it got Paul and me talking about organizing on a grander scale, so it was worth it, more or less, as the good Dr. Stanford would say.

"All those damn meetings," I told the prankster, "all of which were pretty useless, just putting people through the motions, instead of putting them in action."

"Inaction in action," Paul quipped.

"Exactly," I said with a heavy sigh and proceeded to tell him the rest of the story over strong drinks in Helen's backyard.

* 32 *

Every week his refrain was the same and every week his lack of vision had nothing to do with his being blind.

"I've spoken to fifty or sixty people in the community," Lelan would begin, "and there really isn't much interest in voter registration," he would say, gruffly. His only variance being that each week the numbers got larger.

Being sightless as well as witless, he couldn't see how most people around the table, and even his ardent sycophants looked at him like he was just plain silly...which he was. These people were here to try and pull off an event and were happy to have anyone willing to help them do that, even a guy who's into voter registration. Thus, Lelan's weekly rant was disconcerting. Did he want to put me on the spot?

"Yeah, people in this community just love to be powerless. It's our biggest disability," I'd say trying to tease him out of it. It did no good. I was amazed how it came up week after week.

"I've spoken to seventy-five or eighty disabled citizens. I've talked with hundreds of disabled citizens..." If the meetings had gone another week, I'm quite sure he was going to tell me he'd talked to every gimp in the county and could assure me that there was no "real" interest in voter registration.

Consequently, every week I would give him, just a little more emphatically than the week before, what became "the rap." I'd tell him how I had been out in "the vineyards" and how the community seems to be very enthused about registering to vote and taking power, always ending with something to the effect of: "Even if what you're saying is true, Lee, it's incumbent on you -- and all the rest of us, too -- to tell those uninterested people just how important voting is to our community if we're ever going to have any chance of protecting ourselves -- ourselves."

He would get testy and say things like, "Are you doubting my veracity?"

I could tell he was looking for a fight, and I wasn't going to give him one. I didn't take the bait. I'd just sigh, along with many others around the table, and tell him that if he would just invest a little personal capital and let these alleged nay-sayers know how important it was to him personally that these folks get registered and vote, that if he would just do that, not only would more disabled citizens be voting, but maybe a few of them would turn up at his anniversary party.

That moved us along to the greater concern, thank god, attendance. WCIL had sent out 5,000 invitations, had dedicated a whole issue of their newsletter to the anniversary party and the phone still was not ringing off the hook. Hell, it wasn't ringing at all, according to Ted, who was a member of the WCIL's board.

UP sent out a flier to our mailing list of a few hundred, and the reaction was less than enthusiastic. The activists in the community had dismissed WCIL long ago.

Every week people got a little more dismal at the endless meetings.

The truth is, Lelan was projecting his fears. As it turns out, the lack of interest had to do with WCIL, not voter registration. WCIL's lack of community involvement was the most stunning thing about the place. Among the local disabled citizenry, its inaction, its lack of involvement, was what it was most famous for. You'd never know from looking at it from the outside, but, then, that's what window dressing is all about.

WCIL was after all, a bright shiny place, all Frank Gehry avant-garde with the guts of the building showing through here and there, creating the illusion of ultra accessibility and brave new thought, which the Westside's wealthy loved to throw money at. I say illusion, because, in reality, it had no real brave new thought or real connection to the greater community...disabled or otherwise.

In actuality, it did little but raise hundreds of thousands of dollars to pay an executive director and a staff who, likewise, did little more than raise hundreds of thousands of dollars to keep paying an executive director and staff to keep raising money, and on and on and on, ad infinitum.

Lelan, its executive director, besides being a blind guy, was a former record executive who confused record promotion with community organizing and thus was ill-prepared to handle an advocacy organization such as the center was supposed to be. But to the TAB world, he was blind, so he was imminently qualified.

He ran the center from the top down -- corporate style, i.e., with no real interest in empowering individual citizens from the ground up. That was apparent to me by the way he deluded himself, week after week, about the growing disinterest in voter registration. The old corporate apparatchik had no interest in democracy and undoubtedly saw UP's effort as a threat. We were doing what they only paid lip service to. Not only were we advocating the taking of our legitimate democratic power, we were turning others into serious advocates by registering them to vote and getting them to do likewise with still others. In other words we were being proactive. This scared Lelan.

Like most poverty pimps, he tried to stamp out any real progressive change or action, because he feared that it would somehow show him up if they didn't get involved -- and worse -- it might involve real work if they did get involved. Lelan's weekly objections convinced me he shuddered at either thought.

Okay, so Lelan and I weren't drinking buddies. In spite of all that, I never expected what we got on the day of the event, the day I found out that Lelan wasn't just blind or lacked vision, worse, he was just plain mean. That's right folks, Lelan was that most notorious of all things -- a mean cripple.

Now it's one thing to be mean or small to an old boxer like me, quite another when I'm standing outside the center with the President of the L.A. League of Women Voters and a half dozen of her UP/AARP colleagues, all quite enthusiastic about registering disabled citizens to vote.

With my gang of most civil citizens in tow, we meet Lelan at the front door, which he was stiffly blocking with himself and his mighty white cane. Unknowingly, I began to introduce him to Madame President and the others, asking somewhere along in the process, "Where do you want us to set up? In the community room?"

After six weeks of meetings, bitching over voter resignation, food, fliers, etc., where to set up was never actually discussed. I had just assumed we'd use a corner of their large accessible community room.

"No, not the community room," Lelan informed me. "You're welcome to set up in the parking lot."

"The parking lot?" I was shocked and turned to give it a startled once over. There were a dozen beat up, rusty tables and chairs wobbling in the uneven sun-baked, cracked asphalt parking lot. Some had a raging paper table cloth blowing in the wind, held down by that all-purpose centerpiece, a large rock...a seriously large rock. Waiting to fall on god knows who? And in this wobbly crowd, that's foreseeable.

Foreseeable that they could do some very real damage. Foreseeable that is, if you had some real vision, care, and compassion.

Lelan seemed to lack all these -- a true corporate caliber philistine.

"Do you know what the parking lot looks like?" I asked. He was, after all, blind.

"Adequate accommodations have been made for you in the parking lot," he said staring dead ahead.

He may be blind, but I could see that he was just straight out fucking with me. "Adequate accommodations!?" I was stunned, yet again. For a second I forgot that I was in the company of the League President. "You call those adequate accommodations?" I asked sharply. "Man, those tables are a mess, a rusty, ugly, dangerous mess -- worse, there is no shade. It's a parking lot, Lee!"

"Now wait a min--"

"No! You wait," I cut him off. "If this is your definition of 'adequate accommodation,' tell me how the hell we're ever going to get the TAB world to do the right thing and make reasonable accommodations for us? Huh, Lee? How the hell are we going to do that when our own leaders relegate us to parking lots and call that 'reasonable accommodations?'"

"You said you can register people anywhere, right?" he said mockingly.

"Lelan," I said, controlling my anger for the sake of Madame President, "the parking lot is ill-equipped to do voter registration in. It's too damn hot and dangerous."

"Well, I'm sorry. The building has been locked up. Security concerns," he said as straight ahead as his stare.

"Security concerns? What the hell are you talking about 'security concerns?'" This is so absurd and small that I no longer cared that I was standing there with the President of the League. "Lee, we just went through six weeks of meetings," I said through clenched teeth, "and no one mentioned a damned security concern, not once, so don't jerk me around on this."

"At these public affairs, there are all kinds of riffraff. And I can't have them roaming about the building," he yelped back.

Riffraff. That's what he actually said.

"Excuse me, folks," I said to my volunteers, now as shocked as me. "Why don't you go over and have a little refreshment while I work this out. I think you're in luck -- the refreshment table does not appear to be in the parking lot." Everyone was more than happy to go eat, but hunger had little to do with it.

Once they were out of earshot, I really went off.

"What do you mean security concerns," I hissed. "That's the craziest god damn thing I've ever heard of, Lee. This is your damn anniversary party and you're locking up the very center you're supposed to be celebrating. Have I got that right? That's crazy, man! Crazier still, you're making people, disabled people at that, sit out in the hot sun in an asphalt parking lot, instead of in the air-conditioned comfort of the center. That's treating them like riffraff all right, Lee. Tell me, when did we step through the looking glass?"

"How dare you..."

"No, Lelan, how dare you. How dare you waste our time and treat our people like this, like 'riffraff,'" I raged. "This building is your crown jewel and you're locking it up. You're keeping the people out. How dare you! Now, stop being silly and open this joint up. You can't lock your own people out of the very center they're celebrating, damn it."

In a rather ghoulish way, he said, "Oh can't I?" Thank the Great Spirit that he was blind, or else I might have punched him upside his demented head.

It really was another Alice in Wonderland event in my life.

It's one thing when some crazy TAB person discriminates against you and chains off accessible parking, but Mountain was right. It's downright certifiable when a blind fool, one of our own, chains up a disabled resource center. Then it hit me, that's not crazy, nor is it insane, that's sabotage. Lelan preferred to sabotage his own event rather than, I guess, make UP look good...whatever that meant in his small dark squirming brain, only slightly larger than his even darker heart.

Okay, Lelan was more than rhetorically crazy. He was real world whacked, and as I walked away to find a few WCIL board members to express my shock and outrage to, I couldn't help but wonder what was going on with my karma?

I mean how could I, one reasonably decent handicapped guy get locked out of so many different parking lots and centers that were specifically put in place to aid and abet me? How many? Talk of irony. It seemed every time I turned around somebody was locking me out of something else. It was irony verging on perversity. "What's up with that?" the boxer in me asked. Before I could figure it all out, I found Ted and informed him of Lee's insanity.

"Jesus, dude," he said, as shocked as I was.

"Yeah, how's that for planting seeds," I said.

"Of his own demise," he replied. And with that, Ted powered off in his chair to talk to the madman, and I went to apologize and nibble with my civic-minded heavies.

"Don't let it worry you," Madame President said cheerfully. "We can see that he's a stick in the mud." That's about as strong a public condemnation as you're going to get out of a true lady of the league.

They were, all of them, understanding and sympathetic, and, after a bit, with clipboards in hand, they started walking up to the few people at the event and asking if they were registered to vote. Like real activists, even under difficult circumstances, they went to work.

Ted returned after a bit and told me that Lelan had agreed to allow "a tour of the Center."

I was about to tell Ted to tell Lelan to stuff it when Madam President cut in and said she and the others would love to see the center. Once again the diplomatic poise of the League carried the day, and a tour was hastily arranged. Besides, they had already registered everyone who needed it...the eight other people who had been milling about in the parking lot.

"It will give the party time to fill out," Madame President said, optimistically.

I thanked Ted, as the CIL staffers organized the impromptu tour. "I'll tell you, buddy, Lelan is either senile or sadistic. To lock up this minor Taj Mahal and force disabled citizens out into a hot, shadeless parking lot. It's one or the other."

He agreed. "Write a letter of your concerns," he calmly told me. "When Lelan's contract comes up for renewal in a couple of weeks, so will this. It's a real embarrassment."

Enough said. I thanked him again.

I'd like to say that my colleagues returned and that we registered many more people, but the truth is after another hour of polite chitchat and hanging out at the food table, me and my crew registered three more voters.

Just three. Which is three more than before, I'll be the first to admit. But if I needed further convincing that WCIL had no grassroots base, here it was. I doubt that more than a couple dozen people showed up, and of that, we registered a grand total of 11 citizens.

That meant that after twenty years of existence, WCIL's grand anniversary celebration involved less than three dozen people and a locked-up center. As if they needed another reason to dump Lelan, I wrote the letter, and Ted kept his word. It was brought up.

I was told that the letter, as well as a rumored $300,000 dollars that fell through the cracks, upset Lelan so badly that he handed in his resignation...before leaving for one last conference on behalf of WCIL. He got to use the center's dime one more time.

Ted told me later that, upon returning, Lelan had had a change of heart and had tried to withdraw his resignation, thinking his sycophants would rally to his defense, with that favorite defense of sycophants: "How can we survive without him?"

The problem is, sycophants' passions are enthusiastic but none too deep. When they see which way the wind is blowing, they become kites. Even the plump one, who was so outraged at the outrageous Paul, refused to accept Lelan's attempted withdrawal. His resignation was final.

See, crips like Lelan can be small, mean, and exploitive. We are not all roly-poly and all too happy to be helped, and thus it became apparent to me that it's important to speak out against those who use a leadership position to do everything but lead. It is necessary to speak out against those who aren't leaders at all, but greedy little self-serving leeches. For all the BS of WCIL's leadership, some good did come of it. I had found Paul.

"From the insane to the sublime. Is there any other way?" I asked Paul.

"Only in comedy," he laughed.

"I'm just glad you pissed them off, or they never would have mentioned you," I told him.

"No such thing as bad press," he said, chomping on a macrobiotic clump of vegetables. " If they ever say anything positive, it's usually to take credit for themselves."

"Some people lead like that," I offered.

"Or think they do. Lelan's gone, right?" Paul asked with a laugh. "He was a shitty judge of comedy anyway."

"Yes, he was, Paulie," I agreed.

"Hey, bro, you want to see that tape?" he offered. "That red tux is really something."

"Sure. I'm honored to see the offending piece."

2001 never sounded so good. After watching it, we laughed hard. I told Paul I kind of felt sorry for ol' Lelan -- being blind and all -- this whole sight gag was lost on him. "Think about it, bro, the poor bastard was stuck depending on an outraged Dear Abby for a description. Now that's what I call a disability." We laughed harder. "Yeah, without Lelan," I continued, "and his six meetings I would never have met you, bro, so don't be too rough on him. Besides I already did that for you."

"Thanks, but promise me we'll never have six meetings about anything," Paul said. "Lelan must have been blind. Didn't he know that disabled people have enough problems getting to an event, much less six meetings to plan it. Sounds like a lot of hand-holding."

"It was."

"I can see a meeting to plan an event and another right before it to get everybody on the same page, but six! Talk about out of touch with reality."

"It was barbaric," I assured him. As Paul could no longer drive himself, he understood inherently the problems disabled citizens have in simply getting around. He used the county's Metro Access service to get himself to important things like doctors' appointments, comedic gigs and such, but he rarely went out on a whim.

"Do you really think we could organize our community with just two meetings before each big event?" he asked.

"I don't know, what do you think?"

"Why not?" he said. "You saw what six meetings did. There were more people at the meetings than at the event. They sucked all the life out of it. They sabotaged it. All those meetings just made Lelan more and more paranoid. No. Two meetings per event is probably best."

And quite by accident, and with no real understanding of how this would impact upon our future, the "two meeting rule" was born.

Best of all, this discussion was just the beginning, as Paul and I began to seriously think about grassroots organizing. With 2001 playing in the background and Paul's image rising up on the TV like the disability vote itself, I realized I may have just found what I had been looking for all along, namely, another organizer. Paul got it. He was brave, smart, and funny. Best of all, he was bold! And Goethe was right, there was genius in it...in a bright red tux.

2001 never sounded so good.

* 33 *

The 21st century sounded good, but it wasn't long until people started to ask: "What are we going to do next?"

I wasn't sure. Luckily, by design, we had time to think about it. Whatever it was, I was sure I would be doing, if not the bulk of the organizing, then the bulk of the running around, facilitating others' organizing. Whatever that meant.

Such honor was bestowed upon me, not because I was the instigator or well-connected, or even the most qualified, for I was eminently unqualified when it came to all that. I was simply the most durable, even on my crutches.

Unlike a good many of my beautifully broken brothers and sisters, I could take the wear and tear of the hustling about that our fledgling project demanded. I was mobile. I could go to the people. I could fire up the old Ford Granada and hit the road.

Large groups, or one-on-one, it was just easier and more effective to go to them. It afforded me the luxury of being able to hang out. You hang out a lot when you're organizing democratic movements. See, you've got to listen a lot, so consequently you hang out a lot. That is what I was doing that day with the Mountain, trying to recover my energy and enthusiasm from the WCIL debacle.

The Mountain was tickled by the calamity of it all and did everything but say, "I told you so."

"Big waste of time and energy," he said, all-knowingly.

"Yep, you were right," I humbly agreed.

"You are the legs of this thing," he explained, full of good pot and better advice. "Don't wear yourself out. You have to stay narrowly focused, my friend, or you're going to burn out. Don't get involved in organizing too many other people's events. You're just there to register voters and even then, as WCIL showed you, you've got to be careful. Six meetings. Humph!" he snorted with disgust. "I hope you learned your lesson."

"I have," I said,

"Your job," he said seriously, "is to figure out ways to register, inform, and get out the vote of disabled voters, until they get the hang of democracy themselves. And between you and me, brother, that is a big enough task."

"Ain't that the truth," I wearily agreed. Our fondest dream was a real democratic uprising within the community. "Just pulling that off is the miracle, isn't it? Forget all the noble things we're going to do after we take power. The real nobleness of our cause is in the execution of the idea, isn't it?

"Correct. The nobleness isn't in the idea -- it's in pulling it off. It may not be easy," he said in a fresh halo of smoke, which made him look a bit more like a monk, "but if we disabled all made a commitment to register and vote, it really shouldn't be hard. After all, what we're really talking about here is disabled citizens paying attention to their own interests for just a few hours every other year or so and then voting accordingly. Not a lot of time and minimum effort, really, for virtually absolute power. Outside of a little justice, what else could you ask for?"

"There's really no excuse," I agreed again.

"Well, who knows," he said. "It is a powerful message to the most powerless people. Keep at it. You never know...maybe we can spark a democratic uprising yet."

"Maybe we can."

We sat for a minute, taking in the thought and a little smoke.

"It's all so practical," I said softly. "How come it sounds so damned utopian?"

"I think that's true of any idea whose time has come," the Mountain offered. "Just remember, my fuzzy-headed friend, you're not going to win everyone over. Never forget Lelan. And don't waste time arguing with people like that. "

"I know, I know. Don't argue with them, out-organize them," I said glumly. It brought me back to earth. I told the Mountain that I had lost Thompson and that to lose even a half-assed organizer at this point was a depressing setback.

"Get used to it," said the sage. "In this community, we lose people and abilities all the time. Death is just around the corner, man. Truth is, our best people will die, long before you get this crazy community organized and in control of its own affairs. Before you have your uprising. Believe me."

"Shit, Mountain."

"You have to face that," he said firmly.

"Oh man," I moaned, "we're going from the utopian to the morbid."

"Forget keeping people enthused and active, just keeping them alive and in one piece is a major accomplishment. If you can get them to vote in between all that, great! They will make a brighter future for someone else -- because death, you can be sure, will steal many from us before we ever get close to being organized."

"Stop it," I sighed heavily.

"Stop, nothing," he exclaimed. "That's why, with us, time is truly 'of the essence.' Don't put up with the toxic types. They steal too much time."

I had never thought about it before, but it was true. Lungs quit, hearts stop, MS, MD and a hundred other diseases and their acronyms overpower life. Psyches get depressed, medications get swallowed en masse, people grow tired of the pain, the loneliness, the poverty, and, most of all, the inability to do anything about it -- the utter powerlessness of it all.

"This is encouraging," I moaned.

"It's reality, man. That's why it's important to stay focused and not waste time. Don't forget that our lives, on average, are cut short. Don't count on others you've worked long and hard with to wake up in the morning," he said emphatically. "As such, don't waste time playing head games with fools. And meetings," he laughed, "which the foolish love, as opposed to actions, which they're usually afraid to take, only hasten the deterioration and rob you of your troops."

He was right, again. I told him that Paul agreed with him, and didn't wish to work on anything that took more than two meetings.

"Your friend is very wise," the Mountain said. "He's an organizer."

"I hope so," I said, without giving it much thought. "Because I fear I'll never find another organizer in this community."

"You'll find another, and another, and another, as soon as each one of us gets serious about taking responsibility for ourselves, our communities, and our country. Once each disabled citizen does that, you'll have millions of organizers."

Inhale.

"That's what the ancient Greeks intended."

Exhale.

"So, don't waste time in a lot of static meetings; stay in action. Otherwise, we lose people. If not due to death, then to boredom."

And, with a smirk and a toke, we both agreed that boredom was far worse than death.

* 34 *

If one is ready for action, or at least preparing for it, history will do its part, too. "Providence," as Goethe called it, "provides." History sent us, if not an organizer, an organizing force.

His name, like something out of a witch's brew, was Newt.

If you had told us back in 1993 that, within a year, the right wing of the Republican Party would take over Congress, we would have laughed you off. Further, if you'd had told us that these characters -- these "angry white men" -- would start dismantling the social safety net, giving disabled citizens the most compelling reason to register and vote, we would have asked you what you were smoking.

The fact is Newt and his "Contract with America" did just that.

For the first time in sixty years, disabled citizens had a real reason to vote -- their continued physical well-being, which was now under attack.

Newt. His talk alone about cutting up the social safety net really shook people. For the first time since Roosevelt, really, disabled citizens had a serious political problem. Their quest for life, liberty, and the pursuit of happiness, guaranteed by a number of government programs, was under direct threat from Newt and his minions. Funding for low-income housing was slashed. Employment programs and civil rights enforcement were consciously under-funded, or as we like to say, funded to fail.

Enforcement of civil rights law, as my legal battle proved, was virtually nonexistent. Nobody would enforce the law at its most simple, basic and blatant level, a chained-off handicapped parking stall. As has been said before, "Rights don't enforce themselves." Quite the opposite, no enforcement equates to no rights. Which seemed just fine with the new mindset in Washington, D.C.

And there certainly was a new mindset in Washington. They just didn't care.

Such ephemeral things as "civil rights" were overlooked, unenforced, or simply written right out of existence. The business community no longer had worry about issues of access or opportunity. Washington didn't care, so why should they? Throw in a few bribes to building inspectors and the like, and "rights" and "regulations" became little more than dirty words to the angry white guys now in charge.

Self-absorbed, self-serving, and self-righteous, the men who took power in 1994 were, in fact, a distinct minority everywhere...but in the House of Representatives.

"So they are a political problem of our own making," I would tell my audiences. "They are our own fault. Precisely because we did not get our vote out and they did. You know, there are a lot more of us than there are of them," I would tell any crowd of disabled people. "Look about you!"

They would look across the room at all the diversity that made them one. With wide, dark, knowing smiles they knew, regardless of who they were individually, that they shared a common plight of powerlessness and lost potential. They also knew that we, at UP, were right. We had to protect ourselves. Ourselves!

Thanks to Newt, suddenly we were seen as prophets. Organizing our vote really was important...no ifs, ands, or buts about it now. Best of all, we were out in front on this thing. UP had a solution to Newt.

I guess I should be thankful; after all, we were quite fortunate to have the spooky Newt and the very real threat he represented. I reminded myself that this didn't happen by accident, either. Only because we were already out there organizing were we able to take full advantage of the historical and political phenomenon being laid at our gnarled feet.

Were we lucky? Yes. But I happen to believe that luck is merely where preparation meets opportunity. Consequently, when Newt and his buddies started scaring the hell out of disabled people, were we prepared to use the opportunity to organize those same disabled people. Nothing motivates people like fear, but the important thing was to get people to manifest that fear in a constructive fashion, namely, voting. Suddenly, we were in demand! We were visionaries with registration forms.

And register they did. Newt really scared them. The more he talked, the more we registered. The fact is, up to that point, Newt was our best organizer. Talk about finding the advantages within the disadvantages.

Thanks, Newt.

* 35 *

To take a break from the novel life of an organizer, I took a stroll down the boardwalk to the local candy store to buy some sweets for that small piece of sweetness I call a daughter. As I was paying for my confections of affection, I could plainly see a blue international access symbol, denoting a handicapped equipped restroom, on the door behind the young cashier.

Finishing the transaction, I asked if I could use the "gentleman's room."

"Sorry," she said, cheerfully oblivious, "that's just for employees."

"Wait," I said. "A disabled citizen can use a handicapped equipped bathroom anywhere in the county of L.A."

To my astonishment, she said, "That may be, in L.A., but not here. Sorry."

"Lady, this is L.A.!" I said, not realizing the profane profundity of that statement.

This is L.A. all right...with its chained off handicapped parking stalls and (now) locked up bathrooms in seemingly every public place I walk into. Then it dawned on me.

Who owns this building? Without saying another word, I walked outside to the middle of the boardwalk, swirled around as only a guy on crutches can and faced the building.

It looked very similar to the Muscle Beach café in materials and construction.

"How many buildings does Daar own?" I wondered.

This is, like the Muscle Beach café, a relatively new building. It had all the necessary disabled access symbols and signs on the outside of the building as well -- all up to code. Just like the café. I bet it was Daar's. Jimmi said he was the biggest merchant on the boardwalk. Apparently Daar was also the biggest bully on the boardwalk, or, better put, all along the boardwalk.

"Could he actually be denying disabled people the right to piss?" I asked myself. Could he be that horrible?

Not letting people park is one thing, not letting them piss is beyond horrible -- that's painfully cruel...to say nothing of a complete contravention of written public policy, thought the pugnacious paralegal in me.

I laughed sadly at the realization. As Daar had absolutely no empathy for people or respect for the law, how could I expect him to appreciate that the legislature and the courts, as a matter of public policy, had mandated that every handicapped equipped john in L.A. be made available to any disabled person, regardless of whether they were a customer or not?

The legislative intent of such a law was clear. It hoped to avoid the public embarrassment and spectacle of disabled people urinating on themselves. Or worse, on you!

As I walked back to my apartment, I wondered how many disabled citizens this was affecting, many who, unlike me, couldn't make it home to take their long-delayed piss.

I had never been so pissed, while I pissed in my own bathroom. What about all the others who couldn't make it to theirs? Talk about an absolute affront to personal dignity.

And on the boardwalk, too...one of the few moderately accessible beaches in Southern California. Its miles of asphalt "boardwalk" allowed many disabled citizens at least some semblance of a day at the beach. And here was this malevolent bonehead willfully undermining every existing accommodation to make such a day not only enjoyable, but also possible.

Jimmi said Daar was the biggest merchant on the beach, and I'd bet, as I stood there urinating and fuming, that he was doing this at all his stores and restaurants.

If so, this guy was bent, and had to be stopped cold. I buttoned my fly, called my friend Bud, and asked the third year law student if he'd like to walk down to the candy store with me and join me in checking out my unrelenting suspicions. I had suspicions that not only the candy store but all of Daar's properties were busily denying disabled citizens the right to use properly designated bathrooms and parking stalls.

"Man, if this is true, if he's denying bathrooms and such," I told Bud, "my neighborhood is fast becoming the most anti-handicapped area in Southern California, while masquerading as one of the most accessible. No parking, no bathrooms."

"No shitahh...excuse the pun," Bud said, with a sardonic laugh.

"If you don't laugh," I told him, "it makes you cry."

What made Daar particularly despicable was that he liked to have everything up to code. All the necessary signage and regulation blue zones to draw your attention, make you stop, get out of your car, make a specific request, and then after that, after all that -- he denies you.

He likes to screw with people, unnecessarily. How many others had to go through this time-consuming, energy-sapping process only to ultimately be denied? How many walked or rolled by numerous bathrooms with an urgent need, and were denied relief, by Daar's employees?

It was just like the chain. But the bathrooms were different, really different. There you're messing with some of the most intimate and personal needs of citizens with disabilities. It was almost perverse. How could I not stand up against the nuttiness? Truthfully, I could hardly believe I had to fight this fight. This was all so beyond human decency and common sense. Worse, it was all so easy to remedy.

Yet, nobody would make him. "Why is this guy above the law?" I asked Bud.

"He isn't," Buddy shared my indignation and disbelief. "Sounds like grease to me."

"I know, money changing hands."

"What else is new, this is L.A. after all."

He agreed to help me scope out Daar's various establishments, and we got our schedules to jibe a few days later.

In the meantime, I made a second trip down to the Coastal Commission and located all of Daar's beach-front properties. He had three major buildings along the boardwalk, each subdivided into three or four business "stalls" per building. I had a hunch all were up to code, and all were being denied use by handicapped citizens and patrons.

With addresses firmly in hand, we made our way along the boardwalk just as the sun was about to start its twilight drop. First to Daar's notorious candy store.

This was getting surreal. We found that the once properly designated bathroom behind the young cashier was no longer properly designated. The very sign, the great blue orb that designated it, had itself been desecrated. It had been yanked from the door with such force that it cracked the veneer of the door.

Walking up to the candy counter, I asked the similar, but different, young cashier where the sign was, the one that went on the bathroom door behind her.

"That's not a bathroom," she said nervously.

"That's not a bathroom?" I asked again.

"No," she said, her eyes widening with the lie. Poor thing. She was probably a nice kid, but of no real consequence as this was not her fault.

I stepped past Buddy, my silent observer, and went around the side of the counter. Without saying a word, I opened the door. Surprise!

There they were, stashed away like the crown jewels they really are to any weary disabled traveler with a full bladder: a raised toilet, handlebars on the wall, wide stall, adapted sink, and, of course, what was becoming my nemesis's trademark insult, all perfectly up to code.

"So that's not a bathroom, huh?"

She just looked at me with wide moist eyes. Sad and scared, she said, "I'm just doing my job," in a mousy tone.

This guy had a very unctuous way of getting everyone else to do his dirty work, as well as making them feel terribly sad while they were doing it. Well, almost everyone...I remembered the pleasure skeletal John took in his initial bullying. This girl was no bonehead John.

"I'm sorry," she said.

"I know you are, kid," I said softly

Buddy was stepping around the counter to have a closer look.

"Wow, dude, you were right," was all he said.

"Check out the door. They cracked the veneer in their enthusiasm to yank down the handicapped sign from the door." I ran my hand over the three to four inch crack in the door.

The girl was still staring at me. "I'd find a sweeter candy store to work in, if I were you," I told her.

With that, Bud and I walked out to find the next contemptible Daar building. When we arrived at it, Buddy stopped at its corner.

"Look here." He pointed to a small blue orb attached to the building, an orb that featured "Special Ed" and let the public know the establishment is handicapped equipped. This orb itself was disfigured and cracked, with the top half missing.

"Nice pry job," I said.

"You'd think they'd get busted just for being so sloppy," Bud said.

"Or, at least talked to."

It was so blatant. We wanted to explore the inside, but this building was dark. So, on we went. When we got to the next building, we checked for the outside orbs. None were there, just the stiff remains of the adhesive that had once held them in place. Otherwise they had been cleanly removed. This building, the same color and construction as the last two, was actually three shops. We walked into the first one, a cheap tee shirt shop.

Buddy, feigning purchasing power, kept the owner busy while I looked around.

It wasn't hard...just look for the door with the broken veneer, and bingo! They had one! Though these tenants, having some sense of shame, had tried to cover the wound with a large mirror. I reached behind it and carefully opened the door and, you guessed it, another up-to-code john.

This time, though, it was filled with mops, pails, and dress racks. Not only was this store denying use, but they had gone one step further: they had made the accessible inaccessible. They had turned a little oasis of comfort, privacy, and human dignity into a damn broom closet.

The Asian gentleman who ran the store started to get upset.

"Yeah, I'm upset, too," I told him. "Come on, Bud, let's split."

With both of us being scolded (or worse) in whatever Asian language it was, we left realizing that there was a massive, systematic denial of rights going on at all of Daar's properties.

With the sun now deeply set, I told Bud of how the judge had warned Daar in open court to take down the chain. It now appeared that instead of heeding the good judge's advice, Daar went and locked off all the handicapped parking at his other stores and restaurants. He didn't stop there, but proceeded to take down all their international access signage. To top it off, he turned once accessible bathrooms into storage space. In spite of all this, nobody was doing a damn thing about it.

"Talk about being above the law."

"He's a real public nuisance," Buddy said as we walked back.

"Yeah, well, I'll be his private nuisance," I said.

"Stay calm, buddy. We'll get him. I didn't know it was this bad," he replied.

"Neither did I."

"I'll help you, man," he offered, with an infectious Okie smile.

It is the small things, like full bladders, cracked veneer, and Bud's offer of help that keep you going.

"Thank you, Buddy."

Make way for the Bathrooms! We amended the complaint.

* 36 *

He was a photographer by disposition, and a cynic by trade, so he was none too surprised by what I told him. He agreed without hesitation to take the pictures. His "subversive charity work," he called it. I was glad he had a sense of humor, as we would need it.

An old friend, it was Chet's People Magazine cover photo of "Tom and Jane" in front of their house in Santa Monica that clued me in to both Hayden's 1976 Senate campaign, and the Westside neighborhood in which I have lived for over twenty years.

Going back that far, it was only natural for him to "volunteer" to take a few shots of the "actual access symbol desecration."

The telltale signs were all the more apparent in the full light of day, and I wanted pictures. First out front, then a few quick steps across the boardwalk to get a full shot of the actual building, to give everything proper context.

Then the plan was to walk inside and get a picture of the hidden bathroom, its door, and cracked veneer.

"Get a couple of shots of the address, will ya," I told him, as he hunched down on his knee to get a wide shot.

"We got the address, chief, the bigger question is," he said, camera to his eye, clicking away, "do you want a picture of the guy coming out of the address? You want him? I got him," he said clicking off a few more shots. I turned to see a big fleshy guy come charging out of the building, yelling at us.

"Oh boy, company," I yelled to the intrepid Chet. He dropped his camera from his eye for a split second to size up the guy, who, like some great bull, was barreling in on us. He coolly put the camera back to his eye and clicked off a few more shots and, deft as a matador, sidestepped the charging idiot at the last second. Olé!

"Hey, dickhead! This is a public street and we have a right to take pictures in it," I yelled as I inserted myself between Señor Chet and the bull.

The graceless guy said nothing, and I yelled for Chet to split, as the bull had regained his balance and was reaching over my shoulder to grab at the camera.

At one point he got his hand on the lens and from behind my ear I heard Chet click off a few shots. "Now this is a photographed assault and battery," I thought to myself, as the three of us did this crazy dance of aggression and evidence gathering.

With a mighty yank of his camera, Chet broke free and in a flurry of spontaneous snapshots and "fuck you's" dashed off, easily outrunning the bull, who glared at me and slunk back into the building.

"Ever hear of assault and battery?!" I yelled after him.

And did we have the pictures to prove it. Pictures of the charging goon. Pictures of his hands over the lens, only partially obscuring his face. Pictures of me being pushed and tussling.

"All textbook stuff," I told Chet a few days later at his home.

"Oh yeah?" he said, scouring the proof sheet.

"Oh yeah!" I enthusiastically informed him. "If you put anyone in imminent fear of a harmful touching, and then touch them or, by extension, touch anything attached to their person -- like a camera -- you got textbook assault and battery."

"Textbook, huh?"

"Yeah, textbook. This whole case is textbook." I wondered if my life was becoming a textbook study of petty oppression and denial.

After looking at the pictures a little more, I told Charley he should file charges, but he would have none of it. He thought the guy a classless bore, in other words -- a thug...that, and being basically unhurt, he just wanted me to have the pictures.

"I'll help you with your case; I don't need to start one," he told me. "The guy you're suing is truly nuts and you should be careful," he said seriously. "They're getting physical -- you'd better watch it. They'll steal your crutches," he only half-joked.

"I wouldn't put it past them," I agreed. "You know that's considered false imprisonment?"

"What?" he said bemused. "To steal someone's crutches is false imprisonment?"

Oh, yeah, that's textbook.

* 37 *

As though to balance things out again, from battles to breakthroughs, there was a glimmer of hope that this tragic little farce might end sooner than anyone thought. Somewhere between the second and third lawyer Daar seemed to wise up. He dropped the chain. Unfastening it every day during business hours.

I liked to believe he'd grown a conscience, or at the very least got scared. With physical assaults and violence, things were getting out of control, and there is no doubt that Daar began to realize he could lose a lot of money.

Maybe he got some good legal advice. Whatever it was, the chain came down. Should I jump for joy (figuratively speaking -- jumping being one of the few things I really can't do)?

Should I rush right in and have a cup of coffee? I really didn't feel like gloating. Over what? That some guy came to his senses and simply did the right thing? Not much to gloat over, when you think about it. And had he had a change of heart? Or was this just good legal advice?

What about the daily violation of my civil rights, and all the others, over the last sixteen months? What about the bathrooms? And the assault and battery? Daar had made no promises to never engage in such unlawful practices again. And yes, what about the case?

Had they offered to settle?

"No," Harry said. He was my new lawyer, a bit cocky, but I saw that as a plus. "They expect you to drop the lawsuit, though."

"Of course they do," I agreed. "Tell 'em I said to fix and advertise all the accessible bathrooms and parking lots at all their public accommodations and I'll think about it. While you're at it, tell 'em to apologize for bribing me with hot dogs. Then we'll talk settlement. All that, and just compensation, of course, for my lawyers' and my time and expertise."

"I like that," he said. I'm sure he did.

"They won't buy it," I said. "They'll call it extortion."

"Of course they will," he agreed.

For a minute I'm thinking, Harold is cool, he's listening to me. That's good. He is literate and aggressive, and we're on the same wavelength.

"More than likely we're going to have to fight it out," he said.

"You ready to fight the good fight, counselor?" I asked, sitting there on his overstuffed blue velvet couch

"I was born for it," he said airily, "but come on, this is a slam dunk. If Daar's people are dumb enough to fight this out, let's fight!" he said, feet up on his desk, hands behind his head."

"Glad to hear it, counselor," I said.

"I'll transmit your wishes and Buddy will be in touch with you," he yawned.

As I got up out of the couch, he asked, "Did Daar really try to bribe you with hot dogs?"

"Yep! I swear to you counselor, he did."

"I believe you," he smiled, "even though I can't believe it. Happy Holidays!"

"Happy Holidaze, Harry."

As I walked into the beautiful dark blue of that December night, warm and crystal clear, I was happy. I had a lawyer, a smart lawyer, just around the corner from me, a neighborhood guy, who over our first couple of meetings really seemed to listen to me. Good.

Buddy, who had recommended him, was his legal assistant. That was also good. Among the legal egos of Harry and his partners, it was good to have a friend in the mix.

Official Christmas and Hanukkah decorations hung from every lamppost, while those of a more ad hoc flavor blew softly in the wind from numerous windows and fire escapes along the boardwalk. Incense and marijuana mingled in much of the night air as I made my way down to Sal's house.

He'd told me he was decorating his Christmas tree, and to come by for a drink and a little Christmas cheer. I told him I had a little Christmas cheer from the Mountain in my pocket and this made him very happy. He needed "a break from the sameness" of the half-pound he'd stashed under his bed, and had been smoking for the last week.

Merry Christmas, I said to myself as I came around the corner to make my way up the stairs to Sal's. At that moment, as the Fates would have it, from around the other side of the corner came Mr. Daar, arm and arm with a woman I presumed to be his wife. Boom -- there we were, face to face, in the moonlight and street lamps of the Venice boardwalk.

Daar and I looked at each other, quite surprised. I said to him the first thing that came to my mind under the circumstances, "Shalom."

I turned to the red head, his presumed wife, and said, "Happy holidays," with a nice smile.

She smiled back, and said, "And you." Simple and eloquent. Very nice.

Pleased with the poignancy of the moment, I made my way up the stairs as they scurried off. I couldn't help but feel that it may now really be all over. We were humane human beings to each other. There was hope.

Shalom.

* 38 *

I felt lucky that Paul lived in Santa Monica; it gave us a chance to get together over the holidays and do a bit of partying, philosophizing, dreaming, and scheming.

He was good at all that. He took his dreaming and scheming seriously. Besides the Mountain, Paul was one of the first to see that our little experiment in participatory democracy was in fact a legitimate civics project, from which everyone could benefit.

As far as he was concerned, disability had little or nothing to do with it in the grander scheme of things. "Ours is a civic project, not a disability project," he'd say. "When you stop to think about it, if all citizens did what we're doing, getting involved and voting, things really could be different. Greater opportunities for all would abound. Jeez, I'm beginning to sound like you," he deadpanned.

"Egads, it's spreading," I teased. That's what I liked about ol' Paulie, the wise guy, the wise one. I didn't have to explain it to him, none of it; he just got it! But, like all who come to teach, you don't have to explain much to them. The fact that he "got it," that he understood the ramifications of our genuine civic movement, for all citizens, only proved that he was in fact here to teach me a thing or two.

Which he did. Like all great comedians, he had a deep intellect that allowed him to see the pathos in all things and a keen analytical mind that allowed him to break things down quickly. Hence, his wit.

"You could turn this into a good routine, you really could," he laughed, as his tall thin frame, blond and as sparse as his hairline, knocked about the house in his motorized Amigo, punching chunks of drywall out of corners and doors. "Think about it, man. A bunch of gimps taking power and saving democracy has real potential for slapstick comedy. Or better -- divine farce!"

He was living with his own wearying pathos -- in the form of MS, robbing this once healthy sprinter of his muscles and nerve endings, but never his nerve. It was his audacity and his guts, as well as his humor, that kept him going, kept him brave, wise, and unafraid to talk, dream, or scheme on just about anything. In other words, he was great fun!

After the Mountain, it was with Paul that I had some initial discussions about what I was discovering about organizing. Not the rules so much -- as every battle is different -- but, with all praise to the Buddha, what we liked to call the Noble Truths of good organizing.

When we were talking one day, I asked Paul if he was a Buddhist. He said no -- he was a "Bozoist," referring to the orange-haired clown on the kiddie show of our youth. "But I understand," he went on, "they have a lot in common. They loved children, smiled an awful lot, and wouldn't hurt a fly."

I think The Buddha would have appreciated that; and Bozo's never been in such good company.

Whether you look at it from a Buddhist point of view or a Bozoist perspective, here are the hard learned truths that helped us find our way. I hope they help you find yours.

Truth Number One: Invest all people with dignity. This is of particular importance in the disabled community, but we agreed, a universal truth no matter whom you're organizing with. Okay. Invest everyone with dignity. Sounds nice, but how do you do that? How do you take that noble sentiment beyond mere rhetoric, and really invest people with dignity?

You shut up and listen. You become an attentive listener. Right, Paul?

"What'd you say?" he'd ask, in the mock oblivion of a much older man. "Yes, yes, whatever you say. What was that now?"

"The best way to invest people with dignity," I yelled at him, "is to be an attentive listener. Wouldn't you agree?"

"Oh yes, yes, yes, now you listen to me about this. Stop talking!"

People love to be taken seriously and the surest way to do that is to really listen to them. The locals were always glad to tell me of the significant people and resources in their community, as well as the most effective way to access them.

"Invest people with dignity. Just shut up and listen? Jeez!" Paul exclaimed, "I've been telling people to shut up and listen for years in my comedy routine, and now I realize I've just been investing them with dignity," he cracked. Rim shot please.

Truth Number Two: Don't pay attention to numbers. Lead by the power of example, not numbers. Three people or three hundred, it makes no difference, everyone gets the same passionate show if you want to move people enough to do the right thing.

"Ya gotta do it like it's the first time, every time, over and over again," Paul exclaimed. The great Bozoist calls this "the Elvis Presley rule of organizing."

"Remember, three people who walk away 'believers' are the best word of mouth campaign you can have. So, whatever their number, give them the full show. You never know who's in the audience."

Truth Number Three: Don't wait for the money!

"Only hobbyists and political extremists give money to start-up projects," Paul told me.

Good point.

"You know with every voter we register our legend grows," I said. So the money will come. I mean it's a pretty bold idea. The meek really could inherit the earth if the disabled ever voted as one, right?" I asked rhetorically.

"Like they say: 'Boldness has genius in it.'" Paul paused for a moment. "What's cooler than that for the disabled? Be bold -- vote. And the meek really shall inherit the earth! Now there's a slogan for you."

"Yes sir, that's our slogan and our plan," I told him.

"Our plan to bring in the cash to pull it all off, damn it!" Paul responded. We laughed...boldly!

Paul thought about it for a moment. "Invest everyone with dignity. Don't pay attention to numbers and don't wait for the money. Be bold, begin broke!!! Now I know why this movement attracts comedians," he said. "This is good advice for them, too. You follow these noble truths and you may not save the world, bro, but you will ultimately learn how to do fifteen minutes of shtick -- and that ain't bad either."

Granted.

Such are the truths of the Buddhist and the Bozoist.

* 39 *

Paul was a local member of Toastmasters. He told me he enjoyed the camaraderie of other witty people and looked forward to helping the "less verbose, those of a quieter wit than you and me."

This got us to onto the subject of public speaking, which, as we know, some people equate with death.

"Some find it worse than that," Paul would say. Having contemplated both comedy and death, I gave his opinion a lot of weight, as well as his guts. I've had a policy all my life that when it comes to dealing with other people's disability, I followed their lead...just like in organizing.

If they want to talk about their own disability, I am happy to oblige. You find out a lot about people through how they handle their particular situation. You tend to appreciate both the ingenuity and adaptability of the basic person, as well as what they share with you.

However, if they wish not to say a peep about their condition, then so be it. Lots of people with disabilities not only have transcended their situations, but have transcended the need to talk about them as well.

For many it's such a constant part of life that it takes on a mundane everydayness, it is "just part of life." No matter what rigmarole you have to go through to put on your pants and have your breakfast, after a while the sameness of the routine, like all routines, defies pondering -- it just is.

Others don't talk about it because they really do have other things to talk about. They have lives to lead that are full and rich outside of disability. They have work, hobbies, and talents that make them very good chess players, musicians, comedians, and organizers, outside of their disability.

These talents have little, if anything, to do with their disability. Broken or unbroken, straight or crooked, these people would become what they have become, simply because they must. Just as Paul had to leave his job as a designer at some aerospace joint out in the desert and become what he must, a comedian.

Some people don't talk about their disability because they have other things to do -- becoming what they must become -- in order to live up to their full potential. But also, some people are just brave.

Paul was very brave. No doubt about it, as MS doesn't go away until it takes you with it. Some said that his jokes and his devil-may-care attitude were defense mechanisms. Perhaps they were, but they were damn good ones, and it kept the rest of us laughing and doing necessarily bold things.

Death? Death be damned.

Paul would rather tell you about the Jello squid he just sent some boyhood friend through the mail. A very real, very dead, squid...sent overnight delivery. No shit.

He even found a partner in crime. My prospective girlfriend, the lovely Ms. Dee, was only too happy to mix up the slimy Jello mess. They started with strawberry Jello, but didn't care for the color contrast and switched to grape, which they heartily agreed worked much better with the unctuous dead gray skin of the squid.

When that thing started in Detroit at the Red Wings games with some fan whipping a whole dead squid out on the ice, Paul was sure he had inspired it. He had friends in Detroit he had "squidded."

His jokes came out of a purer place than defense mechanisms and denials; Paul was a prankster, a joker, a maker of laughter. A class clown who was also head of the class. Talk about brave. Whenever I think of brave, Paul pops to mind, and not just because he was battling MS. That was the lowly part of it.

No, Paulie was brave because he was, in fact, a comedian. I've always felt that when it comes to show business, and by that I mean having to get up in front of an audience and entertain, the bravest people on the block are stand-up comedians.

When they get into trouble, when the jokes aren't working, they're out there all alone.

When you're a singer in the band, you have a band. You have the music. You have the ability to just keep going. If you screw up in a rock and roll band, the band plays on, before most people even realize there was a mistake.

When you're out there doing jokes, one at a time, and nobody laughs, you have to endure each and every wave of thorny silence -- as well as the audience's acute awareness of it.

To keep going after three jokes bomb, and the silence is so thick that you can hear the clanking of bottles, thugs, and their whores, you have to be very brave. No playing a little louder to drown out the critics, or strutting around like a tiger on Vaseline to tease the girls into approval. No, the only thing you have at your disposal when you're doing stand-up is the next joke.

"Luckily," said Paul, "the audience is rooting for you. If you're sincere, they'll grant you the benefit of the doubt and give you a laugh, even if it is, just a pity laugh."

"It's almost psychological," I agreed. "The human psyche wants to be entertained. It wants to see a good show," I said, flashing back on my wild-eyed days as a saloon singer.

"That's why if you tell ten jokes and seven bomb," the great squidder said, "people will go out talking about the three jokes that provoked real laughs -- not the seven that bombed. It's like baseball, man, hitting .300 counts. Remember, nobody talks about the strikeouts; they talk about the home runs."

"I agree. People want to see a good show and will go to great lengths to believe that they have -- look at some of my rock bands."

No doubt about it.

"Plus man, a couple of good pity laughs can lead to a powerful pity fuck," Paul said in a slight reverie. "That's how much people want to see a good show."

"The stage does have an aphrodisiac effect on people, doesn't it?"

"Yep, no matter what the size of the stage."

"No matter," I agreed. "Six inches or Carnegie Hall, size doesn't matter."

"The important thing is to take the stage," Paul said.

"Just as in other matters of size, it ain't the wand that matters, it's the magician that takes the stage, huh, Maestro?" I asked.

He just kind of looked at me with a big smile and laughed. "Hey, that's funny," he said. "You're beginning to sound like me."

* 40 *

I hope so. I want to think so. Brave and funny is cool by me. And as if to prove that the gods were laughing with us, instead of at us, the next day UP got a seed grant from the Liberty Hill Foundation for $4,000.

"$4,000 bucks," Paul said over the phone, "now we're dangerous."

Exactly.

Liberty Hill Foundation, inspired by Upton Sinclair's speech on Liberty Hill in the 1930's, is one of those rare foundations that supports grassroots community work and will take a chance on first timers. They support projects that have raised little or no money, but are still organizing on passion, brains, and a real need in their community -- projects that many would consider "dangerous" because they tend to challenge the status quo, as opposed to being co-opted by it.

Liberty Hill's intent is to empower individuals and communities as opposed to institutions and infrastructure. They understand that that's what democracy is all about, or supposed to be about. Thus, they dug UP. To the tune of $4,000 bucks.

We broke open the brews and, while Paul read the good news I laid in front of him, I went to the kitchen and got him a straw for his beer. We were happy agitators slugging and sucking down beers.

Paul's initial suggestion on how to spend the money was of course, over the top. "We go get four hookers at a thousand bucks a pop and register them to vote."

I looked at him with a very critical eye.

"What!" he yelled. "Look at us! That's helping the disabled, man."

"Democracy in action?" I asked.

"Just trying to comfort the afflicted," he said.

"Or, as when you upset Dear Abby, afflict the comfortable," I offered.

"Oh yeah, that too!" he said devilishly. "But you know, I've been thinking about that and I don't buy it. That audience was with me. They were cracking up, you can hear it on the tape. They were all having a ball. I can't believe they got so upset at WCIL," he said with a chuckle. "Lelan's an ass!"

"Well that ass has now been 'retired' to the backwoods of Vermont."

"Vermont, huh? Serves him right. He instigated all the ill will."

"That's what you get for pulling sight gags on a blind guy," I offered as he bent his head and took a big slurp of beer. Looking back up at me with that rascal's charm he has when he's scheming big time, he said, "Let's take the 4,000 bucks, fly to Vermont, and personally squid the bastard."

Like I said, Paul was fearless. Death and comedy can do that.

* 41 *

The day before Christmas, Buddy called to tell me that Daar's lawyers had rejected any idea of settlement, much less a cash settlement. "Look at it this way," he said, "at least we know what we're doing next year."

"Yeah, right," I agreed. Fighting the good fight. "Merry Christmas, Buddy!"

"Here's to a chain-free New Year," he said enthusiastically. "Merry Christmas, dude!"

* 42 *

Okay, Maybe I was reading too much Tom Paine. Maybe, after being out on the hustings, I was prone to seeing a greater movement. It was, after all, the holidays, a time of hope. But that's what surprised me -- all the calls we were receiving over the holidays. Full of good cheer and thanks. From all over the state, too! Wanting more information than our brochure could supply. Legitimate interest in our little civic project kept growing. Truth was, the damn thing was taking on a life of it own and thus in need of a larger explanation.

The Steering Committee agreed that UP's first official act of the new year would be to put out a newsletter.

When you consider that we had the editorial help of the Mountain, Paul, and Ted, as well as the graphic artistry of Matthew, we had to think of a reason not to do it. No time for that.

Emboldened by it all -- and the four grand from Liberty Hill Foundation -- we became desktop revolutionaries. Accordingly, it was a slam, boom, bang affair, with no one really sitting down together, face to face and planning it out. No real meetings. No outlines, no agendas.

I did a little running around to drop off a disc or two, but we virtually wrote, edited, phoned, and faxed in the first edition of UPRISING.

The newsletter was a poetic and political reminder to all disabled citizens of our basic belief and main aim: Power is never given, it is taken...Take it! Disabled citizens unite!!!

With the Mountain and I doing "the who, what, and why" of UP and Paul handling the wit and satire, we had more than enough copy for Ted to edit and Matthew to graphically enhance.

All in all, it was a minor miracle that you couldn't help but take seriously when you looked at it. UPRISING was noble in idea and aim, as well as fun to read. Have no doubt, we were very serious in our intent to wage democratic revolution, but I'm happy to say that the piece that everyone liked best in that first edition was Paul's ironic and witty "Top Ten Reasons for Disabled Citizens Not to Vote." With tongue firmly in cheek, he laid our community's apathy to waste. Listed here now for your enjoyment, those ten that set the irreverent tone of UPRISING for all time:

TOP 10 REASONS NOT TO REGISTER TO VOTE

10. It validates my martyr complex.

9. I can live like a king on $500 a month.

8. I think the ADA goes too far.

7. I always wanted to live in a nursing home.

6. I like being the last disenfranchised minority.

5. Jerry might leave me out of next year's telethon.

4. I'm not allowed to use sharp pointy objects like pens and pencils.

3. I might lose my parking spot.

2. It's not part of my rehab program.

1. I'd have to make a decision without the help of Social Security.

Over the months and newsletters to follow, we used poetry, wit, and wisdom from across the political spectrum to demonstrate our non-partisan approach. From the god-sent Goethe to Teddy Roosevelt, to ol' Tom Paine (whom TR called a "dirty little atheist" and thus became our patron saint), what we lacked in resources we made up for in high ideas and dramatic graphics. As democratic revolutionaries and pamphleteers we began through UPRISING to, "begin the world over again," to quote Citizen Paine.

The basic theme throughout all of them: Join us!

As for the occasional typo or missing word...ah, well, our grassroots were showing.

Be that as it may, the free franking privilege for blind and handicapped citizens allowed us to send it out for free. We used it to its fullest, by putting all of our materials in 14-point type or larger.

How big is 14-point type? Go back and read the Top Ten Reasons.

With a minimum of hassle, and free postage, we were marveling at how it was all coming together. The word was out. Citizens with disabilities were actually registering and beginning to think of themselves as powerful. UPRISING spoke to the better angels of their nature and, consequently, the phone kept ringing.

A few weeks later, the Mountain and I were smoking and joking about our ability to organize a "meeting free" newsletter.

"Couple this with our two meeting strategy for events, and you really could organize the disabled, or anyone else."

I told him the three noble truths that Paul and I had come up with. He liked them, and wanted to put them in the next newsletter. "Invest people with dignity," he said half to himself, "don't pay attention to numbers, and don't wait for the money. That's pretty good, guys. A minimalist, action oriented, approach to organizing, that doesn't waste anybody's time."

"Exactly. A minimalist, action oriented approach, I like that," I said holding the smoldering number to his lips. "Damn we're good, huh, buddy?"

"Yeah, we are," he inhaled, "but remember, you're the hub of the wheel."

"Yeah, but if we're doing this right, anybody can be the hub, right?"

"I hope so," he exhaled. "You know me. I think if every disabled citizen takes responsibility and does their own little part, becoming the hub of their own little wheel, you'll have a damn prairie fire, just like the newsletter says."

"Yeah baby, damn straight! An UPRISING!" I gushed at the thought of it, waving a crisp clean copy of our newsletter in the air. "Thanks, Mountain."

"Speaking of prairie fires, do me a favor, will ya?"

"Sure, what?"

"Grab this joint, my beard's on fire."

Fire on the Mountain!

* 43 *

Fools down below. To deal with them I would need both the fearlessness of Paul and the patience of the Mountain. Over the next six months as we prepared for trial, I was to find out, the hard way, that although reasonableness concerning issues of policy was necessary to build consensus, reasonableness in strategy could be a trap.

For fools in policy can be of little consequence, as there is time, when it comes to policy, to nullify or mitigate their affect. However, fools in strategy are deadly because when it comes to strategy, you are in action, and as in all moments of significant action there is little room for error or second-guessing.

Thus, a fool can nullify or mitigate your effect by merely being foolish at a crucial moment. I am not talking about the people you're trying to organize with, either. As I've said before, their common sense and understanding of local people and resources are vital to your success.

The dangerous fools are, by and large, the overeducated and licensed types, you know, lawyers and social worker types, who believe that their narrow field of knowledge somehow makes them smarter than everyone else -- about everything else.

Yes, they're progressive, all right, and they'll help you -- if you do it their way.

They are also very good at making people believe that not to do it their way is the definition of unreasonableness.

See the trap? You're only deemed reasonable if you do it their way. Remember, they've got the license, right? What have you got? Oh yeah, a problem. Worse, the rest of the world buys into this myth that these licensed types know what they're talking about, so it's hard to buck them, to question their authority.

Lawyers count on that.

But remember -- what I forgot -- you're the true expert when it comes to your cause. An expert in the truest sense, because you're getting your information from the community you're organizing in, you're doing your own legal footwork, and thus you really do know better than any licensed outsider just what you're fighting for and how best to win the fight.

You're the real expert. I know that's hard to buy into, as there are no degrees or licenses for grassroots organizing. As such, I know it's hard to go against all them licensed types; I really do, because I failed. And it cost me dearly.

Sad to say everything I learned about unreasonable reasonableness, I learned the hard way, doubting myself. Being less than bold.

"What the hell," I figured. We had Daar. He had admitted in a sworn affidavit that he had been chaining off handicapped parking for years. We had copies of his permits mandating handicapped parking, not to mention, pictures of the chain, the cracked walls, signs, symbols, and doors of all of Daar's buildings. Then there were the "action shots" of the goon charging out of one of them and committing photographed assault and battery.

There was all that, and now, to pile it on, the now inaccessible bathrooms behind those desecrated doors. Add in a guest star appearance by the Assistant Attorney General in charge of civil rights to bolster our argument and one had to say: "Great case."

All we had to do now was educate the jury on the facts, the law -- and the defendant's admissions -- and we win. It was a sure bet! The chains stay down and the bathrooms open up. My neighborhood becomes a better place to live. Not even a fool could blow this.

"This case was a slam dunk," Harry had said. I agreed and really thought he understood. I had worked very hard to bring forth not just a good case, but also a great one. The reason it was "a slam dunk," as Harry called it, was the years of hard work and long hours that I had put into it. I thought he understood and appreciated that.

So it shocked me when Buddy came to me with Harry's first suggestion on the opening day of the trial. Initially I thought he was kidding. But, Buddy wasn't laughing.

"He wants to what?" I asked. I wanted to make sure I heard him right.

"Drop the bathrooms," Buddy answered. And forget about the wrestling match with Chet Anderson."

"Drop the bathrooms. Forget the assault. What's he talking about?" I went to track down Harry.

I found him in the converted mobile home unit that was to be our courtroom.

When I told Harry as reasonably as I could that I didn't think it was a good idea to toss out the bathrooms, he just looked at me. "See, Har," I explained, "though the jury may or may not be able to relate to a disability, all of them know the discomfort of a full bladder. They can all relate to urgently needing to piss. Don't drop the bathrooms," I urgently but reasonably pleaded. "And the assault on Chet Anderson is photographed. How can you pass that up?"

He just shook his head, as though disgusted. "I knew I'd have to go through this with you."

"Hey, Harry, c'mon," I said, not too unreasonably, "locking off handicapped johns is pretty ugly. Don't toss out that cause of action."

"Bud," he called over his shoulder.

This was the start of the trial, and I guess he was going to pull his power trip early and show who was in charge. He was. The guy who seemed to listen so well, now heard nothing I said. Evidently, Bud was to run interference.

"C'mon dude, they're getting ready to talk to Daar's lawyers. They're nervous enough," Bud said, only half kidding. "Let them do the law."

He pulled me outside.

"Yeah, but this is strategy, not law," I told him in the sunshine of the courthouse's courtyard. "Who suggested that we drop the bathrooms?"

"They did."

"They did? Who? Daar's lawyers?"

"Yeah," he said lighting a cigarette.

"Of course they did," I growled, pissed off. "That's the one that scares them."

"Dude," Buddy pleaded, "let's not start trouble on the first day. Give them a chance to be your lawyers."

I should have stopped it right there. I should have said, "Bullshit." Keep the bathroom in the complaint. I should have. But I didn't want to appear difficult or bothersome. I wanted to be reasonable.

I should have known that I wasn't dealing with the quickest strategic thinkers, either, and as such, just shut them down. They could remind me as much as they wanted that they were the lawyers, and they did this regularly, but I should have listened to my gut, and said, "So what."

The locking off of handicapped johns is particular ugly and cruel and showed the malicious nature of Daar's actions and intent.

Why was I explaining this to lawyers? I should have seen them for the fools they were, right there. But being the beginning of the trial, this would have been unreasonable.

When the lawyers came for my approval, I said "Okay" meekly. It left a bad taste in my mouth. I went against my instincts, letting Daar off the hook like that. And that was my fault, this was not about law, this was about strategy and I let fools with law degrees convince me otherwise.

Sure bets can do that.

* 44 *

Somebody made the mistake once of telling Larry that he was funny, and he'd mistaken that for intelligence, or worse, wisdom, ever since. I'm sure as a nervous and puny gimp kid, any little bit of encouragement was absorbed and by necessity, blown out of proportion.

This is why Larry liked to sell himself as a comic, "who happens to be a lawyer -- that's my disability," he liked to joke. At least he thought it was a joke.

He wasn't much better as a lawyer, either. Harry was happy, though, to have a gimp on the team, just to deal with me.

Very funny.

Toward the end of jury selection, I brought up the fact that no one on the jury had a visible disability. The lawyers didn't think I was very funny.

"This isn't a criminal trial. You don't get a jury of your peers," they told me.

"I know that. Still, why not get a few crips on board?"

Harry turned red and told me I was being -- you guessed it -- unreasonable. Larry just stood there in silent assent -- a wannabe. More lawyer than disabled citizen, Larry copped this instant legal attitude when he came on board. 'Larr' was one of them, one of the lawyers. After a moment, he said he agreed with Harry. I was being unreasonable and he too "was afraid of this."

"Afraid of this!" Like he knew me. The asshole. Paul had introduced me to him, inadvertently, and I had made the mistake of telling Harry I knew a lawyer with a disability, Larry, who now gave Harry all the moral authority he needed to get indignant and outraged at my suggestion that there could be some able-bodied bias at work against us.

"You don't have to be disabled to be appalled at Daar's behavior," Harry said in a huff, his able-bodied pride deeply wounded. "Be reasonable."

"I thought I was," I said to myself.

* 45 *

With the work of years coming to a head, guess who couldn't sleep the night before he was to testify.

Problem was, it was all in my head. Everything was a rerun in my mind the night before, and the booze didn't help. Consequently, I was tired on the day that I was to testify to the years of struggle and outrage. To the years of being treated like a second-class citizen in my own neighborhood.

"I guess it's to be expected," I said to myself, trying to find an advantage within it all. "You're supposed to be tired after years of struggle." Yeah, right. When I got out of bed that morning, I realized that this was yet another struggle in the never-ending struggle that was this chain. Just one more.

"Time to make the system work," I said aloud, blinking the sleep out of my eyes.

Common sense hadn't worked, nor common decency. Shalom didn't work. The bureaucracy failed to work, and even the laws on the books had no effect. Now it was time to try and get the courts to work. Now it was time, weary or not, to fight the good fight. I yawned, showered, and shaved. I put on a new shirt, and for the first time in years, I wore a tie, a tie I tried mightily not to get any courthouse eggs on. I almost succeeded, dipping just the tip of it in a little left over yolk on my plate as I got up to leave, feeling a little better now that I had conquered low blood sugar with your basic stroke breakfast. Under the circumstances, I thought it a fair trade off. A little less long-term health for a quick pick me up of more than black coffee.

"Okay. Psych up, not out," I told myself. I knew everything would sharpen once I was on the stand and the initial rush of adrenaline subsided. I would, as in my old stage days, relax and seize the moment.

Or so I thought.

Larry did not understand the concept. It made him nervous. "Don't worry about seizing the moment. Just follow me," he said with grave irritation.

"Jeez Lar, it's just a figure of speech."

I had just found out that he, the nervous one, was going to question me on the stand. "Harry wants it that way," he said, trying to sound tough with a nervous lilt in his voice. Not an easy thing to do. Nor was it confidence building.

"What are you so nervous about?" I asked.

"I'm not nervous," he said, nearly jumping out of his skin, his CP's spasticity exaggerating what was already obvious. Trying to regain a little composure, he said, with saliva forming at the corners of his mouth, "I want you under tight wraps. Just follow my questions."

"Tight wraps. Jeez, Lar, are we in sync here?" I asked.

"You can't just tell your story, damn it. This isn't a press conference," he barked. "We have to lay a foundation for your testimony. So don't go off."

"I understand, Lar. I am a paralegal, and I understand the procedure." And now I really did. Larry was busy being another lawyer at that little white picnic table we were sitting out on the sun deck of the courthouse cafeteria. He had to show that he was in charge. "Maybe he's psyching himself up," I thought, and took a deep breath. "Just ask away, Lar. Lay the foundation, baby," I said. "Lay the foundation."

It was a hot summer morning. Larry was already sweating. "Did you read my legal memo?" I asked, trying to be a calm and helpful team player.

"Yes, yes," he said, "I think so."

"Larry!" I yelled in a whisper.

"Calm down," he yelped. "Everything's fine. You just follow my lead on the stand."

"Okay, Lar."

If only there had been one.

See, Larry was another one of those smart guys. He not only had a license to prove how smart he was, but this crazy-ass gimp took it one step further. Unbelievably, he didn't feel the need to take notes or write anything down, including, but not limited to, the questions he was going to ask me. Consequently, when he froze, in mid-thought, the licensed nimrod had nothing to look at. No legal pad to scan, no chicken scratched notes to gather thoughts from. No questions laid out One through Ten, to get back on track with.

So, after a few obligatory questions concerning name, age, and address, he just froze. Copped a major case of stage fright. I could see it in his face. "And this guy is supposed to be a stand-up comedian," I asked myself. "Joke's on me."

Terrible place to learn that.

There I was on the stand, learning once again the absolutely critical importance of taking care of the small things...like writing down the questions. Talk about a lack of strategic planning. Talk about learning something the hard way. Yep, it's the small things, which make all the difference in the world.

Larry, frozen in the limelight of his own intellectual arrogance, would learn that same lesson -- but at my expense.

So it came down to this. After all the worrying about me, and making sure that I would follow his lead and answer only his questions, he forgot them.

Frozen. He didn't ask about all the calls I made to all the city officials, he didn't ask a question about the assault on me and Chet Anderson. He neglected to ask how it made me feel to be discriminated against in my own neighborhood. He made no inquiry as to my feelings about being a second-class citizen, or about being bribed with hot-dogs. He just froze.

I forget who had enough sense to call for a recess, probably the judge. I was glad someone did, Larry's crumbling -- and that of my testimony along with him -- was a painful thing to watch.

Back in the courtyard, Harry tried to help. "Ask him about the assault, how it a made him feel to be a second-class citizen," he offered to a shell-shocked Larry.

"Yeah, just ask me about that, I'll hit one out of the park for you," I was trying to be encouraging. I figured Larry got it. "Just ask me the questions, bro!"

It was not to be. For, as only the truly arrogant and stupid can do, he neglected to write these questions down as well. And when we resumed, he resumed his previous approach. He sputtered and failed, never asking once how I felt or was damaged by it all. And thus the damage was done. I knew it. Harry knew it. He snapped his pencil in two as I left the stand.

And now I had to face Daar's attorney, Gluckster.

He brought out the faults. And he was very smart. He wrote his questions down.

Did I ever put my complaint in writing to any city official; he wanted to know.

"No, just numerous calls. I did fax them the laws," I offered.

"No record of the complaint, huh?"

This was a mistake, I realized as I sat there on the stand. A mistake that I should have seen and rectified earlier. Alas, such an epiphany, under such circumstances did not do me much good.

Gluckster then asked me some hypothetical questions, which I thought weird, but I answered. "Well, hypothetically speaking..."

The judge got mad and scolded me, which I also thought weird, but then maybe the judge wasn't much for hypotheticals. So be it. "Be humble," I told myself, which was good, because everybody scolded me after that. Lawyers get mad when judges get mad. Everybody was mad. Everybody but Buddy.

"They had you on too tight a leash," he told me. "They really did a shitty job on you. They're supposed to be the pros."

"Yeah, I know. Why didn't he write down his questions?"

"Dumbest thing I ever heard of," Buddy said.

"If only Larry had had the wisdom of a third year law student," I laughed sadly.
"Yeah, if only..."

Harry said he could fix it; he'd tell my story to the jury during closing arguments. Now they would go after Daar. Tomorrow it was his turn to take the stand.

Buddy went home to work on Harry's questions for Daar. The only common sense scholar in the bunch -- he wrote them down.

* 46 *

Proof that simple things do pay off. Harry was at his best. It was his true shining moment, and lord knows we were in need of one. Daar admitted to chaining off the spot, claiming he had official sanctioning. "Building Inspector Parker" gave him the okay.

Forget about what the judge had told him last year. Daar had "official sanction" from the city.

He denied bribing me and claimed that, as the father of a disabled daughter, he understood the problems of the disabled, he just couldn't unlock the blue zone because of the high crime rate in Venice and problems with motorcycle gangs.

How that allowed him to violate disabled citizens' rights had me wondering and I began to believe Harry's assurances that the jury could see right through such tortured logic.

Under Harry's questioning, Daar claimed that it was I who was trying to swindle him -- the bully defense -- and, to add true injury to insult, he swore that he saw me walking down the boardwalk, without my crutches!

This was the greatest lie of all and should have gotten him a perjury rap. The fact is, without my crutches, I can't make it down the stairs of my home and out to the boardwalk, much less walk on it. I figured the jury would be as incredulous as I was, and realize that if Daar was willing to lie about such an obvious thing he was willing to lie about anything. I thought he sunk himself with the jury. They'd be as outraged as me, right? He'd done it now!

Mendacity would damn him.

* 47 *

Their "expert witness" was, as most courtroom experts are, a paid liar. He just didn't make it sound as preposterous as Daar did. He was oh, so reasonable, in tone and manner. "What conflict with the city code?" he smiled.

This sculptor of the truth went on to testify that since there was public parking within 300 feet of the café, Mr. Daar was under no obligation to allow disabled people to use his handicapped spot. It was a complete perversion of the truth, but he was an "expert."

During cross examination, no matter how many laws and regulations Harry would show him, asking, "Isn't Mr. Daar's actions a violation of this law or that regulation?," the paid liar would answer that that was just Harry's "interpretation." His expert opinion was that Mr. Daar's actions were not a violation of the law. Maybe bad taste. But not a violation of the law.

Finally, Harry asked the expert if the handicapped parking zones were there for just decorative purposes, but had to withdraw the question under objection. Argumentative.

It was brought out that he was such an expert that he was paid $5,000 dollars. Daar knew how to spend money to buy the truth he wanted. There was no small gasp in the courtroom, when the price of his expertise came up, but still my legal team thought that kind of money was enough to make one wonder about the actual value of its veracity.

Once again, our attitude was that the jury could see right through this guy.

Perhaps, just in case, we did have a ace in the hole. "Wait until we get our expert on the stand," I thought to myself. Verdi would tell the jury what the law actually was. The top cop for civil rights was our expert.

Daar's expert's opinion was just "an interpretation" of the law, as he was so quick to point out to Harry. But we had the ultimate expert, one who would, with all the gracious authority of the State behind him, tell the jury exactly what laws Daar broke and how that was a violation of my rights, as well as the rights of every disabled citizen who visits Venice Beach. With Verdi there was no "interpretation" of the law. As the Assistant Attorney General in charge of civil rights, his word was the law.

The real beauty was that he cost nothing...except the expense of a subpoena.

* 48 *

As I said, Harry actually did a good job on Daar. He got him to admit on the stand what he had in discovery, that he had in fact chained off the blue zone and denied disabled citizens the right to park and patronize his establishment.

Daar said he was told it was okay to chain off handicapped parking by L.A. Building Inspector Parker.

Henry Parker. I remembered Henry. The first time I talked to him was on a three-way phone call with a Los Angeles District Attorney. The DA was, however, clearly irritated with his time being wasted on what he perceived to be a trivial matter.

I remember thinking, "Good, he'll push the café to take the chain down." Once we got Parker on the line, the DA and I had a vigorous discussion on the various laws at Mr. Parker's disposal in order to remove the chain.

Parker said little or nothing.

This is why I remember Parker so vividly, because his only participation in the whole of the conversation occurred when the DA asked him what he thought, and Parker replied, "This [conversation] has been like an education to me."

An education! I was flabbergasted. The people in charge of enforcing the laws and regulations necessary to protect the disabled public's safety and comfort didn't seem to have the foggiest notion as to what those laws and regulations were or meant!? It was either that, or worse, they just looked the other way -- with or without compensation -- and then played dumb at moments like this.

Now, a much better educated Parker took the stand, and said, time and again, that he found no violation of any laws when it came to Mr. Daar's properties. "It's 'a matter of interpretation,'" and his was, "that it wasn't."

"Was that it wasn't." That summed it up poetically and practically. Forget the law, or public safety -- according to Parker, it seemed that everything down at L.A.'s Building and Safety Office was open to interpretation. And more often than not, when it came to violating disabled citizens' rights, their interpretation of things "was that it wasn't." No matter what law, federal, state, or even the vehicle code (with its one sentence simplicity), Parker never saw a violation. It was astounding. What good were laws when they were interpreted like this? The jury had to see through this guy. He was greasy.

Being that Daar knew how to grease the wheels of the bureaucracy, I couldn't help but feel that Parker's inability to see a single violation had to do with that grease. It got in his eyes. It made him blind.

I comforted myself again, remembering we had Verdi. We had vision.

* 49 *

"Sin of all sins!" The boxer within condemned me, for in the middle of a fight, I did the unforgivable. I pulled my punches. Against Goethe's better advice, I hesitated.

Strategically speaking, I sank to a new low of reasonableness.

And so ultimately it was my mistake. I was listening to licensed fools, who happened to know the law, but knew little or nothing of strategy.

Daar had just put on his "expert" and his "sanctioning authority." Common sense, much less some strategic sense, should have told my lawyers that it was time to put on the ultimate authority, Verdi. Tit for tat, and we had a hell of a tat.

The Assistant Attorney General would correct the nonsensical assertion that Daar was under no duty to provide on-site handicapped parking. Verdi would testify, quite simply, that Daar was under just such a duty -- regardless of the public parking 300 feet away. Verdi would also testify that the very reason the café was mandated to have a blue zone on site, was so disabled patrons wouldn't have to walk or roll an extra 300 feet. He would also let it be known that, as a matter of law, a lowly building inspector does not have the authority to invalidate federal, state, and local laws, including those that prohibit the chaining off and denial of handicapped accessible parking. Quite to the contrary, his job is to make sure that all such laws were observed and enforced.

And again, Verdi would let the jury know that Daar was guilty of violating my civil rights, as well as those of thousands of others each and every day, by creating this public nuisance...which is what it officially became once I put Daar "on notice" by asking to have the chain taken down. As such, Daar could now be held liable for each and every separate violation. That's what our expert was going to say.

How'd I know? Verdi told me. From the start he told me to keep him informed and I had, so I had a pretty good idea of what he was going to say. He was going to tell the jury the truth.

I told Harry early on that Verdi was the only official in the whole damn state who showed any genuine concern or offered any real help. Had anyone bothered to get an Attorney General's opinion? No. "Why not?" I had asked.

"This is a slam dunk," Harry said again. "We don't need the overkill." Overkill?

Luckily, Buddy and I did the next best thing; we subpoenaed Verdi.

And thank God we had. 'Cause we were now playing catch-up and needed a heavy hitter to counter all the crap and half-truths of the other side. The Assistant Attorney General was just that. But unbelievably, Harry didn't want to call him. For some weird reason, he saw it as totally unnecessary.

"Overkill," he said again.

Again, I was stunned.

All of us, Buddy, Harry, Larry, and I, were standing out in the courtyard of the courthouse and thus had to speak in hushed tones, lest Daar's lawyer overhear us and pick up on our divisions. We were all there, but this was mainly between Harry and me.

"Hell, Harry," I yelled in a hush. "Daar's damn expert almost has me believing that it's totally reasonable to send cripples 300 feet down the damn boardwalk to park, and that god-damned blue zones are to be used for decorative purposes only," I fumed in my hushed fury. "And if I'm beginning to believe his crap, what does that say about the jury?"

"Stop it!" he yelled back in a whisper. "You think only cripples can see through Daar and his crew? Shit," he said with condescension, "the jury's not that stupid and uncaring. And even if they were, they still have to follow the law. They can read!"

"Goddamn it, Harry," I said, doubly mad that I had to even argue the point.

"We've got the best expert in the world and you don't want to use him! That's crazy, man," I said angrily, "C'mon, he's subpoenaed. The goddamn Attorney General isn't going to blow off a subpoena." I was no longer at the hush level. "Just make the call!"

"Keep your voice down," Harry shot back. Daar's lawyers were milling about. "Verdi told me he was busy, and not to call him unless absolutely necessary."

I looked at him dumbfounded. Absolutely necessary? Absolutely necessary! "Have you noticed," I exploded, "that you're in the middle of a trial and the other side just made it sound all too fucking reasonable to chain off blue zones. And what's really crazy is how we're debating whether it's 'necessary' to call our expert to counteract all that phony fucking 'reasonableness' with what's real. Namely, the law! But dig this, counselor, in order to do that, we've got to get our expert on the stand first. So, if it's not absolutely fucking necessary right now, my question is: when will it ever be? Huh, Har? Answer me that. Come on Harry, make the call," I pleaded. "It's absolutely fucking necessary," I yelled, in as loud a whisper as possible.

"You're overreacting, damn it, and you're not a lawyer."

"Overreacting! Goddamn you!" I yelled back. The able-bodied bonehead had no idea what he had really said. I stopped and stared at him for a moment. "You know, Harry," I said with considerable contempt, "every time a disabled person gets pissed off, angry, or indignant, we are told we're 'overreacting.' Like we don't have the sense to know when we're being fucked with, or have the birthright to say, 'Enough!' 'Overreacting,' my ass. I'm trying to stop a bunch of guys too bright for their own good from making a big mistake, so don't use that god-damned overreacting crap on me. Call Verdi and get him down here," I said, turning to walk away in a huff.

"Don't you walk away from me like that," he shouted emotionally. "You're not a lawyer," he said, reverting back to a hush. "I make the legal decisions in this case, and we don't need him, it's overkill. The jury is fully capable of understanding the law and how Daar broke it. They get it! They don't need an expert to tell them that!"

And that was it. The sure thing, the bet that couldn't lose, all riding on whether people, able-bodied people at that, would "get it," would understand the outrage, the harm and hurt a disabled person feels when being treated less than equal.

Harry, in his defiant licensed arrogance, was sure the jury would "get it" and be just as outraged as we were. "You haven't cornered the market on understanding suffering," he said harshly. "Christ, man, think about it! How much of an expert do you have to be to understand this kind of conduct is wrong? Be fucking reasonable," he said angrily, walking away in a red-faced huff, his able-bodied pride hurt again. "We don't need Verdi!" he shouted back over his shoulder.

That was Harry's legal decision, his call -- we didn't need an expert. Be fucking reasonable. They, the jury of TABS, "get it."

Honestly? The reasonable thing for me to do, at that point, would have been to say: "I'll stand up in court and fire your ass if you don't bring in Verdi." But I didn't. I blew it. I pulled my punches.

That's where I made my mistake. That was the moment. I should have followed my gut instinct and threatened to fire Harry if he didn't bring in Verdi.

I should have, but I didn't. I hesitated. "Was that it wasn't," I said to myself. I had bought into being reasonable. Stepping back and breathing deeply, I said, "If you're wrong, man, I will corner the market on suffering, dude. I hope you know what you're doing." That was it.

Was that it wasn't...but it was.

Sad thing is, I realize now that I probably wouldn't have had to fire anybody, just the threat of such a thing would have been sufficient. I think now, if I had done that, just threatened him, Harry may have laid down his beast, seen how important it was to me, and backed down.

Maybe.

But I'll never know. I pulled my punches. I hesitated. I doubted myself.

Later, out in the courthouse parking lot, Buddy said to me, "If you're right, if we lose this case because of a lack of expert testimony, you're going to have the greatest 'I told you so,' ever."

I threw my crutches in the back of my car and studied him for a moment, the only legal character who ever took this case serious enough to woodshed, and replied "I don't wanna say 'I told you so,' Bud. Lost causes and 'sure bets' that aren't, are full of 'I told you so's.'"

* 50 *

"Be reasonable," he was always saying to me, as though everything I was telling him was unreasonable. Throughout the whole trial he did this, and now, one final time, he wasn't listening to me, again.

This was his closing. The place where he would sum up our case and, among others things, tell my story to the jury, let them know the kind of person I was, as compared to Daar. He would tell them of my life and past, my work on behalf of the disabled and democracy....how even here and now, I was fighting the good fight, not just for myself, but also for thousands of others. He would contrast that with Daar, who seemingly went out of his way to burden the average disabled beach-goer, or at least their ability to enjoy a Venice afternoon.

I told Harry, "Fine. Go get him. Just be fucking reasonable about it," I joked.

He laughed and made his way to the jury box.

He started out well enough, saying all kinds of nice things about me that don't bear repeating, and then started in on Daar and the moral outrage of it all. The pettiness of Daar's actions were "unthinkable, as well as unconscionable," he insisted, his voice rising, "A disgrace to the community, like something right out of Nazi Germany!" Harry yelled.

"What?" I sat forward. "Did he just compare Daar to a Nazi? Damn! He did!"

I couldn't believe it. It was doubly offensive because Daar is a Jew, and almost incomprehensibly -- so was Harry! I hung my head. "Doesn't he realize how offensive and extreme that is to anybody with half a brain?"

It was suddenly apparent that Mr. B. Reasonable was just another narrowly educated idiot, with no real understanding of history, and, as such, was now misusing it to his full disadvantage -- to say nothing of mine.

He did all this in a high-pitched hostile voice, so it impacted the jury fully. There was an audible gasp from those that understood that calling an Israeli a Nazi was the height of bad taste and audacity. A bad taste and audacity that had come to exemplify Harry's overall handling of the case.

"Daar probably lost loved ones in the ovens of Auschwitz," I said to myself. To compound his thoughtless error, Harry then proceeded to offer advice to the jury on possible damages by explaining that the fine for illegally parking in a Blue Zone was $330, a day, "and if you multiply that by the number of days Mr. Daar chained off the lot..."

Before he could finish the thought, the judge was angrily admonishing him to desist. Such an argument was to be made at the second stage of the trial "when and if there was a finding of liability," he thundered, "and not before."

The Judge made Harry look like the ill-prepared dilettante he was. So Harry foundered, sorely out of his league. He was just a "settlement lawyer," stumbling through a trial that he had underestimated by overestimating himself. No humility, no empathy, no due diligence, just sudden death.

He went on for another sputtering moment or two, completely discombobulated, but I lost interest in the rank amateur. I was busy turning to face my greatest fear. For the first time, I considered the possibility that we could lose.

"Nazis, huh, Harry," I said as he sat down. "Real fucking reasonable."

"Hey, I'm a Jew!" he protested in a whisper.

"That's what makes it so unreasonable, dude! What? You didn't know better? You had no idea?" I asked hotly.

Then he completely blew my mind.

"Yeah, I didn't know better," he said smugly, but neither will most of the jury. Most will have no idea about the comparison."

I didn't know what was sadder, him and his useless arrogance, or the fact that he might be right, and I had to count on that ugly truth.

Some closing.

* 51 *

My belief in common sense and sure bets died the day they brought in the verdict.

Daar was not held liable for a single count. Nothing. Not the ADA, not the Unruh Act, not even the vehicle code. One sentence, it turned out, seemed too much for the jury to comprehend. Forget the law. Forget Daar's admission. Forget common sense and decency. I had been defeated.

It seems that the able-bodied jury couldn't, or didn't, want to understand the very real suffering these chained off Blue Zone and denials of facilities caused disabled citizens. What injustice is worse or more painful than to be denied the very accommodations put in place to assist you?

They had no empathy. My only satisfaction, as I held my head high and took the body shot, was that some day they, the jury, would see it all differently. For at least 83% of them, empathy would be forced on them.

Hope they can find a place to park.

Harry didn't say a word. No apologies either. Just shock. Harry was beyond stunned, not only had he lost, but worst, he had lost a sure thing, and now had no idea what to say. He hadn't planned for this. The jurors would understand the outrage. That was the sure bet, right? Now he was silent. All his licensed intelligence left him. His able-bodied arrogance now scared his legal psyche, leaving him thoughtless as well as speechless. He was, in that moment, disabled.

Larry the wannabe was likewise.

I did as I was supposed to do. In spite of myself, I organized them.

Taking a deep breath as I heard Ms. Bass' voice in the back of my mind, saying in that strong Kathryn Hepburn fashion, "Get up, kiddo," I did. I led the way out to the courthouse steps, for an impromptu news conference with local press. Since I was the only one who could put together a coherent thought, I went before the TV cameras and explained, that, yes, we were disappointed -- but not deterred!

I went on to point out what any student of civil rights already knows, that many times it is history -- and higher courts -- that ultimately right the wrongs done to the common citizens at the local level. "I am sure that this is just such a case," I told them.

No, I wasn't sorry I brought the lawsuit. "Yes, I would do it again tomorrow, and yes," I said, with a glance at my legal team of sniveling rabbits, "we would do things differently." All that brave face stuff.

"Close with a flurry," I reminded myself, and went on to point out that since disabled citizens can no longer get justice in the courts, it is imperative, that we, as a community, organize our vote in order to protect and promote our rights, ourselves.

"We now have no one else to protect us but ourselves, and no one else to blame if we don't." Like I said, all that brave face stuff. I declared my intention to continue my efforts with UP. "We disabled citizens have got no other choice, folks. Thank you."

The lawyers now just stumbled and mumbled. Not knowing what else to do, they went back to speak to the jurors who stuck around to talk to us. I followed them in.

His name was Frank, and he was one of just two or three staunch defenders that we had on the jury. And guess what he asked us? "How come you guys didn't have anybody to back up your legal contentions? The defendant's expert killed us in the jury room," he informed us.

I couldn't believe those were the first words out of his mouth, but they were. He even used the term "legal contentions." This was a smart guy. I seriously thought about saying, "I told you so," to Harry, but he was too numb to even pick up on it. I reminded myself to tell Bud that I got absolutely no satisfaction from even the thought of it.

"Bingo," was all I said to Harry after Frank's frank admission.

They had their $5,000 dollar guy and Parker. They used them.

We had the Assistant Attorney General in charge of civil rights for all of California, and we didn't use him.

And as Frank told it, we robbed our sympathizers of the "expert" testimony they needed to counteract Daar's partisans. As Frank put it, "You tied our hands behind our backs."

We had given them nothing to counter or nullify Daar's expert's BS. Combine that lack of strategic insight, with the legal egos in play, throw in a shitty closing and a jury forewoman who happened to be a banker, and you too can blow even the surest of bets. We did, and I repeat, saying "I told you so" was of no consolation.

It never is...particularly when you let so many people down. Like the whole god blessed disabled community of greater L.A. You know how the mind works when you're in shock. All black.

I had let the whole community down, and all because I had listened to an able-bodied bonehead and one wannabe, who were running on legal hubris instead of a winning legal strategy. Worse, I didn't stop them. I hesitated, questioned my authority more than theirs, and now I had lost.

On the drive home, I came to the realization that the worst aspect of this defeat wasn't that I had failed, but I had failed because of someone else's mistakes...instead of my own.

I saw no good in that. I mean if it's going to be blown, let me blow it. At least that way I can learn something of real strategic importance instead of reaffirming that simple, universal truth that my mother told me early on: "Never listen to fools."

"Face it," I told myself, "chances are, as the present situation amply demonstrates, I wouldn't have blown it." I couldn't have blown it worse than this. I really was the only one who had a basic understanding of strategy, as well as this particular area of law. On my team of lug-heads, I was the only one who was an "expert." And I had doubted myself.

"Remember," I said to myself, holding back a well of emotion, "it is better to go down in flames of your own making, than those of others."

I had failed to question authority. God, that revelation hurt my rebel pride most.

I went home and, after a while, I cried. I admit that none of it was very Buddhist of me.

Finally, huffing and puffing, I took time to remember the most important word in the English language when you're truly suffering. "Endure," I said quietly to myself.

The good stoic in me wiped away a fist full of tears and did just that.

* 52 *

"Where was the advantage in this disadvantage?" I awoke and wondered.

Having progressed beyond endurance, I lay there and proceeded to remember the most important English words ever written -- about anything. "This too shall pass," I said to myself. At least I hoped so. I saw it as a plus that I had progressed from one word to four, philosophically speaking.

Still all blue and pondering, I could see no good in any of it. The bleak dread that I had let the community down was still there. And to think that I had done it on a case that should have been "un-lose-able" only salted the wound in the worst way...with my own tears.

"See what happens when you go with the sure bet," I told myself. "Stick with the long shots."

You don't expect them to pay off, anyway, so there's no real disappointment when they don't. If, however, they do, all the better. With long shots, it can only get better.

With the old "sure thing" that isn't, you can only be disappointed. "Yeah, stick with long shots."

As I shaved, I counted it as a blessing that organizing disabled citizens to vote in their enlightened self-interest was the longest of long shots, so I needn't worry about disappointment, no matter what the outcome.

"Blessed be the long shot and those that take them," I said through a lather of shaving cream and marijuana smoke.

Bloody but unbowed, I had a bad taste in my mouth. Much like that of raw lamb, Karo syrup, and cream, I imagined. I consoled myself with the fact that I had grown strong off that god-awful concoction then, and that I could grow stronger off this god awful tasting mess now.

"They can't beat me," I told myself. "I'm a raw lamb, Karo syrup, and cream sucking man." For the first time in twenty-four hours, I laughed.

Then it came to me in the midst of the thin mirth. Like all good lovers of the long shot and the gamble it entails, I really did have to do what you always do when you lose big. I doubled down.

"We'll organize the whole damn nation," I mumbled through the creamy haze.

* 53 *

Over time, the soul of real life stepped in, too. More than one disabled citizen or friend said to me, "What can you expect from a bunch of TABs?" Yeah, really. What can you expect?

"It's the prejudice of the healthy human psyche; it can't see itself as anything less than healthy," Paul would say. "They can't envision that they are but one slip away from needing handicapped parking themselves."

Exactly.

People in the community have a pretty low opinion of most TABs...particularly when it comes to their doing right by the disabled.

The trial just bore that out.

Then the real results came in. And it is life, not all the nervous pondering, that shows one the ultimate balance of the universe when it comes to justice. For in reality, it is the ripples one creates that ultimately impact the world, regardless of what some jury may say.

And what a wonderful way to find out too -- from Jimmi, down on the boardwalk, just down from Daar's café.

"So, you beat him, huh, my brother?" he said with a big smile.

"Afraid not, Jimmi. The jury said he wasn't liable. Of course, my lawyers were fools," I said half-heartedly.

"Of course they were," he replied with Israeli-accented enthusiasm and knowing. "But you got him, buddy, huh! No more chains!"

Thinking he wasn't getting it, I spoke more firmly than before. "No, Jimmi, Daar beat us in court. I did tell his lawyer that if Daar puts the chain back up, I'll take him back to court. Promise."

"No, there won't be no more courts, my friend! No more chains, no more courts, 'cause you beat him! Look around you, my buddy," he said expansively taking in the boardwalk. "No more chains anywhere. Look."

I looked down the boardwalk, this way and that. It was true, all the parking lots that fronted the boardwalk within eyesight seemed to have their chains down, with nobody having to ask for it. Other merchant's had chains, but they had drop them when asked, unlike Daar. Now, they were all just down...without asking...including Daar's shops.

"Wow, Jimmi, dig that. It is a beautiful day in my neighborhood, huh!"

"Everybody knows you took on the biggest shit on the boardwalk and it cost him $70,000 to fight you."

"Seventy grand," I said, surprised. "You mean seventy thousand dollars! Daar spent seventy thousand bucks on this case?"

"Sure, buddy, that's what they say. You didn't know?"

"No!"

"Oh, come on."

"No, I didn't."

He was busily pulling boxes of merchandise from his car next to his canvas stall. He stopped and looked me in the eye. "Sure, buddy. $70,000 is what it costs to mess with you. So, now the chains are down."

"That was a very expensive chain," I laughed.

"Yeah, right, buddy, like I say, you got him. You got him good. You did it."   Maybe it was just a friend helping a friend feel better, maybe it was a guy in need of a good sign, but you know, my spirits brightened considerably. It occurred to me that with that chain down, I had, in reality, gotten exactly what I'd fought for and more. All the chains were down and the merchant class was not only aware of their responsibility to the disabled, but also put on notice as to what would happen if they violated them. Win lose or draw, they'd spend a lot of cash.

That loss of cash would, more than anything else I hoped, speak to the better angels of their nature and ensure that they continued to do the right thing. Again, I hoped it would. It reminded me of what those old grassroots organizers, the Viet Cong, used to say: Lose the battle -- win the war!

So, an "I told you so" cost $70,000 dollars these days... I could live with that. A few days later, we went to see if the judge would grant us a NOJV and overturn the verdict, in the interest of justice. He would not. There was a smidgen of justice to the proceeding however, when the good judge scolded Harry in an open court, telling him in no uncertain terms that he, Harry, "should have won this case."

That was it. Those were the small comforts I took away with me after three years of hard work. Chains down, the merchant class now well aware of their duty towards the disabled, and an urgent reaffirmation of the need to organize our vote. Fair enough. You've got to play the hand you're dealt.

The lawyers never apologized, either. Oh well, you can't expect miracles from the likes of them. I accepted that, too.

And thus, I was taught that most invaluable lesson of life and long shots. If one is to succeed in them, one must learn to take one's defeats, as well as one's victories, in stride.

That was the trick, wasn't it? I realized that achieving this ability, this kind of grace as a person and as an organizer, is, after all, what makes whatever you're fighting for inevitable. If you can turn your defeats into victories, how can you be defeated?

You can't. Set back, yes, but defeated, never!

"They know you now," Jimmi said, referring to the other boardwalk merchants and bringing me back to my senses. I just smiled in agreement, remembering what Big Mike and Victor, my blessed childhood bullies, had taught me. Namely, when you fight the good fight -- win, lose, or draw -- people think twice before messing with you again. You may have to take a blow or two in the process, but for your tormentors, if there is a big enough price to pay, they tend to leave you alone. Now I had that best of all things for an effective organizer...a reputation.

And a costly one at that. As Jimmi, the wise one said, "Nobody wants to mess with you, my buddy. You're a very expensive problem."

$70,000 to be exact, thank you very much.

From that moment on, I most definitely took my defeat in stride, some might even say with a bit of swagger.

Thank you, Jimmi!

* 54 *

I took it as another fortunate sign when Peter Tart offered me office space down at AARP's Los Angeles headquarters. I thought he was being shrewd, that this was more than friendship; this coming together was all about power...the power of oldsters and gimps. Me and the now dear Mr. Tart -- in sweet collaboration -- taking power!

I mistakenly thought that's what collaboration was all about. Working with friends and fellow organizations that share your goals and objectives, for the benefit of all, right? So I thought.

What I found out, though, was that I still had a lot to learn about collaboration. Socrates was right. The more I knew, the more I realized I didn't know.

"Organizing is a process, not an event, so enjoy the process," I reminded myself.

No doubt, hooking up organizationally with AARP was a godsend for both UP and myself. It offered us, as Goethe said, "all kinds of unforeseen material assistance." And it didn't surprise me that Providence took the form of AARP. After all, they did have more money than God.

As such, they would help us organize disabled citizens in general. We'd help them organize disabled seniors in specific -- a natural alliance. It was near bliss to not have to worry about phone bills, copying costs, or the thousand and one other expenses that nickel and dime grassroots organizations to death. The nicest thing was, I could participate in divinity on their dime.

With such incidental costs out of the way, I was free to appreciate the bigger objective, which I thought was what Peter wanted: to get on with "the big stuff" and, almost unbelievably, to have the resources to actually do it. Let's not kid ourselves; this was a rare chance to accomplish our mission in a big way. Reaching out to hundreds of thousands, if not millions, of disabled and senior citizens was now possible!

Nothing more, nothing less.

Isn't that what collaboration is really all about, the using of another's resources to accomplish complementary goals? Resources AARP had on a scale that I only partially realized, but was never more ready to utilize.

That's why I was quite surprised when Peter got all excited about a mere 76,000 envelopes.

"You need what?" He looked at me with the puzzled alarm of a bureaucrat and his nose twitched.

"Scratch your nose," I told him. "76,000 envelopes, along with the appropriate letterhead, which UP will cover if we have to," I said to soften the blow, preposterous as that sounded to me. Since we had next to nothing and they, along with the money, also had more paper than God. I was to discover that AARP loved paper. The amount of paper they tossed out at one medium-sized AARP event could have handled UP's needs for a year.

That's why Pete's reaction puzzled me. Forget what we're going to use them for, Pete didn't seem to understand that just ordering that many envelopes would make him look like he was doing something. On top of it, he was powerful -- he was going to ensure the registering of thousands of disabled seniors to vote.

"What do you need those envelopes for, again?" he asked.

I loved ol' Pete, but I could see a common practice evolving between us. He was not an attentive listener. I think he thought it made him appear more powerful or busy if he turned away from you while you were talking with him as he continued to work on his computer or take calls. He may have thought it made him appear more powerful; I think it just caused him not to take much in. Whatever the case, I found myself repeating myself a lot around him, reinforcing my belief in the need to be an attentive listener if you're going to be an effective organizer.

I put up with it, though. It was worth taking a little crap from the old blunderbuss due to all the resources he could make available...resources that the ol' tart now seemed to be afraid to use.

I began to explain it to my reticent friend all over again. The great collaboration. Between UP, AARP, and the Union.

I reminded him that it was he, "Pedro the revolutionary thinker" who had first brought up the idea. He had mentioned to me that he wanted to start developing closer contacts with the Union, that their efforts to organize home based health care workers was something that "AARP was interested in."

"Likewise," I told him. I wanted to reach out to the 76,000+ disabled citizens in L.A. county who use attendant care and ensure that they were registered and voting via the Permanent Absentee Ballot. Thus, we had a similar interest in working with the Union on some kind of coordinated voter registration effort.

As fate would have it, all of this was rolling around in my head when I ran into Ruben, union organizer, and humane being, at this or that rally that we progressives liked to rally at. During the course of the conversation, he told me that the Union had the names and address of every person who used attendant care in L.A. County, "Over 76,000 people, man."

"That's a whole lot of voters," I told him. "Maybe we can work together on organizing them."

"We must!" said Ruben, with a bear hug. "We're too poor not to!"

Ruben knew what we were, consumer and attendant alike. We were all of us, poor people.

I'm the first to agree with the unions that we must try to get better wages for the attendants through collective bargaining. Well-paid workers take better care of disabled people, and that helps mitigate the effects of their low-income existence. But, by the same token, thousands of disabled voters who used attendant care could, and I believed would, put a lot of pressure on the Board of Supervisors to put together a "Public Authority" that the union could, then, collectively bargain with.

Reuben told me, "Absolutely, my friend. You are absolutely right. No doubt." In other words, the average union guy understood the potential and mutual benefit.

Consequently, I saw hope in such an effort and was now trying to explain that to Peter, again.

"Okay, dude," I began, remembering Elvis' advice to do it like it's the first time every time. I let the natural shrewdness of the idea rev me up, "If UP, AARP, and the Union worked together, we could conceivably register thousands of disabled citizens by just mailing a voter registration form and application for a PAB to each disabled citizen who uses attendant care. With UP's free franking privilege, we don't even need a postage stamp, dude. All you have do is put up 76,000 envelopes."

"Okay?" he said half-heartedly. He didn't get it. He didn't remember.

"Look, Pete, it works like this," I began again. "If the Union puts up the names and address of citizens who use attendant care and AARP puts up the envelopes, UP will use its free mailing privilege and send each one of those citizens a nice voter registration package. Throw in a nice cover letter of explanation in 14-point type and I'll bet you we'll register a shitload of new voters, cheap, easy, and ethical." I was spinning down. "And all three organizations get some legitimate credit for trying to make democracy work. Cool, huh?"

"Yeah right," he said, "Where do you come up with these ideas?"

"I'm an organizer and I believe in participatory democracy?" I answered in a questioning tone.

"An organizer for democracy," he laughed.

"You said that, I didn't."

"You really believe that stuff?" he teased.

"Got to believe in something, and saving democracy isn't a bad thing to believe in, if you ask me."

"Oh, jeez...saving democracy. Go save yourself."

"I am," I answered. Not being much of a philosopher, he just looked at me.

"Oh," was all he said.

He wanted most, I believe, to be taken seriously. With this AARP gig, I think he saw himself now as a power player -- beyond grassroots organizing. I don't think he understood that "making democracy work" really was his main job, i.e. getting ordinary (senior) citizens to organize themselves. I worried about him. "Titles and power lunches do not a democracy make," I reminded him.

"Don't say nothing bad about expense account organizing," he tried to joke.

I was glad he still had a sense of humor, 'cause I also worried about him due to the fact that he was that rarest of all things: an Irishman who didn't drink. Thus I believe he never really allowed himself to be moved by the power and the poetry of what he was doing, in that truest of Irish fashions. Hell, he didn't even "drink to" such high ideas as "making democracy work." Unlike most Irish, he got no civic pleasure from his efforts.

"76,000 envelopes," he said abruptly. "I don't know if I can request 76,000 envelopes."

"Request. Request?" I am floored. "Those 76,000 envelopes," I said to him forcefully, "are a damn strategic necessity. Don't request them -- demand them. That's power. Use it."

"Power?" he looked surprised. "We're talking envelopes."

"That, my friend, is the stuff of power. The small stuff, I admit."

"Oh, so now 76,000 envelops is small stuff," he said a little ticked.

"Yes it is, buddy," I was a little ticked. "76,000 envelopes should be nothing to you. Particularly when it concerns registering senior voters. Why don't you find out what it takes to order 76, 000 envelopes? Just find out. Use your power."

"I'll use my power. Get the hell out of here," he ordered. Peter was forever throwing me out of his office. It was part of his habit to overreact. Thank god we were good friends and could cackle at each other like old hens, with no real offense taken.

"Just find out what it takes, dude," I said, all but exasperated.

"Yeah, okay. Get out of here before I break your crutch," he said, trying to be funny in that insipid able-bodied fashion. "Hey dude," he yelled after me, "have you figured out how you're going to stuff your voter registration packets?"

No I hadn't. "Listen up," I told myself. Perhaps ol' Pete's got something on the ball.

"Yeah, Pete," I barked, "I thought we'd get 76,000 silver haired AARP volunteers to come in to the office and each stuff an envelope, a real marvel of one-on-one grassroots organizing. How's that for collaboration?"

"You're a genius," my sarcastic friend said. "I know AARP has some kind of mail operations plant from which they do all our mass mailing, maybe we could get that."

My spirits brightened considerably. Mr. Tart was beginning to impress me. "Now you're talking, Petey ol' boy. A stuffing house, wow! Find out what that costs to utilize." A damned stuffing house and 76,000 voter registration packages were not at all out of the question now.

"Yeah, wow!" he mocked. "Now get out of here, I've got work to do."

"Sure, Pete. Just one thing."

"Yeah, what?"

"Look, buddy, would you make the call to the Union, set up the meeting? Somehow I don't think my networking with Ruben is going to secure those names or a meeting. However, a call from AARP's political director just might."

"Yeah, I can probably do that." This was the kind of "let your fingers do the organizing" that Pete loved to do. "But wait a minute," he said, irritated again, "you come in here with this half-baked idea that you haven't even checked out with any other necessary collaborator, insult me and my understanding of power, request 76,000 envelopes on a whim, and then expect me to set up the meeting for you?"

"I told you I was an organizer, didn't I?" I was out the door before he could throw me out again.

"A stuffing house," I thought to myself. "Now, that's bold!"

* 55 *

Northern California was calling. That Mecca of disability advocacy and action was beckoning for UP.

Too cool, for they were already enlightened. They already got it. They understood power and ESI. Therefore, it was easy to sell them on the common sense notion that democracy was our only alternative if we ever wanted to achieve true social justice and self-ensured independence. Best of all, they dug the irony that voting is one of the few things that disabled citizens, as individuals, could do for themselves. And in a community where there isn't a whole hell of a lot of things that we can do for ourselves, voting is poetic justice at its best. Whoever thought that the actual taking of power would be so simple and just?

"And I mean 'just' as in, 'We just have to do it!'"

They would all laugh and agree.

I'd continue, "If we don't, we have no one to blame but ourselves."

Most, if not all, murmured in agreement.

"So, are you ready to take power?" I would ask.

The answer was always the same. They were.

"Step or roll right up, and register to vote!" I would shout, feeling every bit like the ringmaster of democracy.

They applauded just as loud in the north as they did in the south, and many initially wondered, as we had, why organizing our vote hadn't been done long before.

"I think it was waiting for you to do it!" I'd tell them as they registered to vote. It was, after all, the truth.

With many of these groups picking up the tab, I began to travel the state, preaching the gospel about the power of our vote.

"We take consumers and turn them into citizens!" I did not hesitate to tell them.   Together we turned consumers into citizens and citizens into organizers, instantly...all by simply giving them the wherewithal and knowledge necessary to register five other people. Many did not stop at five.

Across the state our elementary ideas about root democracy were taking hold. Hundreds of citizens were registering thousands of other citizens with disabilities and their families. And we did our damnedest to include everyone, to make sure that any disabled person who wanted to vote, and wasn't under conservatorship, got a fair and full chance to do so.

Of course, this ruffled some feathers. It was just a tad ironic that it should happen in Northern California. Again, the dominant myth being that the northern part of the state was so much more organized and enlightened than the lowly south. Just ask Terry.

She found it strange too. She was my lovely Asian-American vegetarian guide for that first foray north. And I'd be the first to admit, I had to focus on "staying focused" on the voter registration chores at hand and not her slinky little hips whenever we were together. The fact that she was married, and happily so, helped immensely.

Still she was vivacious in a high-energy worker bee way, and I couldn't help but be impressed. She was committed and knew everyone in town, and introduced me to most.

I gave that particular speech to three hundred disabled citizens and their families who were as shocked as I, when the speaker before me -- one of the Regional Center bigwigs -- had the audacity to tell three hundred severely disabled citizens that they had to stop being "Medi-Cal junkies."

He proclaimed this not once, but a number of times.

Shaking my head in disbelief, and thinking of Paul and how much I'd like to squid this guy, I started my speech off by introducing myself as the Executive Director of UP and "a longtime Medi-Cal junkie." The place roared. I gave them their numbers.

"Approximately 30,000 disabled citizens of voting age live in this congressional district." I added along with it the fact that their local congressman, who had barely won the last election by a mere thousand votes, was a buddy of Newt's. Enough said.

They hissed. They snarled. They took voter registration forms home with them to register their families.

Earlier, on the trip over to the local community center, I was told that this particular congressman had heard I was in town doing a little voter registration and had gotten quite upset. His margin of victory last time had been so slim that he feared that a bunch of motivated disabled voters were enough to deny him the next election in this rural district. He was right to worry.

He called the director of the Area Board and in a highly irritated state complained about "outside agitators."

Outside agitators? Was this Northern California in the 1990's or the deep South of the 1950's and 60's? I wondered. Outside agitators! How passé.

I was told this so that I could "watch" my remarks. Watch my remarks? Hey, this is Northern California! What are you talking about? You're supposed to be cutting edge, fearlessly pro-active. I was shocked. I thought they knew that this kind of irritation on the part of a local congressman was a red flag of vulnerability and a real gauge of their potential political power within their community.

"All for the price of a postage stamp when you use your Mail-In Ballot," I reminded them. Of course I brought the cranky congressman up.

"Sure he's cranky," I told the audience. "There are enough disabled voters in this room to cost him the election. You bet he's cranky. Don't forget, my fellow citizens, you have the power and the right to upset your congressperson. Use it! Only if you do exercise your legitimate power will your venerable and vulnerable representative begin to do your bidding -- or he won't be your congressman much longer. It's as simple as that."

They applauded vigorously.

I went for broke: "To paraphrase President Harry Truman, if your congressman can't handle the heat, we have a right to kick him out of the kitchen! It's called democracy. Use it. Let's take power together, for a better California, and for a better, more accessible America! Thank you and let's get to work!"

The place erupted.

The executive director hung his head. Sorry, dude.

There was a standing ovation, or what counts as one with this crowd. Elvis would have been proud.

Okay, so there was one disgruntled congressman and one overly sensitive executive director, but, what the hell, I was through with pulling my punches or worrying about what the TAB world thought. I had learned the hard way that that wasn't my job.

My job was to register disabled voters and encourage them to take power. I did just that, walking out of the community center with hundreds of completed VR forms, sweet Terry driving me to the post office to drop them in the box.

"Don't worry about our executive director," she said.

"I won't," I assured her. "After all, this is Northern California."

I came back to L.A. with enthusiasm and an enhanced mailing list, happy as hell to have colleagues to work with up north...even if I had to forget about those slinky little Asian hips...which I had almost done when I got a call from Terry a few weeks later.

"We've been getting some bad press up here. I'd like to send you a tape," she said with evident urgency.

"Sure, go ahead. What's up?" I asked.

She explained that a parent of one of the severely disabled citizens we had registered got all pissed off because he didn't think his daughter was fit to vote, and now the old curmudgeon was raising hell and had called a reporter. The reporter, with much alarm and very few facts, decided to do an investigative piece on voter fraud.

"Jeez, Ter, send down the tape and I'll be happy to respond. Don't worry, we never had any intent to register fraudulent or unfit voters, so this is just a whole bunch of smoke they're blowing up your butt" -- pretty as it is, I thought to myself.

She thanked me with all the sincerity of one who was looking to cover her ass, and that of her bosses'. Understandable. I had to remember that these folks were first and foremost social workers, not civil rights activists, and were just as concerned with case management as they were with voter registration (as well as the budget to do both). They were not used to rocking the boat.

I told her to call up the journalist and ask for equal time. She told me her boss was nervous that such a move would "add fuel to the fire."

Fuel to the fire? My illusions about the almighty avant-garde, cutting edge north were dashed. I thought of telling her this, but her voice was nervous. She needed backbone. So I told her, "I think a press conference or interview that tells your side of the story will put the fire out."

"I don't know."

"Look, Terry, it can't hurt you, 'cause we weren't doing anything wrong or illegal. And if you don't respond, it's going to look like we were. I'd ask for equal time. In any case, send the tape down and we'll see if we can't help you set the record straight."

A few days later the tape arrived. As I figured, it was lazy journalism masquerading as a hard-hitting investigative piece, or, should I say, three pieces.

There was our curmudgeon, the father, bemoaning the fact that his DD daughter was cognitively disabled and therefore unable to vote. They had nice little pictures of the father and daughter around the dinner table, him asking what time it is and her not knowing. This was followed by a "follow-up report."

The next hit piece featured the journalist badgering a bunch of overworked and uninformed workers at the Center. They, being scared, came across as being slightly at their wits' end, looking more like a gaggle of distressed geese than a threat to our democracy.

The grand finale was a report on election day turnout. Our intrepid reporter highlighted a polling place that had been set up in a group home for adults with developmental disabilities...going so far as to put his camera and (bright) lights right outside the voting booths.

With the lights and cameras blazing away, he seemed happy to report that not a single person came down to vote, apparently oblivious to the fact that his lights and cameras were having a rather chilling effect on turnout...particularly when that turnout involved developmentally disabled adults, many who were first time voters.

I'd love to reprint the letter I wrote to this slam, boom, bang mistake of a serious journalist, but due to a computer meltdown many years ago, that is impossible.

He probably still has it. Or perhaps the station's legal department has it on file.

Suffice it to say, I informed him that his "sophistry was showing" when he cast this story as a case of "voter fraud." I went on to point out that, as much as he may not like it, not he, nor I, nor anyone else outside of a judge could take away a citizen's right to vote, and that, as a civic organization, UP had a duty "to expand the envelope" and make a good faith attempt to register as many qualified disabled citizens as we possibly could.

It was better a few unqualified disabled citizens get unintentionally registered than a whole class of citizens get counted out of the process altogether, which is exactly what had been happening up to that point.

I told him to go pick on someone his own size, to contact UP or the League of Woman Voters, and we'd straighten him out. To imply, as his reporting had done, that the incoherent answers of overburdened workers in some way proves fraud was really unfair.

Got a question? Call us. Call UP.

Lastly I pointed out that what his reports portrayed as voter manipulation and fraud -- the empty unused voting booths, all lit up by TV camera lights -- was in reality voter intimidation. All the commotion and controversy of his cameras and lights actually scared people away -- a clear violation of the 1965 Voting Rights Act. It was, in reality, a clear-cut case of voter suppression.

Best regards.

One man's manipulation is another man's intimidation, I guess.

I like to believe, at least in my fantasies, that our ruthless reporter got the letter and ran it by the legal affairs department. They viewed the reports for themselves and said, "Hey, the guy's got a point. Cool it."

All I know is the reports stopped. Terry called to thank me for writing such a well-reasoned letter. "We won one!" she exclaimed. "We'll keep registering people."

I told her, "Make every reasonable attempt to ascertain whether someone is eligible. But remember, we are not immigration agents or mental health experts."

"It was almost too easy," she said. "My boss is still upset, though."

"I'll bet," I told her. I felt like saying, "Tell your boss to go check out the history of social work and social workers. He'd probably be surprised to find that they were a bunch of flaming radicals...radicals and agitators who fought for all the earliest protections of women, children, and workers, as well as the disabled." I felt like saying that, but I didn't. "If that's all, count your blessings," was all I said. I counted mine.

A couple of months later, I spoke to over 1,200 disabled activists at a statewide self-advocacy conference, and Terry was there, all smiles. She, and more than a few disabled voters from the area mentioned the incident to me. Those who had seen the letter I had written thanked me.

It was all very touching. They treated me with such great respect. I told myself to behave.

I didn't drink too much that night, nor think about Terry's slinky hips too much.

She was very happy. The news reports stopped, but our side of the story never really did get out, the side that had to do with disabled citizens having a right to vote (unless a judge says otherwise).

Typical. Even in the enlightened north.

* 56 *

Peter had made the call. "Bob Fox, the union's political director, told me he was coming by," the tart one said nonchalantly, "or sending a representative by."

We waited at the appointed place and time. AARP's big room, high noon. While we waited, we fussed.

"Did you get the lowdown on the stuffing house?" I asked.

"Don't bust my balls on that right now," he growled.

"You didn't, did you?" I wasn't surprised. In fact, truth be told, I was surprised that he had made the offer to call at all. "Dude, whatever you do, don't tell the union you don't know how to access your resources," I said just to piss him off.

"Screw you. I know how to access my resources," he said in a mock whiny voice. "And don't call me dude!"

Before he could bark again, the phone rang. Over the intercom, we were informed that, "The union guy is here."

Pete picked up the receiver. "Bring him down to the big room in two minutes," he said into it. "What? Yeah? Okay," he finished. Now, he was all smiles.

"Your favorite guy is here," he told me, laughing.

"Who?"

"Kenny Ball. See what you get for being a shit head," he said gleefully.

I flashbacked to my last un-enlightened encounter with Kenny Ball and gave Pete the highlights.

"What's he doing here?" I asked, legitimately surprised.

"Didn't you hear? Kenny Ball got hired by the union as their liaison person to the disabled community on all attendant care issues."

"What?!"

"That's right...you were out of town, weren't you? Surprise -- you get to deal with Kenny Ball."

"We're dead," I said. "The guy's toxic. He'll screw things up just to screw with me."

I did not see much hope. Some people you can't win over. But I would try. Talk about long shots.

"Ah, c'mon," Peter said. "Isn't that what collaboration is all about? Working with people that you wouldn't necessarily invite home to dinner."

"Stop talking about yourself, Peter," I moaned. I moaned most because he had a point.

Perhaps, I had it all wrong. Collaborating with your friends is easy. Maybe, the truth is you're only really collaborating when you're working with people you don't like...when you're finding common cause with an adversary.

Kenny Ball would sorely test that theory.

* 57 *

The three of us sat there in the big room of AARP's state headquarters, Peter hoping he wouldn't have to do too much, me, gushing and proposing, seeing the easy wonder of it all, and Kenny, willing to check it out, but displaying his standard reserve for anything even remotely plebeian.

His early remark, that there may be "some privacy concerns about the mailing list," tipped me off that Kenny was already looking for a way out.

Typical Kenny...I could only hope that the ease and simplicity of the idea would carry him. If not that, then perhaps kissing up to Peter would. Kenny was famous for his brown-nosing ways around anyone he perceived as powerful, as well as being quite the contrary around those he did not. Now, the only question was, would the color brown work in my favor?

If nothing else, I hoped Kenny would see that pulling off such a feat -- unionized attendant care workers registering tens of thousands of voters and then putting the power of the PAB in their hands quickly and cheaply -- was in his and the Union's own best interest.

I pointed out that if the Union really wanted to enhance their clout with the (elected) Board of Supervisors and gain a public authority they could collectively bargain with, then registering the people that needed attendant care to vote was one of the surest ways to do that.

"That's real political power that the Board can relate to!" I exclaimed.

He kind of snorted.

"Look, Kenny, everybody's got something the other wants. You got the names. We've got the mailing privilege and technical expertise, and AARP's got the stuffing house," I said, leering at the old tart. "And if we do this right, all three components can legitimately be used to everyone's great benefit. That's real political power. It's a win/win situation, all the way around."

Anybody but Kenny, and I'd have carried the day. "I don't know," he sniveled. "Giving out those names, county social services might have privacy concerns."

"Come on, you guys can get them around those," I cajoled him. "I've seen some of the propaganda the unions have been sending out and, if you can do that, you should be able to send out a voter registration form and application for Permanent Absentee Ballot status. In fact, the Department of Social Services should wholeheartedly support that...supplying yet another service."

"Very funny," he said.

"I'm not being funny," I replied.

"What if they got copied or misused?" he asked, with a little belligerence.

"C'mon man," I said, low key and serious. "Stop being so damn patronizing. We're not invading anyone's privacy, Kenny. We're trying to get them registered to vote, not take a damn AIDS test."

"Yeah, but what if someone copies the list?" he sputtered on.

"Nobody wants copies of your list, Kenny. Nobody's going to misuse it," Peter said firmly.

I flash back to Lelan. Between his "security concerns" and Kenny's "privacy concerns," this community was going nowhere fast. The worst of it being that their concerns were now being raised by disabled "leaders" who didn't seem to want to empower disabled citizens in any real sense of that overused word.

Do that, they seem to be saying, and one of those newly empowered gimps might want their job.

Now, there's a security concern.

"Our intent is to register disabled citizens to vote," I informed my reticent colleague. "Period. Not sell them a damn gimp magazine or bladder bag. All that this concern about privacy has done is hamper our community's ability to communicate, educate, and organize with one another. Let's stop that here and now," I offered.

"I'll run it by Bob," he said. "I'll let you know if it's in our enlightened self-interest," he smirked.

What do you know? He looked up the words.

"I hope you know what's in yours," I shot back.

Remembering I was here to try and collaborate with my adversaries, I tried to overlook his smugness, his air of condescension, around anything involving real people with disabilities. "Check it off to his polio," I told myself, or just your standard inferiority complex. Why not? Maybe it has nothing to do with his disability. Maybe he really does just have a stick up his insecure ass.

He was, after all, famous for his backhanded compliments, not just to individuals, but also to whole rooms full of people. I had seen him walk into meetings of one sort or another and say, in a rather derogatory tone, "Same old faces."

"Same old Kenny," came the response from the back of the room.

Kenny had learned long ago, probably as a defense mechanism, that a toxic remark keeps people off balance. But it also gets old after a while.

Most everyone in the community had dealt with Kenny at one time or another and had had problems with him. It's just that he has the straight world fooled with his brown- nose ingratiating cripple kid routine and they kept giving him jobs. So you had to deal with him.

Okay. I was ready to work with him. I reminded myself that I had actually tried to work with Kenny in one form or another before...just to understand him better. He was after all, smart and verbal, which always impresses the TABs, and, like me, he was fairly durable.

He also lived at the beach. I remembered that when I first went to see him about UP. Having just started it, I was hoping he would pitch in. He could have given a lot of speeches, registered quite a few voters, and gotten quite a bit of glory in the process, but he "didn't like the name," so nothing came of it.

As I mentioned before, he didn't like any idea that wasn't his, which was the current problem.

"Yeah, run it by Bob," I said, coming out of my reverie.

Finally, in that split second of hope that was still left, I thought maybe he'd want to look good in his new bosses' eyes and a collaborative effort with such a beneficial outcome for all couldn't help but do that.

"Hey, Kenny," I said finally, "forget the fact that it will cost the union nothing. This will make us all look good and it's easy, man."

"That's your opinion," he said.

"That's my opinion too," Peter chimed in. Thank you, Pedro.

"Still, I have to check out those privacy concerns," Kenny said. The light reflecting off his glasses aptly reflected the vacancy in his both his eyes and his mind.

"Why don't you do that?" Peter said, a little peeved. Kenny's lack of enthusiasm or even a real discussion of the idea was beginning to even bug Peter. Way to go Kenny!

Peter got up and left without a goodbye. Kenny turned and blinked at me, doing the knucklehead flutter.

I felt like saying: "Thanks, Moe." But I knew that would be unfair to Moe.

Instead, I just sighed and seriously wondered if collaboration was all it's chalked up to be. Collaboration with one's critic was one thing, trying to organize with smug stupidity was quite another.

"Under the circumstances, I await your call," I said to Ken.

"Thanks," Kenny said, much too gleefully, "that saves me from having to say, 'Don't call us, we'll call you!'"

I couldn't believe it, but that's what he said.

I knew this would never work.

* 58 *

With schedules that didn't jibe, I didn't see Pete for almost a week. When I did catch up with the old blunderbuss and asked about the stuffing house, he just walked into his office and slammed the door behind him.

Okay. He was a complex man whom I didn't have time to figure out. Time to initiate.

I turned to his sympathetic secretary, who just nodded in the affirmative when I asked her if she had to put up with that on a daily basis. She did. Now I sympathized with her.

When I asked where the mail operations plant was, she looked at me for a moment and then, in a flash of recognition, said, "You mean the stuffing house." She proceeded to look it up in a humongous AARP directory. "Lakewood," she said, writing down the address, "out near Long Beach -- about 40 minutes south."

It was that simple.

I headed south...wondering all the while if putting up with Kenny's and Peter's caca was really worth it.

It was. I met RJ. And as far as UP is concerned, RJ was the most helpful person in all of AARP. In the real grassroots sense of getting lots of small things done fast, he was the master.

Twenty minutes after meeting this easygoing man, I knew I could learn from him. He had hands-on experience. Plus, he liked to share.

RJ ran the stuffing house and when I told him we needed 76,000 packages made up and what was to be in them, he was little impressed. And well he should be. AARP pumps out millions of packages and tons of literature to its members every month -- and all for "eight bucks a year." 76,000 of anything was small potatoes to him and his crew, regardless of what the uninformed Peter may have thought.

I understood much better when I saw the scale of their operation. It was magnificent, football field size magnificent. And AARP owned it lock, stock, and stuffing machine. They had every kind of stuffing, stacking, sorting, and licking machine possible, and best of all you could customize them to your specific needs. I got dizzy when I coupled all this with the free franking privilege for the handicapped and blind.

76,000 packages, hell! With such a setup, we could conceivably mail voting age cripples in the country their own state's voter registration form and never think twice.

I was getting dangerous. I came back to earth by remembering to bless the millions of senior citizens who sent in their eight bucks every year, as well as the funny, efficient staff and crew that made this place stuff, stick, and lick a million times a day. Thank you one and all!

This was participating in divinity on the grand scale. I reminded myself to mention to Pete that nobody yelled here, either. Maybe I shouldn't be so surprised -- you have to stay calm when you're dealing with millions of pieces of mail every day, all going every which way.

Organization and humanity were big keys here...that and a ping pong table stationed at the far end of the facility. Ping pong was the preferred, as well as the quickest, way to relax and revitalize muscles grown sore or stiff from the rapidity of motion involved in getting out a 33-million-piece mailer fast.

It also led to a good natured, never-ending ping pong game with all sides rooting, for the most part, just to root. When things did get too hectic, or as respite from a major job, RJ was not averse to making everyone go on a picnic.

Yeah, I learned a lot from RJ. And all in just a couple of hours. I learned all the above-mentioned, plus the fact that stuffing 76,000 voter registration packages, "doesn't cost nothing."

"Doesn't cost nothing," I was dumbfounded. Suddenly this little man in dark glasses and smiling mustache was looking downright saintly to me.

"No, it doesn't cost AARP an extra cent to stuff a package, it's only when we put postage on it that it costs us, or that we have to charge for it."

Lighting bolts were striking me in the head. "So, if I had a free mailing privilege that allowed us to mail things for free, it wouldn't cost anything to stuff the packages."

"We've got a full time crew here," he said casually, "and sometimes they're busy, and sometimes they're not; regardless, they get paid. If you had packages you wanted to get out, I'd just throw them in the mix whenever we were less than busy. If you've got a free postal privilege, and it's okay with AARP, it wouldn't cost you a cent. Fact is you'd be doing me a favor. I can use the work as filler."

Use the work as filler! I could have kissed him right there, on both cheeks, like a true collaborator.

"I'd be doing him a favor?" I realized right then and there, who, or perhaps I should say "what," a true collaborator is. A true collaborator never foresees a problem that can't be solved, never thinks up a roadblock (like Kenny), or gets nervous (like Peter) -- he just looks to making your ideas and plans work.

To put it into one word, a true collaborator is: Effective. That was RJ.

"Let me know when you're ready to roll, and we'll throw your goodies into the machine," he said, making his way back to his office.

RJ the magnificent. Not only was he ready to stuff and ship 76,000 voter registration packages but he had taught me a lot. He'd answered the question of "who" it is best to collaborate with, and he didn't even realize it. He was just being very effective.

"You collaborate with the effective," I said to myself. Not your friends, nor your enemies; you collaborate with effective people, regardless. People who get things done with a conscientious good bit of cheer. That's the true sign of an effective person.

"Thank you, RJ," I said, wandering deep into the recesses of the plant, my voice, even at hushed tones, echoing through the vastness. "You're the grand collaborator. You're the one who's going to make this work."

I was not feeling so "grand" about old Peter as I drove home.

That brother o' mine, I thought to myself, he had hung me up for weeks, fought with me numerous times, upset himself all to hell...and why? Because he didn't know his resources. He didn't know what was at his disposal, much less how to utilize them.

I did.

"Goddamn, that guy's a jerk," I said to myself.

Then came a second voice in my head, right behind that thought. It said, "Wait a minute there, hotshot. Show a little mercy, will ya?! Your friend did help you. Didn't he? He set you up, didn't he? Maybe he doesn't know all there is to know about AARP's resources, but then who does? And didn't he, regardless of how ineptly, make it possible for you to find out what you needed to know -- well, didn't he?"

Point well taken. "Then show him a little mercy," I heard my grandmother say in the back of my head. "'Cause someday I might need some, right Nana?" I answered her.

So, on second thought...

Thanks Pedro, you sweet old tart.

* 59 *

He pulled his head up and back like someone avoiding a punch when I told him about RJ and the stuffing house. "Aw, c'mon," he said, disbelieving.

"Dude, it's not going to cost a cent to use the stuffing house."

He said it, again, "C'mon, what are you talking about?" He seemed truly surprised.

"Not a red copper cent," I informed him. "Your stuffing house only charges when they affix postage and since we have a free franking privilege at our disposal, the cost just disappears. Now, how's that for good grassroots organizing, dude of dudes!"

"You're kidding, right?"

"No, I'm not. Call RJ and ask him. By the way 76,000 packages is nothing to the pros down at the stuffing house."

He looked at me, nonplussed for a second, cracked a smile under his salt and pepper mustache, and asked in mock indignation, "What are you waiting for? Let's get those packages ready."

"There you go, Chief," I said, walking out.

"Don't call me Chief," he shouted after me.

"Right, dude."

"Important lesson here," I told myself as I walked back to my office, "Know your resources, and your partners' resources, too." That, and find your RJ.

Now I had to find Kenny. When I told him that we had the stuffing house on line and the voter registration material ready to be shipped from the Secretary of State's office, he started hemming and hawing, telling me that, as he feared, "The privacy concerns were too great. It may violate confidentiality, as well as possibly be against the law. No, the Union wouldn't be able to participate."

"Nobody wants to violate confidentiality," I told him one more time. "Hell, you folks can affix the labels, for all I care, and, believe me Kenny, it's not against the law to send out voter registration forms. And if it is, let's throw a voter registration workshop and get your members to personally register the recipient they work for."

"Oh, so now, we're going to organize your people? I like that," he said with contempt.

"Jeez, Kenny. Don't ya get it, man?" I said with a mix of anger and pity. "I said register them to vote; that's all, dude. They can organize themselves once they get registered and start voting, once they take their power seriously. I just wish you guys would take their power seriously, 'cause most of them are on your side."

"Oh, we take that seriously. That's why we're not getting involved."

Kenny was up to his old tricks. "Figures," was all I said. I knew he had talked the idea down, rather than up. He had no greater vision than to see such an effort helping just UP -- instead of all of us -- and I knew he had squelched it.

He knew I knew. "Look, I have to protect the privacy of those people," he said in squeaky anger.

"Those people? Those people?" I went off. "What the hell are you talking about, those people? Those people are your people, or have you forgotten that?"

"Fuck you," he said defensively.

"Well, fuck you very much too, Mr. Ball!" I said sarcastically. "Face it, Kenny, you're not protecting anyone's privacy since what we are proposing isn't an invasion of anyone's privacy. What we're proposing is setting it up so those people can protect and promote their rights themselves. The Union should do more than pay lip service to that. So, whether you do it with us, or coordinate it through the Department of Social Services, the Union should make sure that every citizen recipient and worker is registered to vote."

"Voter registration, voter registration, that's all I ever hear from you. You've got a one-track mind, man. I can't turn over the list," he said, pissed.

"One track mind," I said, giving it the one-second of thought I never had before. "One track mind, huh? I guess you'd see it like that," I offered the myopic bastard. "I tend to see it as, ohhh, I don't know...how about: singular vision," I said with a laugh. "Great not collaborating with you, Ken. You've done it again -- you've managed to do nothing."

As is true of all toxic people, they do end up doing nothing and I'm sure it gave him great satisfaction.

Well, as we used to say in my old rock and roll daze, "Satisfaction breeds stagnation."

And any more time wasted on such a sadly satisfied Kenny wasn't organizing -- it was stagnation.

Having met his boss, earlier in the year at God knows what event, I tried to go over Kenny's pointed head. I gave Bob Fox a call and told him of our original intent, but Kenny had poisoned the waters...all the while being a cute crip, I was sure. "That's a no go," Fox told me, flatly.

"Is there anything we can do to reach out to the 76,000 citizens with disabilities you're dealing with in order to get them registered to vote?" I asked in final desperation.

"We could probably let you set up a table at all the attendant care meetings," he said quite seriously.

"That's not a very effective way to reach 76,000 people fast," I told him. The silent gloom was palatable.

"Hey," he brightened, "once we get a Public Authority in place, maybe you could sit on the advisory board," he said with oblivious able-bodied enthusiasm. That was supposed to placate me, a seat on an advisory board. Another able-bodied lug-head offering crumbs.

"Bob, don't insult both our intelligence," I told him flatly. "Advisory boards, by definition, are useless, because no one has to take your advice and there's no real power in that, is there, Bob?

He didn't expect that. "You've got to be reasonable, man," he moaned.

"The last time I did that, it cost me dearly," I replied curtly. "In this community, Bob, advisory boards are usually little more than a buffer between the impacted people and the real people in power. They're designed to keep 'the people' out of their public chambers. Radicals in wheelchairs have such a nasty way of marring the fine woodwork, you know what I mean, Bob? In my book, only real power counts. Advice is for Dear Abby."

The reality that was beginning to scare me was that the union hierarchy seemed little interested in working to empower disabled citizens themselves. I had the distinct impression that disabled citizens were perceived as little more then a bargaining chip to them. The necessary cog in the "attendant care industry" wheel, around which workers could organize themselves. I feared we were seen more as commodities than collaborators. First and foremost as a sure way to secure gainful employment for the able bodied. Once again, our rights and real empowerment were given lip service only.

The Union had long been fighting for a Public Authority, which was fair and good, if a number of the members that sit on the PA were, in fact, attendant care consumers with real voting power. That's where things really fell apart, when you scratched the surface of the Union's rhetoric. That's where the problems started. The Union was all for a Public Authority. Again, they needed a Public Authority to collectively bargaining with, but they wouldn't commit to the idea of having disabled citizens -- the very users of attendant care -- on the PA as voting members.

"The Board of Supervisors would never go for that," he said.

"The B of S would go for anything that 76,000 newly registered recipient/voters want, including a Public Authority run by recipients."

Suddenly he was disabled. For my suggestion fell on deaf ears.

"The Union has long supported an advisory capacity for disabled citizens," Fox answered, coldly.

"Gee thanks, that's big of you, Bob. Nice talking to you," I said with disgust. More window dressing. More "cripples as commodity" thinking.

Some TABs get offended when we're not more thankful for this "advisory role." But these are just crumbs of no real power or consequence.

The Union seemed to have a real problem with anything that concerned disabled citizens and real power...be they on Public Authorities or on mailing lists, waiting to be registered and organized. The Union didn't appear to really want a powerful block of disabled voters.

They didn't want to collaborate. Sadly they didn't understand that, on the issues, we were on their side. But no...

That's why Kenny was their guy. "Their little blond beard," I thought, as I hung up the phone in disgust. He wouldn't upset the apple cart as long as he got some apples. Screw that -- he'd settle for crumbs, I realized.

To make it all the sadder, I love unions. My grandfather participated in some of the earliest strike actions in Michigan. Roosevelt was a god in his house. I was taught to honor labor. And I knew, as screwy and manipulative as Kenny and Bob were, there were a lot of members in the Union who were good people, hard working people, who wanted to see disabled people and working class people come together as equals, as true collaborators, for the mutual benefit of all.

As Ruben told me a few weeks later in that unshaved, suntanned, and unequivocal manner of his that inspires, "They are loco, my friend. Don't let them hang heavy on your spirit." I had told him what had happened with Kenny and Bob and the missed opportunity. He sighed. "The suits," he said dismissively, "they want your power. They just don't want you powerful."

Pity Ruben wasn't in charge. I dropped any hope of doing a project with the Union.

When Peter asked, "What's up?" a few days later, I fell to a new low by telling him yet another typical Kenny Ball story, and that I had to apologize for wasting his time. He turned away from his computer screen, swung around in his chair and faced me, rather gleefully.

"Wasting my time, huh?" he repeated back. "How about arguing with me?"

"Yeah," I agreed, "arguing, too."

"And harassing me." He was rubbing it in. I didn't blame him.

"Yeah," I said somewhat sarcastically, "harassing you, too."

"And all for naught," he said.

"Yes, all for naught. Don't go all fucking poetic on me now, Pedro."

"Remember what Frederick Douglass said?" he replied. "Agitate, agitate, agitate!"

"On his deathbed, dude, he said that on his deathbed," I reminded him.

"Well, get up off of yours and find someone else to work with. Pull off your little postal power stunt with someone else. Isn't there anyone else who'd be interested in doing something similar? Do something smaller. Call up someone who's got real power and isn't paranoid."

"You mean someone who's effective," I said.

He dropped his head a bit and looked me in the eye as though he knew I was thinking about him. "Yeah, someone who is effective. Someone who hasn't got a stick up their ass."

"Well, thanks for pulling the stick out of yours, Kemosabe," I teased. "That's a damn good suggestion. We might make an organizer out of you yet." I made my way out, to the sound of his good-hearted obscenities.

I was beginning to think maybe he did understand something about power. He took me right back to my original thoughts on organizing.

Do what you can do for this day and then don't worry about it. Just keep doing the daily things, no matter how small they are, for it is the small things done daily that lead to great things that last.

When I awoke the next morning, I asked myself, "What small thing can I do today that can really make a difference? Hmm. Call someone with real power, who's not paranoid, and who doesn't have a stick up their ass."

While I dialed the number of just such a person, I reflected back upon my original question and chuckled at my knuckle-headedness. "It's the small things that make all the difference."

The real difference this time around came in the form of Dr. Dan, no small man, who ran United Cerebral Palsy in Los Angeles.

Vigorous, with a no nonsense confidence, best described the good doctor, who I had gotten to know over the years of knocking around the community. He was a clinical physiologist, just the subtle side of cocky -- the kind that tends to spark confidence in others.

In other words, he's effective.

"Of course we'd be happy to participate," he told me without hesitation. As long as we didn't use his list to sell magazines, he joked. He had a keen interest in seeing if our free postal privileges would work on such a large mailing.

Cool. I went over to pick up the list that afternoon. 11,000 names. I wrote the cover letter that evening and faxed it over to him the next morning getting it back, with his approval, by lunch. All of which, along with a couple of boxes of voter registration forms and UP return address labels, I bundled together and took down to the stuffing house.

RJ and his crew completed the packages the very next day and before I could call back to see how it was going, they had them in the mail. Mind-numbingly effective.

11,000 was a long way from 76,000, but far better than nothing. Fact was, UP and AARP lived up to their mission and gained a higher profile in the community. The Union got Kenny.

We got quite a few calls from people thanking us, including the good doctor, now a firm believer in Postal Regulation E040. Peter was so happy he didn't even bitch about the envelopes. "Too bad we couldn't have sent out 76,000. That Kenny is such a turd," he said with all the conviction of a repentant foot-dragger.

"Yeah, well, we did what we could do."

"Still, what a jerk off." He seemed more upset than me now that he had seen it all work without anybody getting a visit from the postal authorities.

11,000 voter registration forms and PAB applications went out. Those returned were address corrected, treated just like first class mail. Now Pete wasn't so nervous. With the hearty courage of the tried and true, he damned Kenny all over again.

"For what it's worth," I told him, "you can't fight with toxic people. They know that when you're arguing with them, you're not fulfilling your mission and thus they win."

He shook his head in knowing agreement. "He really is toxic, isn't he?"

"Afraid so, buddy, and the only way to deal with toxic people is not to argue with them -- it's to out-organize them," I reminded myself as well.

"You're right, bro," he said. "Come on, let's out-organize them over lunch."

Ah, sweet collaboration...

"Expense account organizing," he wisecracked. "Ain't it grand! Let's celebrate."

"Celebrate what?" I said, happy to see him happy.

"I don't know...how about saving democracy."

"I'll thank RJ for that," I thought to myself.

"Damn, Pete," I said to him, "you start believing in such high ideas and I fear next you'll be drinking; you know one leads to the other."

"Lead on," he said with a flourish of his arm and bow of his head at the open door.

I did. Who knows, perhaps he'd take both high ideas and high priced booze a little more seriously now.

One can only hope.

* 60 *

The one thing that you can safely say about them is that they are old.

Gray, grizzled, and full of their own history, they are by and large what made this country great...the fearless backbone that got us through the toughest times of the 20th century. And for most of them "back then," they were in the truest sense of the word, the demos -- the poor people.

These are the men and women who peopled the bread lines of the Great Depression, who fought in World War II and, winning it, brought forth such material wealth that they created the modern middle class. That all-purpose class that we all attest to being a part of in America, no matter how rich or poor we really are.

And for the most part they did what all victorious heroes do. They spoiled their children.

These real heroes reminded me of my uncle, who, like many of them, fought at the Battle of the Bulge as a really scared young man, who just kept moving forward.

"Nothing else to do," he told me once. "Courage is simply having no other choice."

Then there were the heroes too old to go to the war, like my grandfather who made it up out of farm boy poverty, and took a whole country with them, bringing about unions and revolutionary ideas like an eight-hour workday, an end to child labor, and the start of Social Security. These policies were brought to you by an organized Labor that ultimately saved democratic capitalism.

These truly brave people now make up the bulk of the membership of AARP. Thirty-three million strong and counting, they don't give participation a second thought, they just vote. As freedom fighters fifty years ago and true believers today, they still champion democracy and have a lot of sway with the status quo because of it. You don't have to tell them to take power. They've got that knack.

You had to marvel at their political acumen and organizational skills, as well as their powerful influence with the status quo, even if you aren't crazy about the status quo. You had to admire them. They understood power. Better, they understood their power and used it to their full advantage.

What they didn't quite understand was that we were one people, the Seniors and the Disabled.

"Get your people and come to the 'Save Social Security' event," they would say to me, sticking their gray heads in the door of my small office.

"Fifty-three percent of the disabled are fifty or older in California," I would remind them. "They're your people too."

"Good...bring them!" they would say in that cheerful way that made you wonder if they were really listening.

Still, they are the 800 pound gray gorilla of American politics. Just saying their name in collaboration with ours gave us a certain amount of cachet with every other organization we came in contact with. It wasn't long before Peter and I came up with the bright idea of bringing all the "heroes" from the senior and disabled community together. We wanted to get them all together to plot, plan, and try to understand how best to mobilize the vote of these two communities which have so much in common.

Thus, the L.A. Mobilization was born.

Peter told me, "You organize it." With that, I realized that, while we could utilize AARP's resources and credibility, I would be doing most of the heavy lifting when it came to the actual organizing -- to mobilize the mobilization.

I looked at it as paying the rent on the office space AARP had given UP.

The first thing I did was invite Madame President from the League of Women Voters to join us in sending out an invitation to dozens of groups, organizations, and citizens to come "powwow" with us.

This time there were no hang-ups about mailing list or privacy bluffs, and lo and behold, over sixty people showed up from a wide range of organizations and programs that served our overlapping communities. We sat in a big semi-circle and introduced each other in that non-profit ritual of name, place, and mission.

It was remarkable to see the different activists look at each other as though looking into a mirror. The disabled seeing the inevitability of age and the seniors perceiving, many for the first time, the near certainty of disability. Faced with the inevitability of their combined fates, as well as a growing awareness (inevitable in its own way) of the political powerhouse such an alliance represented, people from both sides were genuinely excited. Gimps and grumps really could be the most progressive political force in the 21st century.

So there we all sat facing history and seeing the face of our future -- all at the same sublime moment. Many wondered if such a grassroots meeting between the two communities was a first of it kind.

"It wouldn't surprise me," Paul spoke up. "When it comes to political organizing in the disabled community, most everything is a historic first," he only half joked.

Every gimp in the joint shook their head in agreement.

"Welcome to a first," Paul said. "About time."

Rousing agreement there.

Some of the quicker ones figured out that if we reached out to all seniors and disabled citizens involved in our various organizations and services (excluding AARP), we could directly contact over 16,000 citizens and immediately get them registered and involved. Everyone was impressed. Everyone could feel the power. It was right there in the room.

Now we put it out in the streets.

Over the months the L.A. Mobilization trained hundreds of citizens in proper voter registration technique. Many of their organizations and services providers adopted quick and efficient voter registration techniques at the time of intake of new clients.

Not too much bitching either.

The infrastructure was not only beginning to work for us, but they began to understand the power inherent in a program that serves the needs of 600 "disabled voters" as opposed to "handicapped people," and how this change in perception gave them considerably more influence with their local politicos.

The message was getting through. Seeds were taking root.

And for those who still weren't happy about having "one more form to fill out" as though a voter registration form was just "one more form," I would gently remind them that under the National Voter Registration Act of 1993, they had an affirmative duty in Federal elections to make sure that all the citizens they deal with have an ample opportunity to register to vote. I'd slip them a little piece that the League had put out on "voter registration made easy," smile and say, "We're here to help!" Might as well make the inevitable as painless as possible. They usually came around.

During this time we also developed a "GO VOTE" voter's guide for people with disabilities with the help of Mainstream Magazine, and through it we let disabled voters, regardless of their political affiliation, know what questions to ask of candidates and their campaigns on a variety of issues important to our community. Truth is, you can't get credible answers if you don't ask the right questions. GO VOTE allowed people to do that -- over 10,000 of them.

I started doing so many voter registration workshops that I developed a routine that made both the mundane and the profundity of voter registration palatable.

"Just like driving school," I reminded my audiences.

I did dozens of them, for all kinds of organizations, but the best, by far, were AARP gigs, because their local people across the state were fun, interested, and interesting. Plus, the accommodations were always great and accessible. AARP was beginning to understand what "their people" needed -- even ones under forty.

Beyond the hotel room and room service, I liked doing AARP events, because after giving a more-or-less sixty minute voter registration workshop, I could go off and meet with local disabled citizens from San Diego to Sacramento, and I could do it on AARP's dime.

You've got to leverage your resources and good fortune whenever you can. I did.

Everywhere I went, I looked for a local advocacy group to speak with, get on our mailing list, and slip fifty brochures and newsletters to. Plant those seeds.

It wasn't all me either. Paul's "Top Ten Reasons Not To Register To Vote" was a runaway smash with all kinds of people long before I got there. I accepted thanks for him from all quarters of the state. And I would bitch at him to take it out on the road with me, sometime.

"Wouldn't AARP like to pick up that tab?" he would chuckle. "Which category do you put 'attendant care' under on the expense voucher? Hmmm?"

Paul was right. To efficiently move disabled citizens around usually entailed lots of extra time, effort, humans, and money.

"By a factor of about five," the old aerospace designer in him would say. "Put that in your next proposal, me bucko. And maybe then those TAB funders, with their able-bodied mentalities, would understand that five or ten thousand dollars is nothing to an organization of disabled citizens. Hell, that's just the cost of getting us down the hall and safely ensconced on an accessible shitter."

"May I quote you in the proposal?" I asked.

"Absolutely. Thanks for listening."

"I do hope we get to take this act on the road."

"You never know," he replied with a smile. "When's the next Mobilization meeting?" he asked.

"Who knows? We don't do a lot of meetings."

"Too busy mobilizin', huh?"

"Yeah, mobilizin'."

"Good."

That crazy little mobilization, really just a letter, with three signatures and even fewer meetings, allowed us to reach out and work with disabled citizens and activists all over the state...as well as spend a little time relaxing with the local people, which, for the most part, always included a little drinking, a little smoking (of incredible home grown bud), and a little local nightlife...helped along immensely by the heat of the night in Fresno, or Redding, or San Bernardino in mid-July.

Very nice people, too.

They all had stories of how this candidate for mayor or city council won by a dozen votes here, a handful there, and these people, these "locals," knew there were more cripples, gimps, and krinks than that living in their town. "Maybe we should register them, huh?"

"Damn right, you should," I'd tell them. "Then get yourself elected mayor or city council member." More than a few of their eyebrows raised, and a few cracked smiles at the thought. First you perceive, then you believe, right?

I was elated.

We, the gimps and the grumpy -- we were working together, we were actually collaborating. Yes, we stumbled along, here and there, but that was okay, as long as we were stumbling in the right direction...spreading and expanding democracy, one registered voter at a time.

It was also cool that, after many of the workshops, some AARP member would stop me, slap me on the back, and want to have a drink. Ultimately, we'd talk history, their history, and together, over "one too many," I'd gladly let them be heroes all over again.

* 61 *

Speaking of heroes, he was so brave he scared me. Three years in the making, three years in the waiting, and now here he was, "the other organizer."

And I knew he was the other organizer as he was scaring me.

He was thinking bigger than me.

"Can we do it?" I wondered.

"Sure we can, bro," he said, all full of himself and his vision. "Hell, if we start now we can get a thousand crips together to party and vote. No problem. Think about it!"

"I am," I said nervously. He was high on the idea. A big idea.

"A thousand cripples drunk on power!" he said with that short choppy laugh that lets you know he's only half putting you on. "Voting and boasting that they've just cast the first votes of the 1996 elections -- two full weeks before the election! Think about that, man! Who in the community or the media could resist that?" he exclaimed. "I mean, how's that for a symbol of root democracy? Of the meek inheriting the earth, of cripples taking power?! We gotta do it. Let's take the power. And let's have a fuckin' party while we do it!" said the prankster extraordinaire.

"The last shall come first, huh," I said halfheartedly.

"And cum hard, ol' Buddy!" he said, glowing with subversion.

I was sure this was how he looked whenever he was getting ready to squid someone.

"Let's throw a party, dude!" Paul shouted, "a Permanent Absentee Ballot party! With candidates, speeches, voting, red, white, and blue bunting -- the whole nine yards. We can get all kinds of crips to show up," he cheered us on.

"Yeah, why not," everyone else chimed in, the sound of their voices rather sweet and celestial within the enclosed courtyard of Matthew's house, where we were meeting. I tried to see, or should I say hear, this as a good omen.

"Who knows how many we could get interested? Hundreds, yeah, maybe... Why not?" Matthew said as he flipped hamburgers on the grill.

"Hundreds! With an 's'?" I asked, worried, truly wondering if we could get a few dozen disabled voters to show up. I was busy being realistic. "That's a whole lot of cripples, dude."

"Thousands," Paul shot back, "we're going to get thousands!"

"Thousands?!" I was aghast. "You're crazy, dude? We were lucky we got seventy people at the Shelia K. debate, and we had three months to pull that off. You want thousands to show up and you've got less then six weeks to organize it."

"I'll settle for a thousand and one," he said with a cocky smile. "You're going to show up aren't you?" he wisecracked. "Only need a thousand more if you do."

Everyone laughed. The guy's a real comedian.

"Think about it," I pleaded. I was quite nervous at the prospect of handling all the problems associated with getting a thousand disabled citizens together in one room or hall to do anything, much less vote.

I did the list. "First, you've got to find a joint big enough and accessible enough to accommodate a thousand and one disabled people and their families, friends, attendants, and service animals. Then there's the transportation nightmare. Remember, folks, our strategy has been to go to the people. Now we're asking them to come to us. I don't know. That's a big one," I worried aloud. "Then there's all the normal hassles of just pulling off an event this size in less than six weeks."

In those famous words of the truly brave, Paul said, "Yeah, so?"

"Yeah, so..."

He devilishly teased, "You're the one who told me to love the long shots, remember, Kemosabe?"

I was dumbfounded and it showed, 'cause Paul winked at me, and said, "Come on, dude, it will be a ball. You said you've spoken to hundreds of groups. Well, go back to them now that you've got something to invite them to."

"Thanks, Tonto."

"Don't worry," he went on. "Our community loves a party, right? Isn't that what the TABs all say? So let's throw one. A giant Permanent Absentee Ballot party! Hell, we can find a place big enough. Invite some candidates, and other comedians, let the people vote, and serve a little food. Throw in a press that's looking for a good human-interest angle right before the election and before you know it, bro, we've pulled off another 'first.' And all in six weeks," he smiled, pleased with himself.

"Just like that?" I skeptically asked him.

"Yeah, just like that," Matthew backed him up.

"Uh oh," I thought, "Tide's going his way."

"I can help with the transportation," Carrie offered.

"I can help with all the graphic materials and getting the word out," Matthew added.

"Me too," said Margaret, a small gnome-like woman of lovely disposition and politics, who now handled our ever-expanding mailing list.

"I can get the word out in the blind community," Jason, the poet and playwright of considerable reputation said, munching on a piece of corn.

"I'll put the word out to all the CILs in greater L.A.," Ted offered.

"We can do this, we really can." Paul was now fully engaged in his vision and he was rallying the rest of them to what I believed was a hallucination.

"Come on," he said boldly. "Don't hesitate -- isn't that what Goethe said?" he asked me.

"I hate it when you use poetry against me," I moaned.

"I know, but this is powerful, man! Real power and symbolism. How often do you get to do something like that?"

I had to agree. "Not often?" I answered weakly.

"Damn right!" he said with gusto, alive with the idea. "Think of the media this will generate. It'll help UP and get the word out about the Permanent Absentee Ballot like nothing else. It's perfect! Power and poetry all in one, bro! How can you resist it -- it's historic! For the first time ever, disabled citizens will be exercising real power as a community. As an organized political force. Jesus man, how can you not want to do it?! You watch how many voters show up, as well as the candidates. Damn, what are you worried about? Let's just go! Let's just do it, man."

He had a point. Now he was starting to win me over.

They would have questioned my authority if I had said no, and, besides, this being a truly democratic group, I didn't really have any.

"But can we really get hundreds of disabled citizens to join us?" I asked seriously, in between bites of potato salad that were getting harder and harder to swallow.

"Thousands, dude!" Paul urged. "This is the night of a thousand votes!"

"Night of a thousand votes!" I said, exasperated. "Who's going to organize this party and its thousand voters?" I asked.

"We will," they answered instantaneously and in unison.

"I'll personally run this one," Paul said, straightening up in his Amigo and cracking that troublemaker's grin of his.

This was like the squid. I knew he was serious.

"You folks serious?" I asked, looking at the rest of them as they sat there eating barbecue, potato salad, and roasted corn in the sun of Matthew's courtyard.

It was one of those moments. They all stopped eating and looked at me (with the exception of Jason, who munched on his ribs in the affirmative), and more or less said, "Yeah," as one.

Signs from the gods and democracy in action. Can't beat that. Paulie had carried the day.

I thought of bringing up the Mountain, who wasn't with us because he was in the hospital fighting a bowel obstruction, but I knew he'd probably agree with them anyway and say, "Do it." So I just sighed. They awaited a response from me.

"Well, what do you want to call it?" I asked, finally resigned to it. All eyes and ears, that naturally could, turned to Paul.

He was ahead of us. He'd been pondering it all. Being a natural showman and prankster, he had a lot of P.T. Barnum in him, in that he liked to shock and delight all at the same time. "We'll call it, what else: 'Night of a Thousand Votes.' A night of power and politics," he said with appropriate bravado. "Now that's a press release and a hell of a party theme!"

Everyone agreed. It had a ring. It had the power of poetry. Or, perhaps more fitting, pulling this off would be the poetry of power.

"But, wait a minute, people," I beseeched them, "We shouldn't put a number on this! That's too dangerous! If we quantify it, we have something to live up to. If we don't and 150 disabled voters show up, we declare victory and get the hell out of Dodge, too cool for words. Putting a number on it raises everyone's expectations and then -- ask yourself this -- what if only 100 people show up?"

"Don't be an extremist," Jason teased. "You're a better organizer than that."

"Extremist! Look, folks," I went on, trying to be practical, "getting a dozen disabled people together for a little grassroots organizing is a major event. A thousand disabled citizens getting together -- that's unbelievable. I don't know if it's ever been done before...except to institutionalize us...and I'm just not sure UP is up to it -- no pun intended. A thousand crips! Think about it."

"Hey, bro?" Paul said.

"Yeah?"

"Don't pay attention to numbers."

My worst/best dream/nightmare was coming true. A true civic rebel was being born. Not only was he thinking bolder than me, he was using my own words to remind me of it.

I did the only thing a good Buddhist does when he's scared. I turned and faced the fear.

Ruddy Irish red, frail and full of fire, Paul smiled back.

"Can we do this?" I asked, full of doubt.

"We can," he said. "We can."

Being a hostage of democracy, I accepted my marching orders. Okay, "'Night of a Thousand Votes' it is, Paulie. Let's go." Who was I to squelch enthusiasm, and besides, it had taken three years, but UP finally had another organizer who, I was convinced, would keep right on scaring me.

As if to instantaneously bear this out, he said with a wicked laugh, "And this was the first meeting of our two meeting strategy, bro!"

"Oh, Jeez," I moaned. He was taking all this grassroots stuff much too seriously. "Let's not get carried away with theory."

"Don't worry, bro," he said serenely. "One down, one to go -- we're halfway there."

* 62 *

He called me the next morning. Can I meet with him and the President of CBS Studios?

Can I? Hell yes!

The whole next day -- until the ride back, in fact -- I was thinking that Paul and the President of CBS must be friends from Paul's old stand-up days.

They talked away the first half of the meeting like they were bosom buddies.

The President complimented Paul on a recent piece he had in the L.A. Times, and asked if Leno was buying any more jokes.

"I just fax them in, regardless," Paul explained. "Then I watch the monologue to see if he uses anything. It's like playing the lottery every day."

They went on about this show and that; a good friend of Paul's had a show on the lot, as well as a killer drug habit to go with it. The two of them discussed the more sensitive dimensions of that.

Finally, all too casually, Paul began to spell out his plans for the first ever Permanent Absentee Ballot party, his "Night of a Thousand Votes." He explained how we needed vast amounts of unobstructed spaces "to pull off this 'first,' in a way that it won't be our last," he wisecracked.

I had to appreciate Paul's keen sense of the grand gesture -- and CBS Studios offered him that.

"All the world is a stage," he liked to say, "if you can get up on it."

I sat there silently and realized Paul was getting ready to storm the stage. Or should I say, the back lot? "With friends like this, no wonder he's so damn cocky," I thought to myself, "my pro boy!"

Paulie was truly remarkable. I said little 'cause once he started in on it, it took him less then five minutes to seal the deal. The President loved it. He saw the innate coolness of it.

"It's very powerful," the President said. And he meant it.

Unbeknownst to Paulie and me, the President had a son with a disability. He related. His experience with his child's disability colored his world and made him very susceptible to our grand experiment in participatory democracy. He did not think it crazy at all.

"Taking power under those circumstances doesn't sound so Machiavellian, does it?" he said with a well-read chuckle. He is right and he is effective.

"How can I help?" he asked.

One thousand disabled voters and their assorted hardware was no problem to him. He offered us one of the back lots. "Which one?" he asked, "New York City street scene, or The Old West?" Just like that. No hassle. No fuss. Happy to help.

Paul's got good friends.

Both back lots had plenty of room and were mucho accessible. With all the heavy equipment that Hollywood has to lug around, they understand the magic of ramps. To give us an "on-site inspection" the Prez himself drove us over to both. Me and the Prez in a golf cart, Paul right behind us in his hard-working Amigo, hair blowing in the wind, looking every bit the Hollywood anti-hero he really was.

Tombstone was nice, but New York was better. A lot less sand. We took it as a sign when we saw Jerry Seinfeld out on his set at CBS. No question now. In honor of Jerry and that most democratic of cities...we picked New York.

When I told Paul on the drive back that I found it strange that NBC rented a studio and shot Seinfeld at CBS, he laughed. "Maybe that's why this guy was President of CBS Studios," Paul joked. "Let's face it, if the top rated TV show on a opposition channel likes your studio facilities, what does that say about your studio?"

Indeed.

"If CBS was good enough for Jerry, it was good enough for me," I told Paul.

Paul's seriously tattooed driver was little impressed. A true black leather barbarian, he asked "Jerry who?"

"Jerry's here to make shows," Paul said enthusiastically. "We're here to make history."

And then, almost as an afterthought, he said: "And have some fun...some serious fun."

"Serious fun! What else is civics supposed to be about?" I asked him.

"Yeah, serious fun," he cracked, "like making sure a thousand cripples don't fall on each other. Talk about the domino effect."

"At least you're realistic," I assured him, and myself. "So, how long you been friends with the President of CBS?" I asked.

"Friends?" he shouted, "I never saw that guy before today." He began to laugh.

"But I thought you two were old friends."

"Naw, man. If we were, I'd be working for CBS instead of for democracy."

"How lucky for us," I said, surprised. "But, how the hell did you get that meeting?"

His simplistic answer was, in fact, the most profound principal of good grassroots organizing.

"I asked," he said with all the understated grace of the truly heroic.

With that I stopped worrying.

* 63 *

I don't mind admitting that it blew my mind, in large part, because it was so unexpected. It was such a psychic upset, so out of character for them, or at least the image I had of them as the fighters for freedom and democracy fifty years ago. They were so damn fearless back then, standing up to the Great Depression and the Nazis. Quite literally saving the world from certain tyranny.

But I realized as I sat there in growing disbelief -- coming back to my senses, really: That was "back then." This was now; and it was ugly.

As part of our collaborative educational effort, UP and AARP decided to host four Voters' Forums during the last month of the campaign. I figured, "fine." We'd keep an eye on our literature tables and pick up where we left off with the Sheila K. debate of '94.

I was happy to do it. It made good sense to everyone, us, them, and the candidates. It made for good TV, too. And, unlike last time, I wouldn't have too much to do.

AARP had a fourteen-person committee headed by Big Joe, a no-nonsense guy. Gruff, practical, and fairly shrewd, I liked him. I also liked being in the position of only having to worry about UP signs and on-site accessibility, concerns which my aging collaborators were only too happy to leave to me.

Joining them at each of the four sites, you couldn't help but have a good time with them. Jovial, definitely concerned with making sure that the events were accessible to all, and we always had a nice moderate lunch somewhere, on AARP. Who could complain? Not I.

A big part of AARP's organizing strategy involves food, and plenty of it.

AARP knows food does two things: It keeps people content and shows that things are prospering. Power has always been associated with plenty, and AARP had plenty. So I always enjoyed these lunches, along with the worldly views of my colleagues. They were, as I have said before, all good people, all concerned citizens, open-minded, bright, and outgoing.

That's why the strange state of their concern shocked me so profoundly as we sat in the big room of the State Headquarters discussing the actual mechanics of the debates.

Their overriding concern had to do with having actual citizens ask questions of the candidates at the debates.

"You don't want to what?" I shot forward in my chair, answering my own inquiry. "You don't want to have real citizens -- real voters, mind you -- ask real questions of real candidates? I don't believe it," I said amazed. "I thought that's what these Voters' Forums were all about. Hell, I thought that's what democracy was all about...voters questioning candidates."

I looked around the table at my reticent colleagues. "Folks," I said, still shocked, "you've got to let real citizens ask real questions of real candidates. You've got to!"

"Well, now, young man," old Heddy, the gray one, began, "we can't just have anybody asking questions, you know. We can't let this get out of control."

"Out of control? This is a Voters' Forum, not ice hockey," I implored them. Some of the guys on the committee laughed, and I thought I might have an ally or two. "We're dealing with adults here," I said firmly, "people who know how to behave themselves."

They all stared at me like I was an alien.

"Come on, guys, we're talking basic democracy here."

"Democracy will do just fine with the moderator asking the questions," Heddy said firmly.

"That way things run smoothly," a gracious, but misguided colleague of hers said gently.

"Wait a minute ladies," I started again, "the moderator should be like a traffic cop, making sure that everything runs smoothly, so that we may then take questions directly from the audience."

I could see the old ladies digging in, as the old guys fidgeted in their chairs. Where were my World War II buddies now?

Democracy was having a bad day.

"I don't want people making speeches, arousing partisan passions," a lady in large black plastic wrap-around sunglasses said. "You've got to have a tight rein on that kind of thing."

With that bit of wisdom, she starting to look to me more and more like an aging dictator.

Another with frightfully bright red hair said, "Excuse me, it's just a plain fact that people behave themselves better the less they have to do. Let Mr. Cooper ask the questions. He's the moderator; that's what he's there for," she said, smiling like the grandmother she probably was. "Let's stop wasting time. I say vote on it."

Seeing that these old gals were well versed in "ramming one through," I tried one last time to stem the tide by letting out a big, "Whoa! Dear ladies! Let's think this thing through before we vote, shall we?" I said, most diplomatically.

"Oh my goodness!" Heddy exclaimed...

"The fact of the matter is," I cut in, "no one from the audience is going to make a speech. The crowd won't let them. They'd get booed right out of the joint. And furthermore, what's a little partisan cheering here and there? You're going to have that in response to the candidates' answers anyway, not the citizens' questions."

"Can we vote on this matter?" the dictator said, agitated.

I looked at some of the guys at the table, still uncomfortable in their chairs. Nothing. "How did these guys ever stand up to the Nazis?" I wondered. "They won't even stand up to these old biddies?"

"Wait!" I pleaded. "You want to know the biggest reason we should allow citizens to ask questions of the candidates?" Without waiting for a reply, I told them, "It makes for good TV!"

They just looked at me...waiting for me to wrap it up. "It's always more compelling to have a senior citizen ask a question about Social Security, or a disabled person about Section 8 housing. TV news loves that stuff."

One of the old gals actually snorted.

"Look, folks," I said, in a last ditch attempt, "the media has got all the pictures of Bill Cooper asking questions that they want. Let's show them what we look like. Let's let 'em hear what we think."

After I said that, I realized that's probably what scared them.

"Be that as it may," Frightening Red, in a frightening bit of backward logic, cut in, "if the news does show up, they're going to be paying attention to the candidates, not the audience, so let's move on. Let's vote."

I thought about looking them dead in the eye and saying, "Wait one minute! You're the people who fought the Nazis and won! You're the freedom fighters and 'the brave' as in 'the home of the brave.' How can you fear a little audience participation? You who saved Western Civilization are now afraid to let your fellow citizens question their potential leaders? And why? Because somebody might ask an impertinent questions or accidentally drool while asking it? That's what scares you?"

I wanted to ask, "What happened?"

I thought about it, but they were already looking less than heroic, and to fill them with shame would do no good. Hadn't I myself been less than heroic just a few months back? "I thought we wanted to increase citizen participation," was all I said.

It was a bad day for heroes all the way around.

"How about this?" Big Joe said. "We take questions from the audience and give them to the moderator to ask the candidates."

"Now there's a real AARP deal," I said, trying to hide my disappointment. They all laughed.

"I'm just afraid," I said over the chuckles, "that if you don't let citizens ask questions, you lose the power, the theater of the moment...the magic that is so compelling when voters and candidates come face to face. That's what draws one's attention, as well as the media's, that's what's real!" Go down swinging, I figured.

"We believe you, dear boy, but this isn't about the power of theater or good TV, this is about keeping things under control," Heddy said flatly.

"Under control, huh?" I said, irritated. "What does that say about democracy?"

Silence. No philosophers here.

"Speaking of democracy," one of them said, "Let's vote!"

"Hear! Hear!" the other women agreed and the men went along, just to get along.

"I'll second that," the shaded one said firmly.

"All those in favor of citizens asking questions at the debates, raise your hand now," Big Joe said gruffly.

My hand went up, alone

"All those opposed?" All fourteen of their hands went up. I didn't carry one of them.

I sat there on the long side of the table, looking at their fourteen hands up in the air, they looking at my one.

"The moderator will be asking the questions," Big Joe intoned. The vote had been taken.

I saw Peter later and told him about the experience.

"They love security more than they love freedom, man," he told me. "They watch too much local news. It makes them believe that the end of civilization is at the end of their block. Keeps them scared. Makes them believe the worst in people."

"Yeah, but what's that got to do with citizens participating in a Voters' Forum?"

"Where do you think they think the worst will come out?" he said, as he cleared his desk.

"At a civics debate?" I said, exasperated once again. My former heroes were dying hard.

"They don't like to take chances. Remember, security over freedom."

"Well," I said wistfully, "I guess there's something to be said for not believing in heroes."

"At least not when they get old," he replied. "Not when they get old."

That night, as I lay in bed, I said a much too rare prayer. In it, I promised the Great Spirit that I would choose freedom over security until the day I die. Ben Franklin had said, "Those who desire security over freedom, deserve neither."

"Remember that 'til the day you die," I told myself, "hopefully as an old, free man who's still not afraid to fight for it. A very old free man, thank you very much, Great Spirit," I added, just to be on the safe side.

Security over freedom of another form, I guess you could say.

* 64 *

Thank god, I had Paul, and he wasn't old. But then, he never would be, so maybe he could afford to be more daring than most. Maybe never getting old made a difference, maybe not. Maybe it was just him, an ageless prankster no matter what. I just don't know. I don't know if he knew.

What he did know, what he found out "much too late," he told me, was that he was "good at it." He was a good organizer. What's more, he enjoyed it. Now, in the nick of time, he found that out. He was living proof that anyone could organize.

I teased him and called him the "undiscovered truth." If he could do it, then, most assuredly, the common citizen, yes, the common disabled citizen, could be a great organizer, too.

"No experience necessary," he joked. "No special talent needed. Even a comedian can do it." Of course, this was a clown, a buffoon of the most dangerous sort, one involved in some very serious fun.

"Hey, watch it," he would yell back, " I resemble that remark."

He did.

Did he have a knack for it? Sure he did. That was his undiscovered truth -- now all too well known. And that moved him. Like anything new that one is good at from the first, it spurs you on. This happened to him. He found out, with time running out, that he was a really good organizer.

And with less than six weeks to pull it all together, he really did find this out in the nick of time...which is usually the case when you are called upon to do great things. And the pulling together of a thousand citizen crips to exercise their legitimate democratic prerogative by casting the first votes of the 1996 election was, indeed, a very great thing.

"A very great party! Right up there with Boston's tea party," I told him.

"Yeah, but this time we're not going to blame the insurrection on the Indians," he shot back.

After I stopped being afraid of it, or maybe because I was kind of scared of it in the first place, I had to admit that the whole thing appealed to me. The old Yippie in me loved it; it was such a media stunt, such a grand bit of theater.

One night while Paul and I were sucking beers through straws, we agreed that Abbie Hoffman would have loved it.

Paul knew instinctively that everybody else would too. "Who wouldn't want to be one of the first thousand disabled citizens to make real history?" he asked.

"I wanna believe, brother," I told him with a healthy chug of brew.

"You watch," he said with a belch of his own, "ten years from now, there'll be 10,000 gimps walking and rolling around, claiming they were there."

"We can only hope," I replied.

"Yeah, but the really sad truth is," he said, with that throaty laugh he had whenever he was about to shock someone, "most of those 10,000 bastards won't even be registered to vote."

I popped a straw in my beer and sucked hard, laughing at the dark absurdity of it all. I feared he might be right. I laughed so hard the beer shot up and out my nose.

With unrestrained, joyous difficulty Paul hoisted his beer up. "A proper toast up your nose, my brother. Now there's an omen, if ever I saw one!" He roared, "Cheers!"

* 65 *

Bozo may have been his patron saint, but this bozo was no clown. He became instead what we had only dreamed of up to that point -- the "Hub," the almighty Hub. As such, he put his phone and fax number on everything that went out concerning our novel little Get Out The Vote effort. It was rather refreshing to be just another foot solider, just another spoke in the wheel.

Understanding just how precious time really was, Paul wasted none of it, and he didn't let any of us, either. There were the daily calls. Had I "hit up" this funder or that? Had I called this person or that, dropped off this disc or picked up that artwork? Did I line up a postal inspector? Had I talked to the Registrar of Voters? Or tracked down some other "absolutely necessary" ingredient for our civic masterpiece?

Talking with Matthew, Carrie, and Margaret, among others, I found he had everyone in a similar whirl of daily assignments.

We were rolling. Thanks to the practical prankster in the Amigo power chair.

I learned to do my tasks quickly, too. Or else ol' Paulie would immediately crack the whip even if he were funny and profound while cracking away.

"If we're going to have a chance at saving democracy on October 19th," he'd say, stern and mocking all at the same time, "we need to get those invitations to the candidates addressed and out by tomorrow. Dude! Can you pick them up and get them over to..."

"Yes, yes, yes," was always the answer. I didn't hesitate. How could I? There was no hesitation in this guy. He was in full flight. I didn't dare pull back. I didn't want to doubt his magic or look bad in his eyes. After all, he really was pulling off a small miracle with no time to spare.

Along with the daily jokes, good-hearted teasing, and cajoling, there were the daily progress reports. And as an army runs on its stomach, the forthcoming food was always a daily highlight.

Pioneer Boulangerie, Wild Oats, Vons Market, Louise's Trattoria, Co-Opportunity, Denny's, and Carl's were all dedicating food. We had food from across the political spectrum...with Co-Opportunity and Carl's representing the far ends of the political spectrum.

"You might say," Paul, said, "that our food has a very non-partisan flavor."

As this list grew daily, I had to remind him, "We're only feeding the first one thousand, man."

Not only were we ruthlessly non-partisan, but we also had the support of both labor and business. Pacific Bell's Disabled Services division donated a couple thousand dollars. Xerox offered to offset our offset printing costs. The Southern California District Council of Carpenters agreed with me (due in large part to the double bourbons for lunch, and my brother's good standing in the union), that carpenters have a lot in common with disabled citizens. "Fall off one roof and, boom, you're in our club." I stole Paul's joke and picked up another thousand bucks.

Talk of near miracles, Paul's friends in Ventura even found tons of red, white and blue decorations and bunting -- no easy feat in October, as what little is left over from the Fourth of July gets used up by local baseball playoffs.

It was a big whirl with Paul the serene center. He was actually invigorated by it all. He told me he dug civics, said it gave him "a damn good reason to get out of bed." I told him that was the Irishman in him.

He laughed and smiled that "Erin go bragh" smile and said again that he wished he had started organizing earlier.

"You are experiencing the early enthusiasm of actually pulling off a great idea," I told him, "of seeing a great idea come to life. And what's most mind-boggling is that you're doing it, you're bringing it to life. Once you get past that shock, it's invigorating."

"Almost better than comedy," he muttered.

"It's true pathos, baby," I laughed. I told him I had felt the same way when I was out there in the early days of UP. "Don't worry, bro, I think it's a pretty healthy reaction. I think whenever you discover just how really powerful a great idea is, and then start to organize around it, and then see how that affects people, and then see how they look upon you and more importantly themselves afterwards -- you always think, 'I should have started organizing this earlier.'"

He agreed with me that that feeling was probably a pretty good indication that you're on to something. "Action leads to 'And then...'" he joked.

And then he left, almost late for a doctor's appointment. As in organizing, he should have started earlier.

I couldn't help but think about this after he left. In my dear friend's case, it was understandable that he had wished that he had started doing a lot of things earlier, for he had deadlines beyond the date of the event. And now, very late in his still young life, he was finding yet another path...a most ironic path to power -- organizing the poor.

"Given ten more years, how many disabled citizens could this guy organize?" I asked myself. "How much power could he help them take?"

Here he was, long and lanky, with less and less control daily, becoming at the same time more and more powerful in his ability to pull off this monster brag/event of power politics and pure fun, serious fun, literally history-making fun.

So profound and profane, this strange dichotomy of his getting hundreds, if not thousands, of people enthused and involved in being powerful, while conversely every day he lost more and more of the power of his own being, his own body.

I had to stop thinking that it was painful to watch him type at his keyboard...slow, small strokes with fingers that struggled to reach each letter -- I had to remind myself that he was extremely happy.

He was alive. He was an organizer.

Most people that he dealt with never met him. Yet the nobleness of this attempt, this Night of a Thousand Votes, along with his ever-present humor made them want to pitch in and share his vision. They wanted to make it happen.

"I never realized how badly people want to do the right thing," he said one day, as we sucked down beers at his house.

That's the spooky thing about democracy," I said facetiously. "It brings out the best in people."

"And the worst. Ask Jim Crow," he countered.

"Good point, but still, I think most Americans like the idea of the powerless becoming powerful. It gives them hope. That's why we all love to root for the underdog. It gives us hope."

"Who knows that better than you or I?" Paul cracked.

"Exactly," I agreed with a smirk. "All those people you're phoning and faxing are rooting for you. They're rooting for UP. People are turned on because you're turned on. You're powerful, man. You're pulling off the impossible, doing what's long overdue or has never been done. Americans innately love that. You're the purveyor of a great idea whose time has come. Get used to it -- enjoy it!"

"No shit, Shakespeare. I'm just getting used to the fact that people really are impressed with what we're doing, and I don't even have to tell a joke," he said seriously. "By the way, I've got a great idea whose time has come -- the event programs are ready at the printers. You want to pick them up?"

"Gotta have your program," I shouted like a huckster at the ball game. "Back to the small things. Okay, I'll pick them up tomorrow before I hit the road."

And so it was that the most powerless among us was leading us in a most powerful direction. The man who had to be helped getting his hands to his keyboard had his hand firmly on our immediate future. He, who had the least amount of time, was taking the time to organize us.

He was living proof that it could be done. Best of all, he found a way to do it that fit him, his personality, his style. This crippled clown prince, who, up to that point, saw politics and politicians as something to be made fun of was now pulling off a most profound joke on the political establishment.

"Don't worry, dude," he would tell me with that cocksure grin of his. "No matter how many of us show up, we all look alike to most of the TABs. I figure if we keep the crowd moving, they'll just keep recounting us." Then he added with a bit of twisted sparkle, "You watch, me bucko, perception will become reality and the joke will be on them, a thousand times over. The joke will be on them. It'll be sublime."

Just like the powerless taking power.

* 66 *

It wasn't always that exalted. With all the traveling and grassroots enthusiasm for our project, I was having a real problem with certain other aspects of power.

I was becoming a "role model." And after you've given a rousing speech on the need for civic responsibility and enlightened self-interest, you can't just go to the hotel bar and let loose like I did in my old rock and roll days. You know, drinking, flirting, dancing with the muses and so much more. In other words: being all too Irish.

No more. Now people were looking up to me. And not people I knew or would see again, who, if I were to get a little wild, would cut me a little slack or give me time to make amends in the near future.

"Nope. These are complete strangers," I said to myself, finishing my beer as I sat at the bar. The only counter, I realized, I never have a problem getting served at.

I ordered another beer and drank to the Greensboro 4 while reminding myself that people were feeling empowered. People were inspired. They'd buy me drinks, slap me on the back, or give me a thumbs up from across the bar. They were all so damn nice.

No bullies here, just common people wanting to be powerful. And they were looking up to me. Me! Jeez! "Behave yourself," I told myself.

This is the price you pay for being a role model.

Don't flirt.

That will be hard. Whenever you are doing anything powerful and historic, well, that is sexy. A powerful message to a powerless people is a potent aphrodisiac, no matter whom you're organizing. In my sweet case, it was all the more complicated, or should I say all the more profound and sensual, by the fact that I was dealing with disabled women.

All men who love women know how diverse and unique they are. Throw disability into the mix and you have one more splendid and powerful thing to gather strength from, or go crazy over, when it comes to sex and romance.

Man and woman.

I would get offers from disabled women every now and then, for what were obviously more than good wishes...not as often as in the old rock days, but enough to understand the similarities and the needs of all concerned.

Disabled women need to be loved, too. Just like everyone else.

I should understand that. And as a disabled man, I do... better than most men. Everyone loves to be loved.

That's why when Sarah, with the frisky twang in her voice and a lion's mane of wheat blond hair, sat down next to me and tossed her crutches in with mine beneath the bar, I took pleasant notice of her.

She started right in telling me how much she enjoyed my speech, and how she had been fighting with the local authorities in Redding over proper benefits for her and her small son, "for years." Further, she thoroughly agreed, "Everything will be a fight for the disabled until we start organizing our vote and taking power, all thirty-five million of us... I like that!" she exclaimed.

"Damn right!"

Her dark eyes sparkled against her soft alabaster skin. It was easy to be charming around her. She "got it;" she was pretty and she exuded the kind of grassroots moxie that I had been hoping to find up here. She could organize her community.

I bought her a drink.

We chatted. About her kid. About my kid. Then she asked straight out, like a lot of disabled women do, "Have you got a girlfriend?"

"Not at the moment, why?"

"I don't know, sometimes I go a little crazy at these conferences. Wondered if..." She let it hang there.

"Wondered if I'd like to party with a charming young tigress?" I finished.

"Wow! Yeah, something like that."

I fought my first impulse to say, "Usually, yes." Instead, I go with a sincere, "Thank you."

I want to be supportive without seeming lecherous, after all I am a fucking role model. "I take that as a high compliment," I said, "but one must be discreet."

"Must one?" she teased.

I know that one misstep, one intimate misunderstanding and my time as a civil rights activist could be seriously jeopardized, being perceived as little more than a ploy to get laid.

"Yes, one must," I teased back. "What would your roommates say?" I asked, referring to the two friends she had come to the bar with, friends who kept darting off the dance floor and up to the bar to report all the gossip and glamor they could about this or that swirling dervish of a dancing crip.

"Them? You may be right," she said as she sipped her wine.

She never finished her thought, though, for one of the girls was dragging her off to the bathroom, in that feminine ritual of peeing and preening together.

She was down-to-earth pretty, and I had no doubt she was as robust in bed as her personality was. Still, I had my dilemma. It made me think of the other disabled women I had been intimately involved with, from the most innocent to the most sensual.

Vicki, the pretty African-American girl from summer camp of so long ago, who was fashion-girl pretty, coping with a now forgotten cardiac condition. We taught each other to kiss. It was puppy love right up to the last minute on the bus ride home. She did not sit with me and when I went by her open window to say good-bye, she said sternly "Stay away from me."

"Was this my first brush with racism?" my twelve-year-old mind wondered. When I saw her family pick her up, I didn't think so. They looked like church-going people. Very proper. Upright. I don't think she was supposed to be kissing boys -- white or otherwise.

Maybe that's why she had kissed me so hard on the lips the night before.

I hope she is doing well, that her heart is as strong as my memories of that first real kiss.

Then there was another sweet girl, Jesse. She was CP brilliant and ironic, with a lot of anxiety about sex and a great pair of breasts to punctuate her angst.

The fact that she had two good looking sisters, who try as they might to fight comparison, made the magnification of her insecurities all the more complete.

I could not help her or make her orgasmic. Maybe psychology could. She became a very good psychologist and friend.

Finally there was Lucy, which was an Americanization of an even longer and more beautiful Spanish name. Her only disability when I met her that day on the bus, parking my crutches next to hers and swinging into the seat with a salutation of "Comrade," was that she had just lost her life's love, an innocent bystander in a drive-by shooting.

Her red lips against her brown skin, her ability to still laugh through this most recent pain, and the down to earth dignity she carried herself with made her undeniably sexy.

That, and she made the best damn ceviche I ever ate.

She was passionate and virtuous in that way many Spanish-speaking women are.

Polio was not really her disability either, a shaky immigration status was. I thought about offering to marry her as I ate her delicious and juicy ceviche that day down in Manhattan Beach. I mean a woman that could do this to raw fish and limes is worth considering. She told me she knew how to catch the fish too...using her crutch as a fishing pole. "Seriously!"

Such resourcefulness was not enough of a lure to make me pop the question though. We parted as friends, she to Hawaii, where the proper preparation of raw fish is greatly appreciated, and I to figure out what to do with the rest of my life on Venice Beach...besides contemplating her ceviche and what might have been.

So I have known my fair share of disabled woman, to say nothing of the "really crippled" able-bodied girls...the really sick ones, who, in spite of having beautiful faces and bodies, good educations, lots of love and money, still can't figure out what's wrong with them. You know the ones that, like John Lennon said, are "crippled inside," the tiresome neurotics and other assorted emotional cripples that, for a variety of reasons not worthy of mention here, seem to seek me out for advice, consolation, or distraction.

So it is a tricky question. Disabled women in general, have been "dissed" by able-bodied men all their lives, and they do not now need a disabled man to add to the burden. I wanted them to feel what they were -- sexy. I wanted them to feel relaxed and alive. I enjoyed being charming.

But it was an awful dilemma. I was now a role model sitting at the bar, having my one drink before I would slink upstairs and pour a stronger nightcap.

And what should I do about Sarah? Invite her up to my room?

"No one should ever use a democratic empowerment movement to meet women. This isn't a rock band," I told myself.

But what of the fact that these are rare and beautiful women, past the age of consent, who admired what I was doing and wanted to legitimately show their appreciation? Do I shun them?

Do I become one more rejection in their life? I can't please every crippled girl, after all, and I dare say many are happy for that, but what of those who do want to party for whatever reason? Do I deny them?

And what of the not-so-pretty ones, the "Not-Sarahs?" What do I do when I touch them? Am I charming and funny to them, hmm? At times, I felt more than spasticity in their grip, more than admiration in their gaze, and not for sex necessarily, but just the experience of a nice guy being nice to them. I realized that, for some of them, they never got to talk to such a guy.

Outside of family or service providers, many never got to just be around a "guy," to hear a deep voice in jest, a voice that told them how nice they looked in that dress or how charming and funny they really were.

I slugged down the rest of the drink and watched the lame and spastic dancers around me grope and feel each other's bodies on the dance floor, remembering that there is a concept in the disability community about "appropriate touching"...because so many disabled people are inappropriately touched.

Or worse -- not touched at all, which is the most inappropriate form of touching.

I reminded myself of this from time to time and tried to appropriately touch as many people as I could. Still, one must strive for balance. Like all things when it comes to sensuality, it's a sticky wicket, even for an ethical man. A very sticky wicket indeed.

I shouldn't, but I couldn't help but think of Sarah's sticky little wicket. She was so pretty.

She returned and any thought of floating off together into the night had to be put on hold, as the other roommate was getting sick in the john and Sarah had to take charge, naturally.

She gave me a card she got from some other guy at the conference and wrote her home number on the back. "I would like to get to know you," she said firmly, and went off to hold up her friend's head.

I went up to my room, ordered a couple more beers, and lay burping in bed, thinking about calling Sarah and inviting her to my room.

"No, no. Be a good role model and don't fornicate with the citizens you're trying to organize. Besides," I said to myself guzzling the last of the beers and remembering certain other propositions, "why risk sleeping with them, when so many 'on staff' are so willing?"

Power is after all, an aphrodisiac, whether you're crippled or not.

Lucky me.

* 67 *

He called me the night before, after midnight, tired, but full of good humor and wisdom.

"Ready to make American history?" I asked.

"Ready, willing, and disabled," he quipped.

"Let's hope the rest of the community feels the same way."

"Fuck it, we did all we can do. So now, let's have a party!"

"Let's do the show," I agreed, the old stage demons in both of us looking forward to finally getting on with it and actually pulling off this "Night of a Thousand Votes."

"Think a thousand gimps will show up?" I asked.

"If you did your job right, they will," he teased.

"Well, I know you did yours -- so let me say thanks up front, buddy."

"Another UP joke, huh?"

"You certainly are, thanks for pulling this off. I know good things are going to happen tomorrow."

"Ahh, whatever happens, it's a first, and it was fun."

"Go to bed, dude. See you at CBS tomorrow...after I do the last Voters' Forum with AARP.

"Don't forget to invite everyone in attendance to our gig," he said firmly, an organizer to the last.

* 68 *

So this was it. Our great day of sublime haste and sweet execution, of putting our high ideas into action and actually taking power...expressing the will of our people, as a people, in support of all people! And doing so in that most democratic of fashions: using the ballot box and then throwing a party.

And yet, here I was, lover of root democracy that I am, about to subvert the will of the people.

But then, sometimes even students of democracy and questioners of their own authority have to go to extraordinary lengths, make certain philosophical adjustments, and, admittedly, as both an ethical man and an outlaw, do the right thing...in spite of what the majority may have felt or voted.

Besides, this would not be a proper discussion of resurgent democracy if we didn't talk about a little stout-hearted subversion of the will of the majority when that majority is being decidedly un-democratic.

Arriving early at the Voters' Forum, I had intended to just have the microphones set up at both ends of the auditoriums for questions from the audience...as if that had been the plan all along. I figured it would be a fait accompli, simply because I followed that most important rule of good grassroots organizing. I arrived early.

But alas, as they say, there was a better organizer afoot, if you'll excuse the pun, someone who had arrived even earlier and was now in the very process of having the microphones set up.

Big Joe and one of the janitors were busily setting up mics on both aisles. At first I just stood at the back of the auditorium, drenched in red, white, and blue AARP and UP signs, watching the two of them work out the logistics on the large floor space directly in front of the stage.

Big Joe called out in his booming voice: "Make sure you tape down all wires please. I'm going to have a lot of people in wheelchairs down here. We don't need any accidents."

"No accidents, yes sir," the janitor said with the bearing of a military man.

"And let's make sure, can we, that we have mic stands that make it easy for people in wheelchairs to use them," he said to the janitor.

"My hero!" I shouted from my vantage point as I realized what is going on. "Thank you."

He spotted me. "You!" he said firmly. "Keep it down."

He walked up the aisle with a big toothy smile and strong handshake. He turned to gaze over the whole of the auditorium. "Looks pretty good, huh?" he said, crossing his arms.

"Looks great, Joe," I told him sincerely. "Again, thank you."

"Do you think there's enough room down there in the vicinity of the microphones for people in chairs to get in and out comfortably?" he asked.

"I think so," I told him. "Nice job."

"Yes, well, you know kid, more than a few of us knew you were right that day back in the big room, but we also knew it was useless to antagonize those dear old ladies. You know, I have to live with them year in and year out," he said looking at me squarely through his thick glasses.

"Yeah, I know, Joe."

"But I also knew, kid," he continued, "who was going to be here setting up, and it wasn't going to be them. So, as we used to say back in the army, 'The real power is in the hands of the guys who execute the plan,' and today, partner, that's you and me."

He leaned down closer to my ear and spoke in a hush, even though there was no one around. "None of those old gals ever show up to set up or take things down, if you know what I mean. They're meeting mavens. They like the free lunches

AARP affords them. But as for doing the groundwork, they don't want to get their manicures mussed -- and that goes for a lot of men as well. You know, kid," he added in that deep John Wayne-ish voice, "there are those that talk and those that do, and the ones who do get a hell of a lot more done. It's that simple."

"Yeah, it is, isn't it," I replied.

"So I wasn't worried about that vote, kid." The old soldier laughed. "Hell, I hope the average citizen asks a shitload of questions today."

"You're too cool, Joe."

"Conscientious rebellion is ageless, kid. Ageless. Remember that as you get older."

"You can bet on it, Joe," I said, meaning it.

Not only had I learned a few more eternal truths, but I realized that big Joe could be one of the last people to ever call me "kid." I figured I had better enjoy it while it lasted.

"Nice work," Joe yelled to the janitor.

"Thanks a lot, sir!" I yelled.

The janitor gave us a thumbs-up.

I also realized that Big Joe didn't argue with the ladies, as I had; he just out-organized them. A reaffirmation of another small, but powerful, truth.

"Come on up," he yelled to the janitor. "Have a cup of coffee. It's still early."

"Okay. Thanks, Joe."

We walked out to the sunlit lobby, to a large rectangular table in the middle of which sat a large coffee urn. Next to it, looking downright dainty by comparison, was a pink bakery box.

"I brought a box of donuts," Joe said. "The food's not going to be here for another forty minutes." He flipped open the box. "Help yourself."

As I ate an apple fritter, I realized how hungry I was. "Big Joe, you thought of everything," I told him.

"Yes, well, I hope so. It's the small things that will get you. Is there a bear-claw in there?"

"Yeah, the small things," I thought to myself. "Ain't that the truth," I said to him as he fished one out of the box.

"Don't worry, kid. It's too late to worry now. Now we enjoy the ride, no matter how bumpy."

"No matter how bumpy, sir," I told him, again in happy agreement.

And so, willing accomplices that we were, we enjoyed our coffee and donuts, and ended our sweet subversion with discussions of presidential politics and the music of John Coltrane, of whom both the janitor and Joe were big fans.

There is hope for our democracy.

* 69 *

Invigorated by heroes of the past and the present, I made my way over to CBS Studios. I was now anxious to participate in a far more powerful bit of ethical and necessary subversion of our lazy, modern-day, highly qualified, Athenian style democracy.

Night of a Thousand Votes! Root Democracy! Real Democracy!!!

Feeling both the adrenaline and the poetry of the moment, I shouted out "Go Paulie, go! Show 'em what they don't know how, you old Bozoist!"

With the exception of reminding all our families and friends to vote on Election Day, after tonight it was all over for UP as far as the 1996 elections would go. Time to ebb. Time to slink off and ponder. Come what may, the sense of release and long-sought rest was palatable.

"Stay focused," I told myself. "You still have one more show to do. Don't get cocky...yet."

Although the way Paul and his platoon of volunteers were transforming our virtual New York street scene into another bastion of red, white, and blue democracy only added to my confidence.

When I teased Paul that we were wrapping ourselves in the flag, he looked at me in mock surprise, grinned, and said: "We're not wrapping ourselves in the flag, we're taking it back, man."

He shot off in his Amigo to handle some other pressing detail of the moment. I decided I'd let Paul be the cocky one and pitched right in filling balloons with helium...or should I say, fighting off the helium-sucking hordes in favor of blowing up more UP balloons. Not without regret, though. I did think a videotape of everyone saluting and serenading democracy in Daffy Duck voices would be of some artistic, civic, and political significance to somebody, somewhere, someday.

I'm sure Paul would have agreed, but he was now somewhere deep in the veneer of this plywood New York sidestreet executing his master plan. The UP balloons sure looked cool floating in the breeze. Like them, I was floating. I think we all were. It was happening. This was history of some sort and we were all, in our own small way, making it...and what a place to make it -- CBS studios.

This back lot, this life-sized facade, could easily handle "a thousand wheel chairs, plus," Paul joked. "I'm figuring that most folks will show up in a chair, which means we need even more space to accommodate technology. It's either that, or we're playing bumper cars."

A stage, ramp, and sound system were moved into place at the long deep end of the lot and a large banner was strung across the stage. 'Night of a Thousand Votes' blew gently in the wind.

Lights and heaters were strategically set up to avoid burning down any flags or anyone who stopped to salute them. Tables were set up at an angle to enhance accessibility;

literature tables with accompanying lookouts were put in place. Bathrooms were double-checked.

The place hummed with the activity of dozens of people as the food began to show up. I helped lay out flag-bearing centerpieces on row after row of red, white, and blue tablecloths.

Paul had figured out everything, from sign-in guest books to a press table. Even our trash cans full of soda and water had a red, white, and blue motif.

"Now, let's hope the candidates show up," I said to Paul as he whizzed by. "We've got enough red, white, and blue bunting here to choke a patriot or a scoundrel."

"Speaking of scoundrels, wait 'til you see the entertainment," he offered.

"Some of your comedic buddies showing up, huh?

"Yeah," he said, looking a bit weary under his purple baseball cap, "I figured a few real clowns couldn't hurt."

"Really. Hey, look there," I said, nodding towards the far end of the street. The first citizens began to walk and roll in. To our delight and relief, that most important element to any democratic movement -- the people -- began to show up in larger and larger numbers. In cars and vans, on foot, wheel, and crutch they came. Carrie had used her social service muscle with great élan and soon busload after busload of PAB voters were showing up.

Paul was right. The community was responding. They were coming in technology-powered droves. They wanted to be powerful, they wanted to have fun, and they wanted to make history.

And so they did...in a showing of power unlike any other. These most powerless of citizens were proving, in one night of common sense and solidarity, that they could be, with just a minimum of effort, not only the most powerful vote, but also the most just. For the use of their democratic prerogative and influence would ultimately be to the benefit of all.

"A little ESI in action," I thought to myself, and wished Thompson was here.

Still, even without him, it was pretty damn cool. Not a bad bit of organizing. It was good to see all our friends from the workshops and trainings. "All those fifteen minute speeches have paid off," I thought as one after another gregarious voter came up and couldn't thank me enough.

It was the ultimate night of back slaps and handshakes. I began to wonder how many times in one night you could hear the word "great" to describe what we were doing, and not begin to believe it. I told most to go shake Paul's hand. "Paul's the man," I told them, again and again.

Soon, there was music in the air, and people were mingling and having fun, talking, re-acquainting, exploring the "street scene," and singing the praises of UP. More handshakes and hugs. Excited citizens all up and down the street flashed their Permanent Absentee Ballots at me: "I got mine," and, " I brought it," I heard over and over again. It was music to my ears.

"Seeds planted have taken," I told Ted and his wife as they sat together under a heater.

"Got that right," he said happily. "Eve's pregnant, too!"

"That makes me doubly happy, Theodore -- another future voter in our cause," I rejoiced. I left them embracing in the orange glow of the heaters.

Speaking of people who love heaters, many of our friends from AARP and the California Congress of Seniors showed up. And, as usual, they had a good time. They were also experiencing something they weren't used to -- disabled people having a good time.

More than one told me they "never thought of 'it' (i.e. disability) like this." Whatever "this" was, I graciously fought the urge to tell them: "Don't worry, you will." I just told them it was great to have them here, and it was.

Best of all, Big Joe showed up. "Jeez, kid, you've got more red, white, and blue than we do! Spectacular -- like I said, 'There are those that do and those that talk about it. You do it."

"Like you, I got great people, too," I told him.

"I'll say," he replied, opening an ice-cold can of Fresca. "Nice job, kid."

Thanks, Joe.

It didn't hurt that we started things off with a blind a cappella group called "Outt'a Sight" and their rather stirring rendition of "America the Beautiful." As they sang, I looked out at the still growing crowd. "America the beautiful," I said to myself, getting lost in the schmaltz of it all. "They sure are -- it sure is."

From the size of the crowd, I realized how many friends we'd made in all the years of agitating and planting seeds. Then in a flash came the greater revelation. "Look at all the people you don't know, dummy." That was the best part of it...all the people I didn't know.

I was convinced at that point that, as far as civics goes, I'd damn near achieved nirvana...complete release from fear, ego, or desire. And it worked! In perfect harmony with everything but their balance, the people had showed up. The community had turned out in force. In spite of all the health and transportation hassles, the mountain had come to Mohammed, who just happened to be called Paul that warm October night. Thanks to him, and his unrelenting leadership, the beautifully broken had made the scene.

The cripple, the lame, and the blind, the slower thinkers, and all-too-creative doers who understand, if not politics, how to party. They also seemed to realize that, regardless of their physical infirmity or party affiliation, tonight, as a community and a people, we were one -- a slightly fractured "E pluribus unum" I'll admit, but from this diverse many, a most unique one. A "one" that could of its own volition and good will quite literally save democracy.

"What a way to start," I finally told myself, as candidates began to show up and sign in. More than a few having to stop and think about what to shake as they tried to "work the crowd." I laughed. Again and again that night, I would see the mundane smack dab up against the profound. You've got to love this community.

Talk about pathos. I mean, what words do you use to explain the movement in one's head and heart when a dozen "vent quads" -- guys who use ventilators to breathe, and who never go anywhere on a whim -- show up to exercise their democratic prerogative.

The only word I can think of is: Powerful.

It was. We were.

And all because of a guy who had trouble getting out of his bed that morning.

Paul didn't feel great and told me it was because he had trouble sleeping the night before. "The excitement, ya know." I hoped it all hadn't been too much on him. Wrapped up in his royal blue jacket and purple baseball cap, he did seem in a frailer than usual condition.

When Paul told me to emcee the event, I started to protest.

"I got enough to do down here," he cut me off. "We still gotta feed this horde, man."

I was glad he threw that in -- to save my psyche -- because this guy loved the stage, the limelight, and the chance to be funny. When he doesn't want to storm the stage, I worry about him being more than tired. Enough said.

"Okay," was all I said. So I opened the show. Walking on stage to a hero's welcome that I didn't really deserve, I nonetheless called forth: "Are you ready to make history?"

An affirmative roar rose from the crowd. "'Cause that's what you're doing tonight -- making history! Dig this! For the first time ever in American history, disabled citizens are getting together as an organized political force and delivering their vote as one community and one people! A people committed to social justice and plenty for all. Give yourselves a big hand!"

They did. Some used two, some one, others just hooted and whistled, happy to get on with it.

"How does it feel to take power?" I asked enthusiastically. They roared back in the positive.

"I thought so," I said quietly. Once they started laughing, I went into standard emcee mode, walking everyone through the night's procedure and just playing the moment, thanking everyone for coming, pointing out this and that person who had in some way been crucial to the success of the evening, introducing local dignitaries, making a big deal about the postal inspector, Mr. Crockett, who, looking resplendent in his best postal blues, was there to officially pick up the ballots.

Once inside his standard issue leather bag, our ballots would be considered officially mailed. "So don't miss this guy," I told the crowd. "He's the one you have to give your ballot to in order for your vote to be officially mailed. He is our personal mailman tonight. Take a bow, Mr. Crockett!"

Mr. Crockett waved to the crowd.

"I repeat, give Mr. Crockett, the postal inspector, your ballots in order for your vote to be properly mailed. Can I have another hand for Mr. Crockett and the US Postal system, folks! They're here tonight to make democracy work!"

The crowd couldn't have agreed more. There's nothing like a uniform to add a little legitimacy to the proceedings.

I got Peter up for a speech, as well. He'd gotten AARP to put up a thousand bucks for our thousand votes, as well as last minute use of a thousand little things like flags, print jobs, ink pens, etc. So the old tart had righteously earned his three minutes before the none too rich and all too powerful.

I even made Paul take the stage for a few moments, overriding his protests by simply pointing out that the people wanted to thank him. I was right; he got the longest, loudest, applause of the night -- over a full minute, no urging necessary.

Without getting too maudlin, I realized that Paul was a hero -- a real hero. He made us be more and do more than we ever thought we could. He laughed in the face of our fears and made us want to go along with his most profound joke. He brought our high idea to life.

I watched him take in the crowd's thanks and say a few words in response. I knew he was moved because he didn't tell a single joke. Not one. I leaned over and even asked him if he wanted to tell a few jokes.

He said, "No," he didn't want to "blow it with a joke." He must have been moved. "See you guys in 2000," he said, firmly, "and don't forget to vote, huh?" The place went wild.

Was it working because of the innate justice of what we were doing, or had it all been dumb luck? I wondered. Were we in harmony with the universe, or just a great cosmic joke? Was this a fluke, or just the first step in a process that would finally allow the "truly meek" to inherit the earth?

Before I could figure out what side to come down on in my philosophical quandary, Paul was rolling off stage, and it was time to start introducing candidates and letting them make their three minute pitches. We were going to give everybody five minutes, but due to the large turnout of candidates, we had to cut them back to three, with the exception of the presidential surrogates.

Paul allowed only the presidential candidates to send in surrogates, realizing that our chances to get those guys were next to nil, "even if Bob Dole is a gimp," he said.

The candidate turnout was so big that I told Paul, "We have to organize the whole state by 2000, and hold the first presidential debate on issues of interest to disabled citizens." I was a bit giddy and half-ass joking, which is never a good thing to do with a comedian, particularly a fearless one.

He lit up. "Now there's a long shot," he shouted at me over a manic candidate's amplified ass-kissing that passed for a speech.

"You bet, buddy -- a very worthy one," I shouted back

"I'll organize that with you," he grinned at me from under his baseball cap.

"It's worthy of your talents, buddy," I said happily. It was good to hear him speak of the future, so far in the future.

"Yeah, it would be, wouldn't it?" he said with some satisfaction.

"Look around, Paulie," I yelled as I took the stage. "Look around you. If we can do this in 1996, imagine 2000."

No doubt about it, debating presidential candidates in 2000 would really be cool, but right now, in 1996, we'd have to settle for surrogates, who showed up as if on cue, right after the above conversation.

Dole's campaign flew in their disability guy from DC, who thanked us profusely for pulling off such an event...actually explaining that it gave him and his position in the campaign "some validity."

Paul and I looked at each other with stunned grins when he told us, "You guys are the only ball game in town." His thanks were sincere -- "Or as sincere as a Republican gimp can be," Paul joked. "He was a gimp, wasn't he?"

"I don't know. That gray suit's sure a disability, particularly with this crowd."

"All hail those outside the cosmetic norm," Paul declared as I walked off to introduce a few more candidates.

Shortly thereafter, Clinton's campaign sent over a UCLA professor and presidential advisor on disability, a swankily dressed Hispanic gentleman with matching cane. Paul and I agreed that Clinton's campaign had it all over the Dole campaign...in terms of the disability fashion vote.

The President's disability consultant also told us that this was the biggest group of disabled citizens he'd talked to during the campaign.

"Boy, do we have our work cut out for us in 2000," Paul said almost happily.

"Yeah, but tonight we party! Look at them, pretty wild crowd, huh, bud?" I said with a sense of now serene satisfaction. It was true; the community had come out in all its colors. The community not only responded, it got dressed up. I began to see a thousand disabled voters easy.

"Pretty wild crowd," Paul agreed. "Outside any norm."

We had tried to get a representative from the Perot campaign, but they never returned our phone calls, and since no one felt like speaking for them, or knew much about what they stood for, well...so much for that so-called people's campaign.

Luckily, there were a couple of "old lefties" in the audience who offered to speak for Nader, and we were most happy to oblige them.

We figured the more the merrier, but you did have to respond in advance. For those candidates who did, it was great fun watching them all swearing allegiance to the ADA, talking about their experience with someone they know who has a disability, or pleading ignorance, and looking to us for guidance. That kind of honest pandering got the best response.

The alternative candidates also added a lot of color and humor to the proceeding. An old actress friend of mine was running on the Natural Law ticket for the State Assembly. She got up and talked a little politics, but spouted more poetry and, as a result, was a big hit. She got quite a few votes, from what I heard...more proof that poetry, if properly used, really can help you take power.

Besides the poetry of power, we purposely invited all the third-party candidates in order to send a message to the Democratic and Republican parties that they can no longer take our vote for granted. Fact is, an organized disabled electorate could give any candidate, third party or otherwise, a real shot at doing what I seemed to talk about most -- taking power. UP as an organization was hell bent on letting both voters with disabilities as well as the political establishment know exactly that.

We do have other options -- and the power of our vote gives those options credibility.

As you can imagine, this upset some of the partisan hacks in the audience, for there were many of those, who came mostly just to see what was up, as the "obvious joke" went all night long.

One, in a more inspired state, yelled at me behind the stage: "To offer our community anything but major party candidates was a devious mistake that the major parties won't forget," she scoffed.

What she didn't seem to grasp was that I hoped they would remember. "Just be happy that the Natural Law party didn't send a candidate for president," I told the crass hack, "'cause we'd all be doing transcendental meditation right about now. Ommm!"

I was too busy to argue further with her, for at that moment the Los Angeles County Registrar of Voters, herself, made a guest star appearance along with a very nice speech saluting our efforts. All very cool, as well as very unexpected.

And still more local candidates were showing up from all over the county to bask in our fresh limelight. We knew that some of the local races were so tight that it was conceivable that a few candidates might just squeak through on the votes they got this night...particularly those sharper ones who pleaded ignorance and asked for our guidance. It was quite possible.

"Who cares who yells at you," I told myself. "Being the balance of power, or just the perception of being that, in any number of local races, was, in fact, real power."

Needless to say, I was happy to get on with the voting. That was the real symbolic moment. And they got it on tape. Paul had done right by that, too. Every damn TV station sent over a crew to catch our historic moment.

Who says symbolism doesn't count? It does when you get it on the eleven o'clock news. TV and radio news crews were everywhere.

I made sure that Paul and the voters did the interviews. I was just a traffic cop getting one to the other. This was not false modesty. This was just an excellent opportunity to show that UP was more than a one-man show.

I wasn't going to blow a chance to do that. There's no such thing as one-man democracy. Lots of members of UP, from Paul the master organizer to the common disabled citizens who came to vote, eat, drink and do the wild thing on the dance floor, were fighters for democracy, too, and I wanted that on the eleven o'clock news.

The TV stations obliged me.

And so we were to come to the great moment. The vote.

The powerless actually exercising power. The last coming first! All that great biblical stuff that, dare I say, we were righteously putting into action. Right there, right then, and forever more, we were taking power! And best of all, a full two weeks before the election!

In accordance with state law, we asked the candidates to leave the party before the voting started. They did, having for the most part now figured out what to shake and not shake. Ahh, sweet progress!

"So, you're ready to take a little power!" I shouted out to the audience. The power was in the reply. They shouted back with democratic unanimity -- they were!

"The Boston Tea Party has got nothing on us," I shouted back. "Lets get started, 'cause there's a whole 'nother democratic revolution out there waiting to happen. Let's make it happen."

I heard the civil sound of envelopes being opened.

"Okay now, my fellow citizens, it's up to you!" I began. "The only thing I want to do is remind you that after each of you has voted, be sure that you get your ballot over to Mr. Crockett the postal inspector -- that's him in the shining blue uniform. Remember folks; your vote can't count unless you give it to him. Mr. Crockett, take another bow," I urged.

Mr. Crockett came back up on stage to re-acquaint himself with the audience. I deliberately made a big deal about him, again, because he was essentially our human mailbox. Depositing their ballots with him made it official. With that, their vote would be properly signed, sealed, and delivered, relieving us of our burden to make sure that everyone's ballot was safe, secure, and reflected their honest intentions. Mr. Crocket did all that for us. He was a big deal. "Give him a hand, folks!"

They heartily obliged again and again. They, who had never seen themselves as powerful, were now -- even without alcohol -- a little drunk on the fact that powerful people were paying attention to them. "They were 'under the influence' of having influence," Paul said after, summing it up beautifully.

"Okay, my fellow citizens, the candidates have left, the food's on hold, let the voting begin!" I yelled into the mic.

And just like that, things quieted down. Suddenly all you could hear was the ripping open of PAB envelopes and the minor hush of assistance. Now was a time of great concentration and thought. That, or they were just behaving for the cameras. Whatever it was, it was a most profound quiet.

Disabled citizens began to vote. Some on their own; some with help from their attendants and friends. Others, who had punched out their ballot earlier at home and now merely came to the party to drop it off, sought out Mr. Crockett first. Then they were followed by those who waited specifically for this public moment -- before the cameras -- to cast their ballots.

While all this history was being made, the food, with the help of those same attendants and friends, began to be served.

As mentioned before, power and plenty go hand and hand, and this was a powerful gourmet feast from beginning to end, whatever your taste. There was eggplant Parmesan, quiche, and a variety of salads from our gourmet providers, as well as burgers and fries from our drive-thru supporters. Something for everyone, all very democratic.

Everybody raved about the food, which I was happy about. Being so busy, I didn't get a change to sample it, and to this day I regret that. Still, eclectic and plentiful like our people, that night we powerfully fed the newly empowered.

With political and physical hunger abated, it was now time to be entertained and Paul's comedic buddies took over.

One of the comics from the old "Fridays" comedy show started the festivities off by doing one of the funniest impersonations of Bill Clinton I'd ever seen. "Bobbing and weaving Billy," he called him as he bobbed and weaved through his routine, "feeling your pain."

A few lesser knowns did their own bit on the state of affairs of this or that, and, of course, when in desperate need of a laugh, got a little raunchy. That always goes over big with this over-sexed and under-loved crowd.

It was hard for me to pay attention as I was always lining up the next act. But I heard the howls and applause. Everything was going along so smoothly; I admit I was feeling cocky.

We had actually pulled it off. Everyone had done his or her civic duty and voted, as well as been fed and entertained, and it happened without anyone falling on anyone else. Talk about perfection on a tightrope. But, seeing as how we consciously courted long shots, we had a male nurse on stand by just in case. Thank you Mr. Luke.

Okay, so the bathrooms were accessible and nobody had crashed into one another. That, along with the help of hundreds of good civic-minded people, had allowed us to pull off our little PAB party. Paul really had thought of everything.

This wheel, of which he was the hub, was rolling along quite nicely. The community got it. They understood that it was democracy, and their involvement in it, that would bring them power and justice.

Thinking of justice brought to mind the chain. The blue zone, the denial, the court case and the loss. I realized, standing there in all the red, white, and blue hysteria, that all that had led up to all this. Talk about turning weakness into strength, disadvantages into advantages...

"If you're tenacious enough to stick it out," I reminded myself. Then it hit me. Isn't that the key to tonight, to grassroots organizing, hell, to life itself? Hang tough, and you'll figure out a way to turn things around. Just don't be afraid and don't hesitate once things begin to turn. I looked over at Paul, who was thick in the middle of a bevy of friends and admirers.

And don't be afraid to play the long shots. Sometimes they do pay off.

What a payoff! Proof positive that it could be done, citizens with disabilities could organize themselves -- themselves! We really could be the most potent force for social justice and civic responsibility in America. No doubt now! This time the thought literally sent a shiver down my backbone as I stood there in the off-stage shadows.

Our friend Wendy Sue, a comedic folk singer, was wailing away melodically on stage.

I closed my eyes and took a deep breath. With it, I realized, "We could create 'the promised land' right here, right now, and on into the 21st century. 35 million disabled citizens/voters could actually 'begin the world over again.' And all for the price of a postage stamp. Wow!"

The beautiful and ironic assumption of such power brought a smile to my face. It could be done. Night of a Thousand Votes was just a harbinger of things to come. Another shiver, not of fright, but of enlightenment, verging on anticipation shot up my spine. Sweet chuckle of satori.

With the klieg lights of the stage burning and the music and the crowd wailing away in a slightly fractured unison, almost Om-like, my senses and mind became one and clear.

Feeling the full measure of my breath, I saw what was possible, what was in store, if we, as a humane people, lived up to our full potential. I exhaled easily. We surely would respond to Thomas Paine's call "to make the world over again." I knew that when I opened my eyes I would see the future.

It was dancing and whirling around on canes, crutches, and wheels, in front of me -- full of life, laughter, and power. No doubt, the common sense, compassion, and tolerance imbued into this crowd was exactly what America needed more of.

"Nice job, Paulie," I thought to myself. "Nice bit of history making, dude."

I had to tell him that later. As right now his glowing admirers surrounded him. Cool. Let him bask. "Wait 'til 2000," I said to myself, as I stepped out of the shadows. "Old Paul and I will be unstoppable."

I was cocky. I didn't realize it just then, but I was. And of course the second I was -- the gods punished me.

"We've got a problem here, sir," I heard, off to my side, as I came out of my civic swoon.

Mr. Crockett came up next to me, with a handful of ballots. There was the glint of legitimate concern in his eyes and I thought maybe somebody had gotten hurt, or worse, tried to mutilate or otherwise screw with someone else's ballot.

Would I have to make a citizen's arrest? It's a crazy thought, I know, but it's the one I had. So much for nirvana.

"What's up, sir?" I asked.

He opened his bag so that the light from the stage illuminated the now cast ballots within...the real votes of disabled citizens, the ultimate fruits of our long labors...the manifestation of our efforts and our power all wrapped up in one postman's leather bag. These mail-in absentee ballots represented the first hint of our power properly exercised...of our power yet to come. They were as close as I ever hoped to get to something sacred, other than a child.

The ballots themselves were kind of beautiful under the stage lights as they emanated a soft celestial blue from his bag...stage lights that also made Mr. Crockett's postal uniform stand out in a similarly striking fashion. It all looked perfect, except for his eyes.

"The problem is," he said gently, "I can't accept these ballots."

"Can't what?" I gasped.

"Not without stamps."

"Not without stamps?"

"These ballots," he said, holding an un-stamped handful up, "I can't accept these ballots without stamps."

Stamps! It hit me like a ton of lost votes. None of these ballots could be mailed without a stamp! Without stamps, my kind and immaculate blue postal inspector couldn't accept our mail-in ballots. Without a postage stamp, my much-ballyhooed mail-in ballots could not be mailed in.

"Oh my god, postage stamps!" I gasped, my eyes now widening with the same fear as his. I looked in the bag. There were hundreds of ballots, with many in desperate need of a stamp. "My kingdom for a horse!" came galloping home to me as did, "For want of a nail."

I was about to blow our historic moment for the lack of a god-damned postage stamp. The afterglow and wisdom of near nirvana was now completely trashed.

In one of those grotesque seconds that flash through your mind -- when you must imagine doing the unimaginable -- I was horrified, horrified at the thought of having to go back out on stage and announce to everyone that they had to take their ballots home, affix a stamp and mail it themselves. No mass mail-in. No coordinated action. No shit! OH, SHIT!!!

Talk about destroying the very meaning of the event. The whole point of the damn thing was that we were voting -- and mailing in those votes -- as one community, but idiot boy that I am, I forgot the stamps. I thought we were finally wakening the sleeping giant of American politics and instead, by forgetting the postage, we were just nudging it in its sleep...just enough to irritate and depress it.

This was far worse than losing the court case.

When I lost the case, disabled citizens expected nothing new from the TAB world, and so were not too hurt or even surprised. Here I, one of their own, one of their "leaders," would have to break their newly empowered hearts. No TABs or system to blame, this was my own stupidity that blew it -- and I wasn't even drinking (though I knew I would be sucking something stronger than beer through a straw for at least a month after such a tragedy).

This was far worse than a loss of nirvana; this was complete hell. I broke every rule. I was afraid. My ego, my pride in myself as an organizer, came crashing down around me. My every desire for a second bloodless American revolution through the use of the ballot box was defeated by the simplest of oversights.

I lost faith. I wanted to run and hide, but I could not.

What would Buddha do?

I turned and faced the fear.

Mr. Crockett looked back at me, and smiled. "If you don't mind, sir," he said softly, "I'd like to take care of the necessary postage."

"What?" I said like a drowning man who had just been thrown an unexpected rope.

"It'll be my contribution. I'll take care of the stamps, sir," he said with that dignified smile.

I had been saved. UP had been saved! Saved by a simple act of kindness, by a profound and decent "common citizen." Why had I doubted anything less?

"Bless you Mr. Crockett," was all I could say. I almost knelt.

I felt like the Buddha, Jesus, hell, all the gods and goddesses of all religions, plus Goethe himself, looked down on me at that wrenched moment and took pity on my doubting soul...a soul that had been so quick to forget all the hard learned lessons over the past three years, a soul that didn't deserve redemption. But, a soul they took pity on, nonetheless, and saved.

And the pity they took manifested itself in the split second conscience of Mr. Crockett, who, with his generous and timely offer saved Night of a Thousand Votes -- all by himself, making his postal blue aura all the more resplendent in his role as lifesaver.

In that supreme act of human kindness, Mr. Crockett saved us all. With no urging from anyone, he saw an unmet need, and he met it. He may not have saved the world, but he sure as hell saved UP's place in it.

I know now that, of all the kindness and honors that have been bestowed upon UP and myself, of all the omens, perceived and believed, this single act on the part of Mr. Crockett was the surest sign of UP's ultimate success...because his generosity was so necessary at that exact moment. Without that simple humane act, our grand effort in root democracy would have been pulled up by its roots. It would have fallen on its face, in front of the whole world, like a foolish cripple who forgot to replace a well worn crutch tip.

"Bless you, Mr. Crockett," I said again.

"My pleasure, sir," he said with simple dignity. "My pleasure."

With that, he walked over to the side of the stage and leaned over the lip to accept still more ballots. "I think it's great, what you're doing," he turned and yelled at me, as I watched him make his way back into the crowd.

"He thinks it great what I'm doing?" I said to myself. I realized, yet again, it was the simple things that can make you or break you.

Stamps.

Just as importantly, I also realized, that when you're suddenly "at the brink," it is the ordinary person, doing extraordinarily simple things, that most often saves you.

Mr. Crockett proved that. I looked over at Paul and realized I was the luckiest of men to be surrounded by the likes of him and Mr. Crockett -- real heroes, not tough guys or movie stars, or even anyone wanting anything out of it except to do the right thing. "How could I have ever doubted?" I asked myself again as a chilly breeze hit me in the face and brought me back to my senses.

It was almost nine thirty, and Marsha Sue now had cohorts up on stage. A few of our newly empowered having made their way up on stage, were now singing back-up to "Rolling On The River," as well as lending provocative and very unchoreographed dance moves to both the song and the moment. Marsha Sue sang and laughed along with everyone else at the vitality and joyful raunchiness being expressed by her impromptu background singers.

I let myself be happy again. A near miss is, as Churchill said, "exhilarating."

Just when I figured it could get no better, it got better. The Mountain made it. Fresh out of the hospital by a day or two, he came and voted. Amazed at the striking red, white, and blue effect we had achieved, as well as our numbers, he was most taken with the food. As a gourmet, he was extremely happy to eat something beside hospital food. Even if he had to do so sparingly.

"We did it in two meetings, too," I told him gleefully, "with the second one taking place this morning."

"Did you actually meet?" he asked, savoring a little eggplant Parmesan.

"Kinda. I just listened to Paul. He was the hub."

"You guys did a great job," he laughed. "I should go away more often."

"Paul did a great job in spite of not having you around," I informed him. "I'm just glad you're here, else we might have had to dedicate this whole damn night to you."

"Dedicate it to Paul," he said. I knew what he meant.

"I'm betting on the long shot," I told him. "We'll all be registering millions of voters and pulling off a presidential debate in 2000."

"You think big," he said, as his attendant of the moment wiped his mouth.

"Paul does too," I laughed. "Hell, he's thinking big enough for all of us."

"That's cool. Here's to 2000!" the Mountain said with gusto as his attendant readied his drink.

"Here's to bloodless, democratic revolution overnight!" I exclaimed.

Matthew walked up just then, happy to see Mountain, and between us we tried to figure out whether our little experiment with the demos was more of a political event or a cultural one. I went political. Matthew went cultural. The Mountain said it was a toss up. We finally decided that Mao was right. Just as one had to be both, our Night of a Thousand Votes was both and more -- it was plain revolutionary. Gan bei!

With both revolution and fall in the air, I made my way back to the stage to announce the last song, thanking everyone and directing them over to still more TV cameras that were just arriving.

"Please feel free to tell the press what you think about democracy," I urged them. "On the way out, folks, feel free to take a little red white and blue memento home with you. Maestro, if you please," I said happily. And with that, we pumped Iggy Pop's "Lust for Life" over the PA system.

I, too, have a bit of the cultural revolutionary in me. With the noble tom-tom drums of the old iguana pounding into the night as well as my psyche, I quickly made my way to the far end of the long narrow fake street that we had turned into a giant voting booth.

There, at the far end of the lot, was a slight sloping cement hill that, when stepped upon, gave one an excellent vantage point from which to see over the heads of all our friends and fellow organizers. Taking full advantage of it, I stood there and looked out over this unique and historic gathering, with its rainbow of disabilities, and realized that Paul was right again.

Hundreds of disabled citizens, along with all their necessary machinery, attendants, and animals looks, to the naked TAB eye, an awful lot like a thousand people, regardless of the actual number.

Paul was right about everything -- we had turned perception into reality. It looked like a thousand voters, so for all intents and purposes, it was a thousand voters. Michael Deaver would be proud.

As I walked back through the crowd one more time, saying thanks and goodnight to the departing masses, the clean up crews began to "strike the set." I found Paul sitting under one of the glowing heaters, quite by himself now, having given out the last directions to the clean up crew an hour ago.

The orange light on his satin blue baseball jacket and purple cap gave him a rather sagely air.

When I told the wise one about the heart attack I practically had over the forgotten stamps, he started laughing wildly, "Jeez, dude, now that's funny! Damn, I would have loved to have seen your face. Damn stamps! Whattaya know? It is the small things! So, what happened?"

I told him how the most noble Mr. Crockett had "saved the night, our movement and our reputations with his strategic generosity."

"What'd you expect?" he asked.

"What'd I expect?" I asked back, surprised.

"You're always saying the 'the gods are with us.' Believe it," he said rather serenely. "'Believe and don't hesitate,' right? Sounds like that's what Mr. Crockett did."

"Thanks for reminding me, Chief. Nobody does that better then you," I informed him.

"See if this heater is on high, will you, bud? I'm a little cold. Thanks!"

I reached up and gave the valve a small turn. Heat and light increased.

"You did it, Paul," I told him. "Even cleaned up after yourself, too -- you fearless bastard."

"Hey," he said with mock indignation, "I resemble that remark." The increased light and heat gave him a big smile. "We did it," he replied, as the buses pulled out from the parking lot. "Strike that, they did it. All of them -- think we got a thousand?" he asked.

"Sure looked like it," I replied. I told him what I had seen -- nay, perceived -- at the far end of the lot. "You turned perception into reality. And not in just getting a thousand disabled citizens to show up. For once, buddy, disabled citizens were perceived as powerful and influential -- and that in and of itself is really revolutionary. Watch the late news tonight and see."

He just kind of smiled. "Perfect," was all he said.

"The ancient Greeks would be proud," I told him.

He kind of smirked and said, "As long as the geeks are."

This geek was. Particularly after I saw the lead on the local evening news.

With pictures of disabled citizens voting, the voice-over tag was "The first thousand votes of 1996 have been cast."

That put it nicely. Channel surfing, we found that every local broadcast had something about our "Night of a Thousand Votes." Channel 7 had an extended interview with Paul, with him talking about "the tip of the iceberg," and all.

"One thousand down," I told myself falling off into a blissful sleep, "thirty-five million to go."

"Talk about long shots," I thought to myself. "I'll take those odds," I said, quiet as a prayer.

* 70 *

We didn't intend to save democracy. That would have been presumptuous and not in keeping with our firm belief that it takes the vast majority of citizens to save a democracy.

But we were in the afterglow of our civic masterpiece, and feeling expansive. If we hadn't saved democracy last night, we felt we had kicked off the process. There was no turning back now. California first, and then America next, right?

"Why not," said the relaxed master organizer.

"Why not, indeed," I agreed, sitting there on his small enclosed balcony. "You know me, bud. I love to think big. Next time, we'll do a thousand and one."

"No joke -- history made, must be pursued," Paul said with zeal, having gotten a little rest.

I thought that was pretty wise. "One must be tenacious," I told him.

"Like my love life, baby!" he shouted. "Like my love life."

After his tour de force, or because of it, Paul was taken home by some young pretty, and, as tired and ill as he was, he had a "nocturnal emission" in her hand.

"I think it was her hand, man. I had my eyes shut so damn tight when I came, I don't know for sure." And he laughed.

"Further proof that Providence provides," I teased him. I was happy he got laid after the gig...or close enough to it to satisfy the need. "The perks of inspired organizing," I chuckled.

"I've gotten laid for my jokes before, for making people laugh, but, dude, I've never gotten laid for inspiring someone," he marveled.

"Ain't it grand, Paulie? Ain't it grand!" I declared. I like to think it was the lingering effects of such muses that got us thinking so big.

Whatever you may say about the wild bit of fate we'd just shared, or our mutual love of long shots, we had just gotten out the first thousand votes of 1996, hadn't we? We had just made history.

"Damn cool," Paul said, and he was right.

"Better than a hand job after the show?" I asked the profound prankster.

"Much better," he laughed. "Hand jobs come and go, history's forever, bro."

Add a few beers to such circumstances, and for at least a few moments, anything seemed possible as we sat there in the warm afternoon sunshine.

"Who'd of thought democracy could be so much fun?" the grand organizer asked, chewing on a straw.

"Who'd've thunk," I heartily concurred.

"I'm glad we got it on tape. Looking at it, I realized everybody really was having a ball," he said happily.

"Yep, they were. You did it, you old Bozoist. Abbie Hoffman would have been proud."

"Who'd have thought," he said again after a moment.

"You did, brother, you did."

He half smiled. "It worked," was all he said.

I cracked open a couple of beers for us.

We watched our (taped) history on Channels 2, 4, 7, 11, and 13. It was almost a clean sweep. Paul was right again; pictures of the powerless becoming powerful were just too much for the press to pass up. Not only had perception and reality become one, but it had been broadcast all over Southern California.

It was now evident for the world to see that our brothers and sisters knew how to count, so, why not take power and truly begin the world over again?

Why not? But, since I didn't want to sound presumptuous, all I said to Paul again, was: "Who'd've thunk?"

"Maybe we can save democracy by throwing one giant party, have a night of a 100 million votes, invite everyone. Why let the gimps have all the fun?" he asked.

"Why indeed," I agreed again. "Just think what would happen if every citizen in this country voted."

"Mass chaos?" Paul quipped.

"Only for the powers that be," I answered. "If voting was mandatory, I'd bet you'd have a bloodless democratic revolution overnight. Make voting a duty instead of a right and I'd bet you'd have affordable health care, an accessible society, and an expanding middle class in very short order."

"How can you be so sure?" Paul asked, contemplating it all between sips on his straw.

"Because those things are in most people's interest," I reply.

"Ol' ESI, huh?"

"Exactly," I answered. "We've just got to get most people voting. Common sense and decency will do the rest, once everyone does their civic duty."

"That's the trick, isn't it, getting people to see voting as a civic duty?"

"There should be no trick to it. It should be the law of the land."

"To vote?" he asked slightly surprised.

"Hell, yes," I said with an emphatic chug of beer. "If this is a democracy, i.e. government with the consent of the governed, then it seems only logical that the government has a duty, itself, to require all citizens to vote by secret ballot -- in order to ascertain that consent."

"Mandatory voting -- is that what you're talking about?" he asked with a grin.

"You catch on quick, Kemosabe," I said. "Mandatory universal suffrage is the key. Anything less and the deck is essentially stacked against the common citizens."

"Meaning every citizen has to vote?" he asked, closing his eyes and looking directly into the sun, soaking it up.

"Meaning that if you're a citizen you have a duty -- not a right -- but a duty to vote. Just like the Ancient Greeks intended when they invented root democracy."

"They forced you to vote...the Greeks, that is?" he asked.

"Oh yeah, bro," I assured him. " In the first democracy, that root democracy, every citizen had to participate, had to vote. That's real democracy," I said with a quick swig.

"Our Athenian-based American democracy, with its need to register and the right to not vote, is sham democracy. It does little more than allow the oligarchy to thwart the will of the people and breed apathy and contempt. Of course, you could fix all that just by making it the law that all citizens have a duty to vote, by secret ballot, in regular elections. And, for the record, Paulie, it sure would end any attempts at voter suppression in the South once and for all. One less thing for the DOJ to worry about."

"I've never thought about it before, but I guess if all the citizens had to vote -- if we had full participation -- the people, for good or bad, would really be in charge. Wow, do you think the great semi-washed masses could handle it?"

"Yeah," I said with another quick swig. "After all, common people do have common sense, don't they? They are the ones that work the jobs, raise the children, pay the taxes, and make America run on a day-to-day basis, aren't they? If they can handle all that, I think they're smart enough to vote in their best interest. I trust them."

"But don't you have a basic right not to vote?" Paul asked quite seriously. "Shouldn't you have the freedom not to vote?"

I wasn't used to him playing it so straight.

"I used to think like that, too," I assured him. "But upon reflection, I had to ask: 'Is that really freedom in a democracy?' Or just an excuse to be lazy? Hmm?"

"Good question," he agreed. "Damn good question."

"You bet it is. Why shouldn't the government demand that all citizens take the time to vote. They demand your tax money. Shouldn't you have the freedom not to pay your taxes? They make you register your car. Shouldn't you be able to forgo such police state tactics? Hell Paulie, both you and I know there are all kinds of things that the government makes us do."

He nodded.

"Why then," I asked in a liquid rhetorical flourish, "Shouldn't the government -- allegedly 'of, by, and for the people' -- require all its citizens to vote in order to protect their own freedom, and transmit their societal wishes to their duly elected government. I maintain, ol' bud, that in a real democracy, mandatory voting is what guarantees the freedom of the people, not what denies it."

"Man, you are wound up today," he chuckled.

"The success of high ideas and strong brews," I said, "a concoction fit for the gods."

"And nobody telling you how to vote, huh?" he asked.

"Heck no, man," I reassured him.

"The American people wouldn't put up with that?"

I laughed. "No, mandatory voting doesn't have anything to do with telling people whom to vote for. All mandatory voting requires is that you've got to vote...you have to participate. Voting itself would still be done by secret ballot. You could vote for anyone you choose, or for that matter, 'None of the above.'"

"None of the above?"

"Yeah, why not. 'None of the above?'" I asked, not waiting for an answer. "I mean if a majority of the voters are dissatisfied with the caliber of the candidates and vote 'None of the above,' you could have fresh follow-up elections. That's much better than not participating just because you're disgusted with the whole lot of them. It's important to remember that apathy sucks because it allows the less than enlightened to take over. It plays right into their cynical self-serving hands."

"You have a point there," Paul agreed.

"I really have come to believe," I continued, "that if a citizen really loves America, you prove it by whether or not you take the time to vote."

"Not running around waving the flag," he added.

"Voting -- not just saluting the flag -- is the supreme act of a real patriot in a real democracy and, if you don't vote, I'm afraid no amount of flag waving is going to save you -- or your country."

"I never thought about it like that, Doctor Democracy," the master organizer teased.

"Sorry, dude, I get carried away sometimes."

"That's okay," he reassured me, "at least you're passionate about something -- something most of us have never really sat down and given much thought to. I mean, shit, democracy, really? I hadn't thought about it 'til I got involved with UP. And I had always voted...I just never thought about democracy itself -- root or otherwise. So don't apologize -- I wouldn't."

"Thanks, Paulie," I told him. "You don't make me feel so crazy about wanting to believe. Thanks a lot."

"Likewise, buddy," he said. We sat there for a moment, just listening to the neighborhood.

"You know, Rousseau? The great French philosopher asked the most intriguing question of modern western political thought ever," I said after a bit. "And we, my dear friend, have stumbled upon it, right here, right now."

"Way to go, Rousseau!" Paul chuckled and then asked with deadpan seriousness, "What's that? What's the question?"

I smiled at him and burped. "Can you compel man to be free? Think about that. That's the question. Can you compel man to be free?"

He thought for a moment. "I don't know, bro," he said finally. "Can you?"

"That's what root democracy and mandatory voting are all about. Compelling people to be free."

"You've really been thinking about this," he laughed. "I'm kind of impressed, you've done your homework."

"Yeah, well, I like talking to you about it, buddy, as there aren't a whole lot of people you can sit down with and have a rousing good discussion about democracy."

"What does that say about America, that you have to find a clown like me in order to have a thoughtful discussion about the big D with?"

"There's hope yet...?" I said facetiously. "You know, with all apologies to Tocqueville, we as a people haven't talked about democracy in over two hundred years."

"What about the elections? We talk about politics -- almost too much."

"I agree with you, buddy, we do talk about politics, elections, the culture, current events, the economy, and on and on and on, but ask yourself, when was the last time you sat down and talked with anyone about democracy? Just like we're doing here."

"Never."

"You're damn right, never. When was the last time you talked with anyone about what it means to be a citizen in a democracy?" I asked him, as he squinted at the sun.

"Never."

"Right again."

"When was the last time any of us, crips or TABs alike, talked about, or thought to ask just what are the rights and responsibilities of a citizen living in a healthy democracy?"

"I can't remember."

"Again, never!" I said with eyebrows raised. "We don't inculcate our people with any sense of civic duty or responsibility. It's all just a bunch of 'Me, Me Me-ism' and soulless materialism, with no real sense of the greater community. It's not the way it's suppose to be."

"They wonder why we're all neurotic...or worse," Paul said, breathing deeply. "We're all so damn lonely and detached from the larger community. Wasn't it Aristotle who said that 'Man is a social animal?'" he asked.

"Oooh, Aristotle," I teased him. "Now I'm impressed."

"It wasn't all rocket science and bathroom comedy in junior high," he informed me.

"Apparently not, you social animal, you." I was really enjoying my dear friend, his cold beer, and the warm balcony. "Truth is, dude," I continued, "I didn't think about it either, 'til I started researching 'the big D' for our voting project. That's when I stumbled upon the founding precepts of that first root democracy. And the more I study it, the more I am convinced that mandatory voting, by secret ballot, in regular elections, is the only real solution to our apathy."

"But could it really work, man?" he asked, "Could you get all the independent, crotchety citizens of America to do it, to vote? I mean really, could you mandate such a thing?"

"I don't see why not. Did you know that citizens of modern Greece, Australia, and a variety of other mature democracies have mandatory voting? They seem to have made the best of it."

"You're kidding. In rough and tumble independent-minded Australia, voting is mandatory?"

"Oh yeah. It's the law. You *have* to vote. And I think it's safe to say the Aussies have progressed. After all, they put a damn opera house on the beach, didn't they?"

He nodded.

"Mandatory voting is an accepted fact of Australian life, as well as most other sophisticated democracies. Citizens have to vote or pay a fine. Most people follow the law and, consequently, they get election turnouts in the high nineties."

"No shit. Those crazy Aussies," Paul said. "I always said that when Britain sent the criminals to Australia and the

Puritans to America, we got the raw end of the deal. This proves it. They got real democracy and we got the Christian Coalition."

I laughed. "That's right! We got the Christian Coalition 'cause they vote, and we don't. Remember, most of the powers that be don't really want 'root democracy' and the fully participating electorate that that entails. Why, if that happened, there's half a chance that their predatory economic power and avarice would be held in check. The way the ancient Greeks intended...and I'm afraid the corporate elite legitimately fears that."

"Root democracy, huh?"

"Yeah, root democracy, the rule of the poor over the rich, through their superior numbers."

"We're getting really dangerous now," he said. "I love that. This is bigger than just gimps."

"Oh yeah, buddy, this is about 'We the people' actually meaning all the people. You know, earlier you were wondering if the people really have the ability to govern themselves. I believe that with just one simple law, we could ensure that they do."

"One simple law, huh?" he said, with a less than sincere laugh. "If only it were that simple in America." He sucked up a little beer.

"But it really is, me bucko," I informed him. "One thing I've learned from history and grassroots organizing is that the most profound things often happen because of simple things."

"Hear, hear," he said vigorously, "PAB parties do lead to hand jobs!"

"Well, yes, you could put it that way." Trying to pull his mind back to more civil affairs, I went on, "It's the powerful who want us to believe that all our problems are bigger than we are, that they are beyond simple solutions, when, in fact, nothing is farther from the truth...as I learned again at your civic masterpiece the other night. This helpless mindset is just a way to keep the common citizen feeling overwhelmed and powerless...to the point of mass apathy."

"Do you really believe that that is their plan -- I mean, the powerful -- to keep us dazed and confused?" he asked.

"With rare exceptions, yes! That's always been the objective of the powerful. To create fear, confusion, and powerlessness, mostly by doing little things, things you hardly notice. That's how they stay in power over the long run. Guns and cops take care of the momentary crimes and insurrections, but to hold institutional power, real power, you have to take care of the small things, the things that people hardly notice until it's too late."

He was chewing on his straw. "Okay, don't go all conspiracy theory on me now, bro."

"Oh, okay, let me ask you, buddy: What do you think was the worst thing President Reagan ever did to undermine our democratic processes?"

"I don't know," Paul said with a fresh grin, and the last gurgle of his beer, "run?"

"Well, that's a close second, but that ain't it. Neither was the military build up, the attack on the social safety net, the savings and loans scandal, or the 1980 tax breaks."

"He did something worse than all that? Say it ain't so, Ma," Paul moaned.

"Oh yeah, all that was just politics, bad as it was. He had to pay off the power elite, i.e. those angry white men. But, like I said, that was just politics, the spoils going to the victor and all."

"Okay, so what was the worst thing Ronnie did, man?" Paul asked, anxious to find out what could be worse than all that.

"I love it when you're excited," I laughed. "What Ronnie did to undermine our democracy -- his greatest of all sins -- was that he got rid of the Equal Time Doctrine."

"The what?" Paul asked, surprised.

"See, like I said, it's the small things. Have you ever heard of The Equal Time Doctrine?"

"No, I thought that was a rule in the women's john or something," he wisecracked.

"Very funny, my friend, but, no, that's not quite it. Before 1980, if you had someone on a TV or radio show from one side of the political spectrum, you had to have someone of an opposing opinion on the show to at least give the appearance of balance. Remember "Point, Counterpoint" on 60 Minutes?"

"Shana, you ignorant slut," Paul said in the deep gruffly voice of the old right-winger on 60 Minutes.

"Exactly, bro," I laughed at his reasonably good impersonation. "That all came about because of the 'Equal Time Doctrine,' which Reagan got rid of very quietly by executive fiat."

"But wait a minute, how could he do that? The law's the law," Paul declared, as indignant as that old right-winger.

"The Equal Time Doctrine is, or was, a doctrine -- an agreed upon procedure -- not a law, and, as such, Reagan was able to get rid of it by Executive Order...with the mere stroke of his pen."

"And nobody bitched?"

"Nobody bitched," I said sadly. "I only know about it because I saw a blurb on it in one of the news magazines in '81. Its costly demise merited a mere sidebar. Since then I've seen nothing on it."

"No wonder all those right wing wackos have taken over the airways," Paul said, disgusted.

"Exactly," I agreed. "The marketplace of ideas -- so important to a vital democracy -- was closed with the mere stroke of a pen. Now broadcasters don't have to give equal time to talk of inequality or poverty, much less what could conceivably be done about such problems. Getting rid of the Equal Time Doctrine allowed the big media corporations to dominate the public airways, set the public agenda, and put on people and opinions that solely support the corporate party line."

"Damn, man," he said, shifting in his chair. "I can't believe the press wasn't up in arms. Journalistic integrity, First Amendment, all that."

"I know, man, makes them all look pretty shabby," I sighed. "Sadly, no one in the mainstream media said a thing. They got bought off. They just rolled over and pandered to their corporate masters. It was either that or lose their place on the guest list of the power elite's dinner parties."

"I'm afraid status is what counts in America," Paul said. "Ask Dear Abby. Equal Time Doctrine, huh? Amazing. Where'd you find out about root democracy and all?

"The Encyclopedia of Philosophy to begin with. Throw in a little Will and Ariel Durant for context."

"Oh yeah, context," he said, I guess that's what the Equal Time Doctrine is all about...context, right?"

I thought about that. "You're right," I said, after a moment. "If the Equal Time Doctrine was simply reinstated, or, better yet, became law, you'd have at least a couple of opposing view points -- some context -- with which to make your political decisions, and that couldn't hurt." I sighed. "Hell, if you gave the voters more opinions and context within which to make informed decisions, the people would be able to govern themselves quite nicely."

"Think about what it would do to the candidates," Paul said as the sun began to fade. "If all citizens had to vote, wouldn't it be incumbent upon all candidates and campaigns to educate all the people on their views and policies, instead of catering to the same small bunch of unusually angry white men?"

"Jeeze, that's a great point. You got the hang of this philosophizin', dude. You got real potential."

"Well, I'm just trying to do my civic duty," Paul said with an impish grin. "So let me see if I got this straight, Kemosabe..." he said with sudden glee.

I can't help but feel that I'm being set up for something, some transcendent joke to go along with the transcendent ideas.

"...By simply making voting a duty and re-instituting the Equal Time Doctrine, you contend that we really could have a healthy democracy and a better America, right?"

"You got it, Tonto -- it's that simple," I said feeling like a successful philosopher, having pulled the veil of ignorance away from my gifted friend's eyes.

"That, and lying to the polls," he said with a smirk.

"Lying to the polls? What?" I asked, not at all getting his point.

"Lie to the pollsters, man," he chortled, "you know, be less than forthright with the machinery that takes America's pulse...plus or minus three percent. Those asinine opinion takers and makers claim to tell us who's up or who's down, but usually do so in a faulty fashion. I say fuck the polls. Lie to them; undermine their credibility so nobody believes them."

"Wow! I never thought about that. Lie to the polls."

"Hell yes," he said with a passionate grin. "I mean, can you believe it? We let a few thousand yahoos, who aren't smart enough to hang up the phone, tell us who we should and should not be voting for. It's crazy! Really crazy. I say lie to them! Undermine them so badly that nobody believes in them or pays them any attention whatsoever! Then," he said, looking right at me, his eyes widening with excitement, "guess what we can all do?"

I didn't know if this was a new routine, or if he was serious, so I just said, "Don't stop now."

"Then..." he said slowly, with impish glee, "then we could all go to the polls and vote our conscience! Think about that! Wouldn't that be cool? Just voting your conscience!"

"Hell, yes!" I yelled in happy agreement with this great democratic prankster, who, with real humor, was making uncommonly good sense. "You're the one who's dangerous," I told him. "You'd do away with an industry. Political consultants and pollsters would have to get real jobs selling soap or something."

"That's right! Wouldn't that be great," he laughed. "And just think of 'we dear citizens' all gathered together around our TV sets until the wee hours of the morning -- waiting until the last vote is counted -- to see who really won, instead of finding out at 8:01 from the exit polls. I think that would be lovely and a hell of a lot more fun."

"How long have you been thinking about this?" I asked him.

"Three minutes," he said without missing a beat. "See what happens when you're an attentive listener?"

"No kidding, political genius. Lie to the polls, huh?" I marveled at its audacity. "I have to admit it would be great fun to throw that kind of good-natured monkey wrench into the machine. That could be a real movement, Paulie."

"If you have a problem with lying to the polls," he offered, "at the very least, tell the pollsters that you're voting your conscience, and therefore can't participate in their stupid poll...how's that?"

"Pretty good, dude. Pretty good. You've made the voting rights crowd proud, to say nothing of Dr. King, Mother Parks, and the Greensboro 4."

"That's heady company that I'm not too sure clowns like us belong in," he commented. "But, nonetheless, I say end the fucking popularity contest that American politics has become," he continued, only half tongue in cheek. "End the racehorse mentality that now infects our politics. Lie to the polls and vote your conscience on election day! Damn, I like that!" he said, legitimately pleased with himself.

I agreed. "You really could start a movement," I told him. "Like in the movie Network, 'I'm mad as hell and I'm not going to take it any more!' You know, 'I'm voting my conscience so leave me the hell alone!'"

I don't know if he heard me. That wicked grin told me he was contemplating more than the sunshine's shift on his patio.

"What if the politicians couldn't trust the polls?" he said conspiratorially, as it all unfolded before him. "God forbid they'd actually have to vote on principle -- if they could find one -- instead of polls. I mean, what would happen if they had to lead, instead of being led by the polls? What if they actually had to stand for something?" he asked.

And I thought I was deep! Now who was dangerous?

"Those are heavy questions, you old Bozoist," I offered.

"Know what else is cool about lying to the polls?" he asked rhetorically. "It's an action -- or should I say in-action -- that everyone can participate in...by not participating. Talk about sweet irony."

"Talk about balance," I said.

"Call it what you want," he smiled, content with himself and his three minutes of sheer political wisdom and mischief. "I think it would be a healthy thing for our democracy if the citizens decided to decide the next election by simply voting their conscience."

"Yeah," I said, "now there's a bit of revolutionary thinking."

"How do we do it?" he asked mockingly.

"I don't know man, but keep drinking and dreaming," I said. "But whatever else you do -- act decisively."

"This really could be a prescription to save our ailing and apathetic democracy," he said as I pulled another beer from the ice chest for each of us.

"Mandatory voting by secret ballot, restoration of the Equal Time Doctrine, and lying to the polls. Not a bad prescription for democracy in the 21st century," I said, sticking a fresh straw in his brew.

"We're going to save democracy, dude," he said with a now serene smile, "or at least every gimp in it."

"Bravo. Bravo!"

Maybe it was the headiness of having pulled off our Night of a Thousand Votes, maybe it was the powerful ideas rolling around in our heads, maybe it was the humane bravado of it all, but suddenly we began to really talk about how it could really be done.

Throwing off our hesitations and sucking up our beers, almost by force of habit, we began to look at -- how?

"First things first," I offered, "you'd have to get a law passed that made voting a duty, and I don't think the Congress or the state legislatures would go for that. Most of those characters would probably be out of a job if they had to really pay attention to all their constituents. Getting something like that through the Congress or a state legislature is going to be no easy trick."

"Screw the legislature," Paul said, without a trace of humor in his voice. "This is California, isn't it?"

"Yeah," so..."

"So, dude, think about it. California has an initiative process, doesn't it? Let's put the question on the ballot."

"Hmmm..."

"How appropriate," he laughed. "Put the question on the ballot and then put it to a vote. Let the people decide." Put the question of voting to a vote.

"Should it be the law of California," I said in a loud authoritative voice, "that each and every citizen of the state of California has a legal duty to vote, by secret ballot, in regularly scheduled elections?' There. How's that?" I asked in a more subdued tone.

"Very good, very good. Keep it simple," he said, with his usual enthusiasm for that which has not yet been done, or even attempted.

"Exactly. Exactly," I responded equally enthused. "That should be the length of the whole initiative. One sentence! One sentence long."

I could see the organizer in him beginning to mull over the possibilities. "You know we could do that," he said seriously. "We could organize a ballot initiative."

"Dr. Democracy, damn it, nice to know you," I teased him now. "We could put it up to a vote here in California, couldn't we?"

"Damn straight, man. You know this issue would drive those less than democratic types crazy. If they came out against it, for once they'd be seen as the hypocrites they are."

"You've got something there, Paulie. Hell, the debate alone, as to what are the responsibilities of citizens in a healthy democracy, would be great for this state, regardless of whether we win or lose on the initiative itself."

"The state?" he exclaimed. "Hell, dude, such a California initiative would spark a nationwide debate on civic duty. Talk about some serious fun."

"You'd redefine patriotism, man," I said, full of admiration for his high idea and unique plan of execution. "I love it when you think big, big guy."

"If it ain't big, why organize it?" he said with a wink.

"Exactly," I agreed with the democratic monster I had help create. We sat there for a minute in the relative quiet of his neighborhood and, listening to the trees rustle, we imagined pulling off the greatest civic debate ever. I said after a time, "What a campaign that would be. It would be great fun."

"You bet it would," he said too seriously. "I'd give it a go just because we'd have so many powerful people shitting in their pants. Imagine how they'd have to pay attention to poor people -- poor people, dude -- if those poor people had to vote. What great campaigns those would be."

"Now you're sounding really dangerous," I told him. "Powerful people shitting in their pants, all poor people voting...oh brother!"

"This is about saving democracy," he laughed, "through using democracy! I love it! I want to do it!" he said with true heart.

"I want you to, do it, Paulie," I assured him. It did my heart good to see him so revved up and thinking of the future. "You're a natural organizer, buddy."

"Let's have another beer," he said spitting out his straw. "This is something to celebrate, something to look forward to!"

Now I knew he was excited as this was his third beer. I had to go to the kitchen to retrieve them, as the ice chest was empty, a real first for Paulie and me. As I went, I couldn't help but marvel, once again, at the fact that the guy with the most precarious future was again seeing the future and leading the way.

I have to admit that, after what he had just pulled off, I didn't think that pulling off such a campaign to revitalize democracy was such a god-awful long shot. Not with Paul as our all too fearless leader. I was sure that win, lose, or draw, we'd have some very important and serious fun.

Returning, I kissed him on his sunburned forehead. "The Ancient Greeks have got nothing on you, Paulie," I told him, cracking him a brew. "I think you deserve yet another new straw, dude!"

"Long as it's not the last straw," he said. I wasn't sure what he was referring to, and because of the upbeat mood, I didn't ask.

Which I now regret. Had I known it would be our last beer together, I would have told him that I loved him and been quick to get another one.

* 71 *

And so another election came and went with 1996, and you pretty much know the results of that, so there's no need for me to comment on it here, except to say that during the ebb many of us went our separate ways. Matthew, Ted, and I went back to being dads or becoming ones. Carrie started an ADA consulting business.

Margaret, in between classes, kept updating our mailing list and Jason's play was a hit.

The Mountain, the grand ol' Mountain, moved up north. His sister lived there and, having made a pretty penny in the gold rush of the Silicon Valley, purchased a second house as an investment. She now wanted the big guy to come live in it. Who could stop him? His latest attendant had a schizophrenic episode and took off in the middle of the night, leaving the ol' Mountain with a rather "dour" morning to face. His health was slipping too.

I told him he wouldn't like the cold. He agreed, but said his next crop would be great. He was right about that.

"Look at the bright side," he told me when I went to visit him the night before his departure, "UP now has a Northern California organizer."

"To go along with our east cost organizer," I said referring to Paul, whose health went into an abrupt decline shortly after we agreed to save democracy, forcing him to fly back to Virginia to be with his family.

As smart and witty an organizer as Paul was, even he couldn't get good, conscientious help and, like the Mountain, this had a detrimental impact on his health. Just as abrupt as Paul's health change was his brother's insistence that he "come home." Finally when Paul was talking out of his head from sickness and/or the drugs to fight the sickness, they came and got him and took him home. Good brothers.

Under the circumstances, it wasn't that unusual not to hear from him for quite a few days, particularly if he was "resting and writing jokes." But there was a long pause. I worried...particularly since the next time I heard from him he was in a hospice somewhere in Virginia.

He had arrived in such desperate straits that his family was prepared for the worst.
They actually gave last rites to the golden joker.

But -- and I am sure this was done just to fuck with the doctor's head -- he woke up a few days later and started cracking jokes about needing a beer and a straw. With that, he began a rapid improvement. He told me, "All things considered," he saw no sense in sitting in a hospice when he felt so good.

Par for the course, he put a new spin on things when he rolled out of the hospice, quite literally having cheated death.

"For at least a few minutes," he liked to say, realizing what a gift any extra time was.

Was there time enough?

"I've got things to organize," he said during a call and, without missing a beat, he began to talk about 1998. "Statewide," he declared, "we'll have one big statewide Permanent Absent Ballot party. All three and a half million of us. All I need is a fax machine, a phone, and a couple of hookers and I can organize this thing from anywhere in the world."

"Don't I hope so," I thought to myself.

"I love the 21st century," he wisecracked. "You can be everywhere, when you're nowhere at all."

"You know, me bucko, what the real question of the 21st century, is?" he said, all full of never-failing bravado, always ready for his next big idea.

Already loving it, I just said, "No, bro, what?"

"Technology, brother, technology and how we use it. Do we use it to liberate humanity or enslave it."

"Good question? What's the joke?" I asked.

"No joke. Just get me a phone and fax machine and I'll show you how to use technology to liberate humanity -- hookers and all -- one vote at a time."

"You got it bro," I happily told him. "We'll fly you in a couple of weeks before the gig, put you on the ground, and you can pull it all together, in person if you want. Can you do that?" I asked, happy he was feeling his oats and still dreaming.

"Do that! I beat death to do that, man!" he laughed.

"The best ones do," I said, thinking back on my birth. "You're a survivor, Paulie."

A few weeks later, I got an e-mail from him. There had been another close call.   He was at the breakfast table, and had passed out. "Head first into my corn flakes, bro. Ever try to pick soggy corn flakes out of your nose?" he asked a few days later on the phone. "Breakfast in the twilight zone."

He sounded weak.

Over the new few days I worried that my dear friend had only gotten a short reprieve, and, almost as if upon cue, the phone rang. It was him. His voice was stronger than I ever heard it. He was robust in sound and plans and ready to send me an outline of our statewide effort for 1998. He even brought up the ballot initiative, "Think we could do both in '98 – a twofer?" he asked.

He sounded so damn good that my fears of losing my friend and long-sought fellow organizer were laid to rest.

"You ready to foster democratic revolution for the price of a postage stamp?"

"Nothing more I'd rather do, my brother."

One of my fondest hopes was to see the 21st century with ol' Paul and work with him to foster the most democratic of revolutions. "Across the whole damned United States," I told him.

"Thirty-five million voting gimps can't be held back, can they?" he laughed.

"Hell, no, bro! Not with you in the lead."

"Yeah, we'll show 'em."

"We'll have some serious fun, huh, you old Bozoist?"

"You bet. Hey," he exclaimed, "whoever thought democracy could ever be so much fun?"

"Who'd've thunk?"

I got off the phone with a yelp of joy and relief.

He was right. If thirty-five million citizens with disabilities took the time to cast their own votes, they couldn't be held back.

A few days later there was a message on my answering machine from Matthew, who had heard from a mutual friend of Paul's brother, that Paul had passed away. He had been rushed to the hospital in the early morning and, with his family all around him, holding on to him, the big lanky guy, the best, boldest and funniest organizer I ever knew, left us.

It was simply wicked, the way death worked. He sounded so great, so full of life, just a few days ago, raring to go, ready to organize the whole damn nation.

Death had suckered me. He had sounded larger than life. And now he had transcended it.

"Is that how death works?" I wondered. It makes you stronger right at the end so you can say your goodbyes? But he didn't say goodbye. His was a healthy hello, an urge to get on with it -- he was looking forward to "2000 and beyond."

Now he was beyond.

The best organizer UP ever had, someone it took three years to find, was gone.

The Mountain was right -- in our community, we are short-lived and our best organizers do die much too young.

I was truly sad. My friend, my teacher, my comrade in busted arms, was no more, and, to compound this saddest of all funks, I wondered if the last time we spoke, I had told the old Irish bastard that I loved him. He had sounded like he was going to live forever, so I wasn't sure.

Shit!

I would have sat down and cried, but I was still in shock. That would take a few days.

Then I remembered. He was a clown -- the worst, and best of it being that he was a brave clown.

"Time for me to be one," I told myself as I blew my nose.

Okay.

I went and got a beer out of the fridge and stuck a straw in it. I re-read Goethe. Then I walked outside and, sitting down on the porch, I took a deep breath of the fresh ocean air. Since it was a cement porch out to the sidewalk, I poured a little of my brew into the earth of a large planter hanging off the window. "For you, Paulie," I told him one last time. "Thank you, my brother."

I looked up at the bright blue sky of Venice Beach. "What do I do to honor you?" I asked of him and myself. I knew I wasn't going to Virginia and didn't really want to. I don't like funerals...and I couldn't think of anyone worthy of sending a Jello squid to.

Damn!

I dropped the straw onto the puddle of beer in the planter and, finishing the rest of it in one healthy slug, I belched loudly. "I'll miss you Paulie. You were the gutsiest gimp of them all. You weren't afraid to think big and then act on it."

I looked towards the sky over the ocean and blew him a big kiss.

I hoped they buried him in his red tux so that he would look sharp wherever he ended up fomenting democratic revolution. I smiled at the thought of that. I breathed deeply and steadied myself to begin again...to register someone to vote...to find the next organizer...to do the small things. "Don't hesitate," I told myself.

And you, my fellow citizen, disabled or otherwise -- don't you hesitate, either. Be bold! Go register to vote, and then register someone else to vote and make sure they follow through. That way, history will be made and pursued, and this thing called democracy will never end.

Who knows? Ultimately, we may even get it right and make it work the way the Ancient Ones intended: For the people...all the people.

Yeah, I know it's a long shot, but --

About the Author

Shawn Casey O'Brien is the former Executive Director of the Unique People's Voting Project (UP) and was instrumental in registering and getting out the votes of a hundred thousand disabled citizens and their families. He is also the former lead singer/songwriter of the 1980's Los Angeles punk band The Cripples. He lives in Santa Monica, California where he brews award-winning beers and premium dry meads.

err
16
20
38
125 Content, we're
222 (2) palpable, palpable
287 then = than

209 SA Conf.
23.5 months. (than m, the now (up)
72-6 Dr. Wh.

CPSIA information can be obtained
at www.ICGtesting.com
Printed in the USA
FSOW01n2305041215
14220FS